D1566703

DATE DUE

THE NORTH CAROLINA STATE CONSTITUTION

with History and Commentary

THE NORTH CAROLINA STATE CONSTITUTION

with History and Commentary

With a New Foreword by the Author

John V. Orth

THE UNIVERSITY OF NORTH CAROLINA PRESS
Chapel Hill & London

The North Carolina State Constitution, with History and Commentary,
by John V. Orth, was originally published as *The North Carolina State
Constitution: A Reference Guide,* No. 16 in the series, Reference Guides
to the State Constitutions of the United States (Greenwood Press,
Westport, CT, 1993).

© 1993 by John V. Orth

First published by The University of North Carolina Press in 1995
New Foreword © 1995 by The University of North Carolina Press

This edition by arrangement with Greenwood Publishing Group, Inc.

Library of Congress Cataloging-in-Publication Data
Orth, John V.
   The North Carolina state constitution : with history and commentary /
by John V. Orth ; with a new foreword by the author.
     p.   cm.
   Originally published: Westport, Conn. : Greenwood Press, 1993.
  (Reference guides to the state constitutions of the United States ; no. 16).
   Includes bibliographical references and index.
   ISBN 0-8078-4551-5 (pbk. : alk. paper)
   1. North Carolina—Constitution. 2. North Carolina—Constitutional
law. I. Title. II. Series: Reference guides to the state constitutions of the
United States ; no. 16.
KFN7801   1971.A6077   1995
342.756'02—dc20   95-14496
[347.56022]   CIP

*The paper in this book meets the guidelines for permanence and durability of
the Committee on Production Guidelines for Book Longevity of the Council on
Library Resources.*

Manufactured in the United States of America

99   98   97   96   95   5   4   3   2   1

For Noreen

"Hey, old pal . . . "

A frequent recurrence to fundamental principles is absolutely necessary to preserve the blessings of liberty.

Constitution of 1971, art. I, § 35

Constitution of 1868, art. I, § 29

Constitution of 1776, Declaration of Rights, § 21

Contents

Contents

Foreword to the Paperback Edition

After decades in the shadow of the federal government, states are today claiming a larger role in national politics. Local problems have always demanded local solutions, but even problems of national extent, such as poverty, racism, and inadequate education, may be better solved by individual states. Closer to the people and rooted in local history, states offer the possibility of more responsive and efficient government. Local solutions, even of similar problems, may vary from state to state. Justice Louis Brandeis long ago likened the states to laboratories in which social and economic experiments are conducted. The results in one state may prove instructive elsewhere.

Renewed interest in state government will necessarily mean greater attention to state constitutions. Bulwarks of civil rights, constitutions embody many of society's deepest convictions, such as belief in freedom of speech, press, and religion, and in safeguards against abuse in the prosecution of criminals. Americans' "chartered liberties" are not all to be found in the federal Bill of Rights: state constitutions contain their own, sometimes more expansive, declarations of rights.

Because many well-known constitutional cases involve limitations on government, constitutions are too often thought of in purely negative terms: government shall not do this or that. But the fact is, constitutions are empowering documents. First and foremost, state constitutions *constitute* state government, determining who shall make the laws, who shall enforce them, and who shall resolve disputes.

State constitutions do more than organize state government and safeguard civil rights; they also proclaim some of society's highest aspirations. A particularly clear example is the North Carolina Constitution's declaration on education: "The people have a right to the privilege of education, and it is the duty of the State to guard and maintain that right." Along with such grand policy statements are also found some quite detailed provisions concerning matters more commonly, and sometimes more appropriately, dealt with by ordinary legislation. The North Carolina Constitution provides, for example, that the net proceeds of all fines, penalties, and forfeitures shall belong to the county school funds. Both the grand declarations and the mundane details of a provision raise tricky problems of interpretation and implementation.

Perhaps the most famous advice on how to read a constitution was uttered by Chief Justice John Marshall: "We must never forget," he said, "that it is a *constitution* we are expounding." His point is that a constitution deserves a different, presumably more generous, reading than the limited construction put on lesser documents like statutes or deeds. But emphasis must be placed on the whole text as well. A constitution is an interrelated whole and must be read as such. There is no greater error (except an ungenerous construction) and none more easily made than to read a constitution as if it were only a series of unrelated propositions. And constitutions themselves seem almost to encourage this mistake: they rarely contain any cross-references or indications of related provisions.

This book is offered as a means to encourage an informed reading of the North Carolina Constitution. A historical essay puts the current constitution, which went into effect in 1971, in the context of its two predecessors, the Revolutionary Constitution of 1776 and the Reconstruction Constitution of 1868. The size of the book permits the reader literally to grasp the whole document: the book can be held easily in one hand. Both the constitution and the associated commentary can be read in a manageable amount of time. Copious cross-references to related sections are included to facilitate a comprehensive understanding. Finally, a bibliographic essay provides a guide for further reading if more details are required.

State constitutions are notoriously amendable. Since 1971 the North Carolina Constitution has been altered twenty-two times; by contrast, the federal Constitution has accumulated only twenty-seven amendments in two centuries. The state constitution may today stand on the verge of still further amendment. For example, the long-debated question of whether North Carolina's governor should be given a veto on legislation will at last be put to the voters. Other questions, such as whether the state's judges should continue to be chosen by direct election, are sure to follow. To spare the constitution hasty or ill-informed alterations, the voters must be prepared to give them thoughtful consideration. An informed electorate is the constitution's only, and best, safeguard.

John V. Orth
Chapel Hill, North Carolina
February 1995

Foreword

Not since Henry G. Connor and Joseph B. Cheshire, Jr.'s *The Constitution of the State of North Carolina Annotated,* published in 1911, has there been anything comparable to this treatise by Professor John V. Orth on the Constitution of North Carolina. As anyone familiar with the resurgence of state constitutional law during the last decade well knows, this is a book whose time has surely come. During these years state courts across our land in criminal prosecutions and civil litigation have "dusted off" their respective state constitutions and used them in lieu of and in addition to the federal constitution to resolve individual, or civil, rights issues. And, in the words of a former Associate Justice of the Supreme Court of North Carolina, "during the past decade, North Carolina has been at the head of the movement to energize state constitutional law."

These words appear in an article by retired Associate Justice Harry C. Martin titled, "The State as a 'Font of Individual Liberties': North Carolina Accepts the Challenge," published by the North Carolina Law Review in September 1992 as part of the Law Review's symposium on North Carolina Constitutional Law. That the North Carolina Law Review devoted its entire September 1992 issue to this subject is strong evidence of its timeliness and importance.

State constitutions generally and North Carolina's Constitution in particular are rich sources of fundamental principles of democratic government and guarantees of individual liberties. The North Carolina Constitution begins with a Declaration of Rights, which comprises thirty-six sections of Article I. Some of these provisions have origins in the Magna Carta; others, in the 1689 English Bill of Rights. Subsequent articles in the constitution outline the powers and responsibilities of the three branches of government: the Legislative, the Executive, and the Judicial. The constitution then proceeds to deal more specifically with various aspects of state government.

The North Carolina Declaration of Rights not only contains a longer list of rights described in more detail and with more specificity than the Federal Bill of Rights, in many instances the state document also speaks in terms of the rights of the people rather than in terms of prohibitions against government infringement of those rights. This difference may be important on the issue of whether "state action" is a prerequisite to the redress of a state constitution rights violation. Finally, the North Carolina Constitution contains provisions for which there is no federal counterpart.

Today North Carolina lawyers have an obligation to be conversant with the North Carolina Constitution and to urge upon the courts consideration of its provisions in the resolution of issues to which they pertain. North Carolina courts have an obligation to deepen their understanding of the great document. Its intelligent use requires at a minimum that lawyers and judges know its text, its structure and, above all, its history.

Professor Orth's treatise covers all of these things. In addition, it contains a comprehensive bibliography of valuable sources. The legal profession, indeed all citizens with an interest in the law and its development, will welcome this book as a thorough, scholarly, and singularly helpful contribution to the development of North Carolina's organic law.

James G. Exum, Jr.
Chief Justice
Supreme Court of North Carolina

THE NORTH CAROLINA STATE CONSTITUTION

with History and Commentary

Part I

North Carolina Constitutional History

To the intelligent lawyer or layman who cares to know not only what the law is, but the reasons upon which it is founded and the causes which have, either through legislation or judicial decision, contributed to it, there is no more instructive or interesting study than constitutional history.

Honorable Henry G. Connor
United States District Judge for
the Eastern District of North Carolina

North Carolina's three state constitutions chart the evolution over two centuries of a modern representative democracy. The Independence Constitution of 1776, adopted by a provincial congress rather than by direct vote of the electorate, organized a republic of free males with full participation reserved for property owners. As settlement on the westward-moving frontier shifted the demographic center of the state, pressure for political reapportionment steadily mounted. Serious civil unrest was avoided only by extensive amendments, ratified at the polls in 1835.

While advancing democracy eroded the privileges accorded to wealth, race emerged as a new qualification for voting. With only one further amendment the state's first constitution endured until defeat in the Civil War necessitated a new organic law, adapted to the reality of the end of slavery. Despite continuities, the 1868 Constitution marked a greater caesura in state constitutional history than even the 1776 Constitution. The Republican draftsmen took the opportunity to introduce many humanitarian and forward-looking provisions, but the "Carpetbagger Constitution" was not finally accepted by indigenous white males until extensive amendments were adopted in 1876.

For almost a century, from the end of Reconstruction to 1971, the state's second constitution (as amended) provided the frame of government, although further amendments accumulated in the second third of the twentieth century. To consolidate the gains of the prior hundred years and to introduce a number of much-needed reforms, the state's third constitution was approved by the voters in 1970, effective July 1, 1971. While significant, the break with the past was not dramatic: The changes introduced did not compare in magnitude with those made in 1868.

THE CONSTITUTION OF 1776

[A]t the time of our separation from Great Britain, we were thrown into a similar situation with a set of people shipwrecked and cast on a marooned island—without laws, without magistrates, without government, or any legal authority— . . . [B]eing thus circumstanced, the people of this country, with a general union of sentiment, by their delegates, met in Congress, and formed that system of those fundamental principles comprised in the Constitution, dividing the powers of government into separate and distinct branches, to wit: The legislative, the judicial, and executive, and assigning to each several and distinct powers, and prescribing their several limits and boundaries. . . .

With these observations in 1786 Judge Samuel Ashe opened the celebrated case of Bayard v. Singleton. Although the country Ashe had in mind was North Carolina and the congress the Fifth Provincial Congress that met at Halifax in November and December 1776, his general description would apply to any of Great Britain's rebellious thirteen colonies. Once independence was declared on July 4, 1776, Americans were like so many Robinson Crusoes, "shipwrecked and cast on a marooned island." Having cut themselves off from the Crown, the historic source of constitutional legitimacy, they were strictly speaking "without laws, without magistrates, without government, or any legal authority."

Like the self-reliant pioneers they were, North Carolinians immediately set about the task of rectifying the situation, finding a new source of legal authority in the people themselves. When delegates to the provincial congress appointed a committee (including Delegate Samuel Ashe) on November 13 to prepare a declaration of rights and a constitution,[1] the committee reviewed rather precise instructions from Mecklenburg and Orange counties,[2] but it profited most from a letter from William Hooper, North Carolina's delegate to the Continental Congress, enclosing copies of recently adopted constitutions from other states.[3] There were even two pamphlet-sized letters of advice from John Adams, already a renowned authority on constitutionalism.[4]

After barely a month's work, the drafting committee presented proposals to the full congress which, after making some more or less important changes, speedily approved the final product. The declaration of rights, considered at four sessions, was passed on December 17, 1776,[5] while the constitution, which was given somewhat more extended consideration—at six sessions—was passed on

December 18, 1776.[6] Although treated separately, the two documents form a single whole, the latter expressly declaring the former "Part of the Constitution of this State."[7]

Like all other contemporary state declarations and constitutions, neither was submitted to the electorate for approval. In part this omission may be explained by the exigencies of the time—a "shipwrecked" people needed speedy rescue—but it also reflected an unfamiliarity with constitution making: The distinction between ordinary and fundamental law was not yet clearly marked. When the North Carolina provisional government had announced the election for the Fifth Provincial Congress, the resolution informed voters that "it will be the business of the delegates then chosen, not only to make laws for the good government of, but also to form a Constitution for, this state."[8]

The declaration of rights and the constitution (narrowly considered) form an effective blend of revolutionary theory and practical politics. The relationship is not that exhibited by the U.S. Constitution with its appended Bill of Rights, the latter adding civil rights to a document establishing the basic institutions of government. Instead, North Carolina's declaration of rights, like those of her sister states, is logically, as well as chronologically, prior to the constitutional text, providing a statement of general and abstract principles given particular and concrete realization in the constitution proper. The abstractness of the declaration has allowed most of it to survive (with modifications and additions) in the state's later constitutions, where it appears in the body of the text as Article I.

The declaration of rights began, appropriately enough, with a categorical assertion of popular sovereignty: "That all political Power is vested in and derived from the People only."[9] Effective political power, however, was confined by the constitution to certain "Freemen of the Age of twenty-one Years": To vote for members of the senate, one had to possess a freehold of fifty acres;[10] to vote for members of the lower house, the house of commons, one had merely to be a taxpayer.[11] Annual elections ensured accountability. To be eligible for legislative service there were higher property qualifications: Membership in the senate was restricted to men with "not less than three hundred Acres of Land in Fee,"[12] while each member of the house of commons had to have "not less than one hundred Acres of Land in Fee, or for the Term of his own Life."[13] The governor had to be a man of still more substantial property, possessed of "a Freehold in Lands and Tenements above the Value of one Thousand Pounds."[14]

Similarly, the declaration of rights provided for separation of powers: "That the Legislative, Executive and Supreme Judicial Powers of Government ought to be forever separate and distinct from each other."[15] In practice, however, it was the bicameral legislature, the General Assembly, that was supreme. The General Assembly, not the voters, chose the governor[16] and members of the Council of State,[17] the treasurer,[18] the secretary,[19] the attorney general,[20] and all the judges,[21] as well as the officers of the state militia.[22] This contrast of principle and practice did not escape contemporary observers. Reviewing the situation a decade later, during debates on the adoption of the U.S. Constitution, James Madison commented in *The Federalist*:

If we look into the constitutions of the several States, we find that, notwithstanding the emphatical and, in some instances, the unqualified terms in which this axiom [separation of powers] has been laid down, there is not a single instance in which the several departments of power have been kept absolutely separate and distinct. . . .

The constitution of North Carolina, which declares "that the legislative, executive, and supreme judicial powers of government ought to be forever separate and distinct from each other," refers, at the same time, to the legislative department, the appointment not only of the executive chief, but all the principal officers within both that and the judiciary department.[23]

The lesson the Founding Fathers drew was that separation of powers needed to be qualified by checks and balances lest one branch become overpowerful.

Not only was the governor elected by the General Assembly, but also his executive authority was hemmed in on every side. While he could succeed himself, he could not serve more than three years out of six.[24] He could fill no executive posts; even the local justices of the peace were named by the General Assembly, the governor merely commissioning them.[25] He could make no important decision without the advice of the Council of State.[26] Lacking a veto, he took no formal role in legislation; bills became laws when passed by both houses and signed by the speakers.[27] Overbearing colonial governors had generated so strong a reaction that the republican office was handicapped for years. To this day North Carolina's governor has no veto.

On the divisive subject of religion, the declaration of rights roundly declared "That all Men have a natural and unalienable Right to worship Almighty God according to the Dictates of their own Conscience,"[28] a principle realized in the body of the constitution by the disestablishment of the Church of England.[29] Nonetheless, clergymen in active service were barred from the General Assembly and Council of State,[30] and a religious test for office remained: "That no Person who shall deny the being of God, or the Truth of the Protestant Religion, or the Divine Authority either of the Old or New Testament, or who shall hold Religious Principles incompatible with the Freedom and Safety of the State, shall be capable of holding any Office or Place of Trust or Profit in the Civil Department, within this State."[31] Although the section was aimed at (respectively) atheists, Roman Catholics, Jews, and Christian pacifists such as Quakers and Moravians, it prompted a later commentator to observe tartly that "it would be difficult to formulate a statute more obscure in its terms or inviting more controversy as to its meaning."[32]

In fact, the constitutional stricture was relaxed in practice. In 1809 Jacob Henry, a Jew elected to the house of commons, was challenged on the basis of his religion. The house, which under the constitution was the judge of its members' qualifications,[33] refused to exclude him, apparently on the ground that a seat in the General Assembly was not an "Office . . . of Trust or Profit" within the meaning of the Constitution,[34] an appealing decision that nonetheless puts one in mind of the ingratiating query of the old Tammany Hall politician: "What's the Constitution between friends?"[35]

More soul-searching was provoked in 1833 when the General Assembly elected the learned, but Roman Catholic, William Gaston to the state supreme court. Gaston had served previously in the General Assembly, profiting apparently from the precedent set by Henry. Two years later, this problem was resolved more straightforwardly by an amendment substituting "Christian" for "Protestant" in the religious test,[36] a change that did nothing to clarify the position of Jewish officeholders such as Jacob Henry.

That the North Carolina drafters in 1776 could have completed their work with such celerity is due to the availability of models from other states, as well as to the arsenal of political arguments accumulated during the frequent quarrels with colonial governors. The revolutionary manifesto with which the declaration of rights began, for instance—"That all political Power is vested in and derived from the People only"[37]—apparently emerged from the deft wielding of an editorial blue pencil on the second section of the Virginia Declaration of Rights: "That all power is vested in, and consequently derived from, the people; that magistrates are their trustees and servants, and at all times amenable to them."[38] Similarly, the section on separation of powers is almost identical to that in the Maryland Declaration of Rights,[39] while the section on freedom of religion follows almost word for word a section of the Pennsylvania Declaration of Rights.[40]

American constitutionalism, as the revolutionaries themselves loudly protested, was nothing new; rather, it was deeply rooted in English tradition. When North Carolina declared "That excessive Bail should not be required, nor excessive Fines imposed, nor cruel or unusual punishments inflicted,"[41] it was not merely repeating the antecedent declarations of Virginia[42] and Maryland.[43] It was also deliberately echoing the English Bill of Rights of 1689,[44] a product of the Glorious Revolution that checked Stuart absolutism. (In due course, the provision was to make its way into the U.S. Bill of Rights as the Eighth Amendment.)

Some sections were of even older provenance. For example, North Carolina declared "That no Freeman ought to be taken, imprisoned or disseissed of his Freehold, Liberties or Privileges, or outlawed or exiled, or in any Manner destroyed or deprived of his Life, Liberty or Property, but by the Law of the Land,"[45] a provision traceable, by way of the Maryland Declaration of Rights,[46] all the way back to the Magna Carta in 1215.[47] Although the "law of the land" as a phrase was often supplanted elsewhere by "due process of law," for instance in the Fifth and Fourteenth amendments to the U.S. Constitution, it was—and remains—North Carolina's guarantee of the rule of law.

The nature of the English contribution to American constitutionalism must be expressly recognized. It was a legacy about how power ought to be exercised, not about what ought to be done with it or who ought to have it. How things ought to be done—for example, that neither bail nor fines should be excessive; that punishment should not be cruel or unusual; that life, liberty, and property should be protected by the law of the land—these were the immensely valuable lessons of centuries of struggle over power's inordinate claims. The proper exercise of power earned the government respect and affection; it focused attention on immediate and practical problems and minimized disputes about the process itself. What ought to be done was the concern of day-to-day politics, while who ought to have power was an exceptional question—indeed, the ultimate constitutional issue. When in dispute, it could not be answered by ordinary means; if peaceful resolution failed, a revolutionary situation arose. When North Carolinians and other Americans declared the people, as opposed to the Crown, the source of sovereignty, they seized for themselves the highest power in the state, but by solemnly affirming the traditions of English constitutionalism, they showed they had learned the lessons about power's proper exercise.

Not every section of the 1776 Constitution was concerned with creating the new institutions of government or with setting the ground rules for its operation; some set broad legislative goals, calling for later action by the General Assembly. For example, one section modeled on the Pennsylvania Constitution required "That a School or Schools shall be established by the Legislature for the convenient Instruction of Youth, with such Salaries to the Masters paid by the Public, as may enable them to instruct at low Prices; and all useful Learning shall be duly encouraged and promoted in one or more Universities."[48] In partial discharge of its duty to provide elementary education, the legislature subsequently chartered numerous academies, but their masters looked in vain for state salaries: For years the extent of public support was limited to exemption from taxes and perhaps authority to raise funds by conducting a lottery.[49] It was not until 1839, after constitutional revision had unleashed progressive forces in the state, that a recognizable public school law was passed.[50]

Higher education was first addressed during an important legislative session in 1784 when the General Assembly considered chartering a university, but it was not until five years later that an actual charter was granted.[51] Again avoiding an appropriation of public funds, the cost-conscious legislators endowed the new institution with the state's right to escheats[52]—that is, the property of those who died without an effective will or known heirs—a provision that was to result in an important lawsuit two decades later.

In 1784 the General Assembly redeemed another constitutional promise, also drawn from the Pennsylvania Constitution: "That the future Legislature of this State shall regulate Entails in such a Manner as to prevent Perpetuities."[53] Entailment provided a means for tying up land in a family, the basis for a hereditary aristocracy. Colonial North Carolina law permitted the practice, actually giving it more leeway than the aristocratic Mother Country then allowed.[54] The 1784 statute, part of a wide-ranging reform of property law, prevented limitations on the descent of land in perpetuity, justifying the change in political terms: "entails of estates tend only to raise the wealth and importance of particular families and individuals, giving them an unequal and undue influence in a republic, and prove in manifold instances the source of great contention and injustice."[55]

The 1776 Constitution generated little judicial interpretation. "Prior to 1868," it has been observed, "the Constitution was so simple in its provisions, leaving so much administrative detail to the Legislature, that few questions involving either the validity of acts of the Legislature or of constitutional construction were presented to the courts."[56] A nationwide dearth of constitutional litigation might also be added: The frequent recourse to the courts with constitutional challenges, a characteristic of modern American constitutionalism, did not develop until the second half of the nineteenth century.

Nonetheless, one of the most famous constitutional cases in North Carolina history was decided in the eighteenth century. Bayard v. Singleton (1787), the case in which Judge Samuel Ashe likened Americans after the Revolution to a "set of people shipwrecked," involved one of the first recorded challenges in America to the constitutionality of a statute. Despite the guarantee in the declaration of rights of due process of law ("law of the land") and an even more specific guarantee of trial by jury in "all Controversies at Law respecting Property,"[57] the General Assembly had adopted a statute in 1785 directing that suits brought by claimants of property confiscated during the Revolution should be dismissed upon a showing by defendants that they derived title from the commissioners of forfeited estates.[58] When forced to choose, the court preferred the constitution over the statute, thereby establishing judicial review in North Carolina more than a decade before Marbury v. Madison (1803) established it at the federal level.

In 1805 the lesson was repeated when a legislative attempt to deprive the University of North Carolina of property it had acquired pursuant to its right to escheats was declared unconstitutional. In Trustees of the University of North Carolina v. Foy (1805), the state's highest court reasoned that title had vested in the university and that the law of the land protected it from subsequent divestment. The court added that the creation of the university had been directed by the people assembled in constitutional convention and drew the dubious conclusion that the General Assembly could not deprive the university of this means of support. Although it acquiesced in the result, the legislature demonstrated its authority by promptly altering the university's charter, making the governor chairman of the board of trustees and empowering the legislature to fill vacancies on the board.[59] After the Civil War the governance of the university was again to become the subject of dispute, provoking a constitutional amendment in 1873 to restore legislative control.[60]

While the 1776 Constitution generally avoided details better left to the legislature, it lapsed into specificity in one important regard: political apportionment. Each county was given one senator[61] and two representatives[62]; in addition, six named towns, the "borough towns" of colonial days[63] (Edenton, New Bern,

Wilmington, Salisbury, Hillsborough, and Halifax), were granted a representative apiece.[64] Fayetteville was added to the list by act of the constitutional
convention that met there in 1789. The General Assembly had asked the convention to consider, in addition to the momentous question of reversing North
Carolina's prior rejection of the U.S. Constitution, the propriety of extending
representation. The convention voted in favor of joining the Union[65] and adopted
an ordinance amending the state constitution.[66] It was apparently thought unnecessary to refer the matter to the voters, the convention (like the Fifth Provincial
Congress) having plenary power. The fact that the legislature had not felt competent to act on its own is, however, evidence of the recognition of the distinction
between fundamental and ordinary law.

As the demographic balance in the state changed, shifting toward the western
frontier, a political imbalance resulted. The smaller eastern counties continued
to preponderate in the General Assembly. The recurrent battle of west versus
east that raged in many of the seaboard states flared in North Carolina as well.
No further piecemeal adjustments were made, and civil disturbance was only
narrowly averted by wholesale change in 1835. It is noticeable that North Carolinians chose to resolve their constitutional dispute by amending the existing
document, rather than by writing a new instrument, the chosen path in many
states. Perhaps it testified to the inherent soundness of the first constitution, but
it also represented the state's constitutional conservatism, a trait from which the
second constitution was eventually to benefit as well.

Since the 1776 Constitution made no provision for amendment, the General
Assembly improvised a process based on that used in 1789. A special election
was held to call a constitutional convention that would propose amendments
regarding the basis of representation and other specified topics.[67] All persons
qualified to vote for members of the house of commons were eligible to vote on
the convention, and delegates were to possess enough property to serve in the
house—as well as being of the white race, an ominous indicator of things to
come.

As to representation, the convention was to consider restructuring the senate,
to consist of 34 to 50 members chosen by districts based on the amount of taxes
paid, and the house, to consist of 90 to 120 members (excluding borough members) chosen by districts based on population. In addition, the convention was
to devise a method for further constitutional amendment, should that become
necessary. At its option it could consider, among other things, ending borough
representation, disfranchising free blacks, altering the religious test, lengthening
legislative terms from one year to two, providing for direct election of the
governor, and prescribing the governor's term and eligibility for reelection.
Finally, the convention was forbidden to consider dividing a county between
two or more senatorial districts, depriving a county of at least one representative
in the house of commons, reducing the property qualification for senatorial voters
or for senators, or disfranchising anyone presently qualified to vote—except, of
course, for blacks.

The voters approved, and delegates were elected who met in Raleigh from June 4 to July 11, 1835. Whether the limitations on the powers of the convention were valid or not remains unsettled since the delegates chose not to disobey their instructions. They did, however, engage in preliminary debate about whether it was proper for the General Assembly to prescribe an oath requiring them to abide by the restrictions.[68] The mere fact that the legislature included the oath suggests doubt concerning its power to control the convention. In the end the majority voted to cut off debate, and all delegates took the oath.

The principal amendment they proposed dutifully eliminated the county as the basis of representation. Senators were to be elected by districts based on the amount of taxes paid, although no counties were to be divided,[69] while representatives were to be elected by districts based on population, with each county being guaranteed at least one representative.[70] For purposes of apportionment the relevant population would be the so-called "federal population," a concept borrowed from the U.S. Constitution—that is, the number determined "by adding to the whole Number of free Persons, including those bound to Service for a Term of Years, and excluding Indians not taxed, three-fifths of all other Persons."[71] The obvious effect was to count slaves as three-fifths persons for purposes of representation. The size of the senate was fixed at 50 members and the house at 120, the maximum allowed by the legislation calling the convention—and a size that survived into the second and third constitutions. Borough representation was ended, and legislative terms were lengthened to two years, also changes that have endured. Breaking with earlier practice, legislative sessions were made biennial rather than annual.[72]

Exercising their discretionary powers, the delegates proposed to define the electorate on racial lines for the first time since pre-Revolutionary days. Although colonial law and practice had prohibited blacks from voting,[73] the 1776 Constitution had granted the franchise indiscriminately to all "freemen" who met the property qualification, including free blacks. While it is now impossible to determine whether black voters were admitted to the poll in every North Carolina county, it is certain that they voted in some and that their numbers in a few places were substantial.[74] Disfranchisement was extensively discussed in the 1835 convention and carried by only a small majority: On the key vote, delegates were divided sixty-six to sixty-one.[75] An 1835 amendment excluded all non-whites, substituting a biological for a status qualification: "No free negro, free mulatto, or free person of mixed blood, descended from negro ancestors to the fourth generation inclusive (though one ancestor of each generation may have been a white person) shall vote for members of the Senate or House of Commons."[76] The effect was that free blacks and other non-whites counted as whole persons for purposes of representation, but could not themselves vote.

Property qualifications were to be retained for the senate: To vote, white males still needed a freehold of 50 acres;[77] to serve, they still needed to possess 300 acres of land in fee.[78] The new scheme of apportionment represented a compromise between the regions. Basing representation in the senate on taxes and retaining the property qualifications ensured the wealthier east a continued majority in that chamber, while basing representation in the house of commons on population (as qualified by the federal three-fifths rule for counting slaves) meant that the more populous west would gain a majority in the other chamber.[79]

A second principal amendment broke the General Assembly's monopoly on power: The governor was to be elected directly by the voters qualified to vote for members of the house of commons.[80] His term was to be two years, and he was limited to two terms within six years.[81] Despite this apparent shift in the balance of power, little changed in reality. As the doughty Nathaniel Macon, Revolutionary War veteran and still a political power in the state in 1835, bluntly put it: "Where the Governor has next to nothing to do, it is of little consequence who elects him."[82]

In addition, a procedure was established for future amendments to the constitution. A convention could be called by a two-thirds vote of each house[83] (no mention was made of submitting the product to the electorate), or a specific amendment could be proposed to the voters by the General Assembly if adopted at two successive sessions, with an intervening election, by majorities of three-fifths and two-thirds, respectively.[84] Finally, the religious exclusion was altered from non-Protestants to non-Christians,[85] a change that would eliminate doubt concerning the Roman Catholic justice of the state supreme court, William Gaston.

The proposed amendments were submitted as a single issue to the voters in the fall election, the first time ordinary North Carolinians had been given an opportunity to decide a constitutional issue, black voters presumably being eligible to vote on their own disfranchisement. Ratifying the compromise worked out by the politicians, the electorate approved the amendments, with an overwhelming majority in favor in the west being joined by a small minority in the east.[86] Following the precedent established by amendments to the U.S. Constitution, the state appended the 1835 amendments to the 1776 Constitution, rather than incorporating them in the text, the practice with the state's later constitutions.

No other change was made in the constitution for two decades, until political rivalry between the Democratic and the Whig parties raised the possibility of eliminating the property qualification in voting for senators.[87] After years of debate the issue was put to the electorate in 1857 and approved.[88] The result was perhaps a foregone conclusion since the voters on the amendment were those qualified to vote for members of the house of commons; that is, those meeting the minimum tax-paying qualification were invited to permit themselves to vote for members of the upper chamber as well. The effect was to double the number of senatorial voters.[89]

Now that the electorates of both houses had to meet identical property qualifications, it might have been questioned whether the upper house was any longer needed, but the senate continued to be based on districts laid out according to the amount paid in taxes, and senators themselves continued to have to meet a higher property qualification than did members of the house of commons. When even these distinctions were abolished in 1868, the senate nonetheless survived. Bicameralism, based on colonial and ultimately on English practice, had put down deep roots and maintained itself as an institution.

By 1857 North Carolina had transformed itself into a republic of tax-paying white males twenty-one years of age and older. It is a legitimate subject of inquiry when, and whether, the state would have extended the franchise beyond that group. The experiment with a non-racial republic, one based on free status and at least enough property to pay taxes, had been officially abandoned in 1835. There is no reason to think, given the heightened passions about race and slavery in the period, that North Carolina would soon have reversed itself, if left to its own devices. Landless white paupers, unable to pay taxes, were equally unlikely to be admitted to the franchise; whatever was happening in other states, North Carolinians still adhered to the conservative political theory that the propertyless were not stakeholders in society and therefore not entitled to a voice in public affairs.

Women, too, seemed permanently excluded from politics. Although a women's movement almost wholly limited to Northern circles had sounded a call for female suffrage in the Seneca Falls Declaration in 1848,[90] no observer of antebellum North Carolina would have thought votes for women any more realistic a prospect than emancipation of the slaves. Lowering the age of majority from twenty-one to eighteen had not yet been anywhere proposed. The most that such an observer might have forecast would have been a reduction, or perhaps the complete elimination, of the property qualification for (adult white male) officeholders, although, as we shall see, even this relic still had defenders in influential circles.

In any case, secession and defeat in the Civil War soon set in motion a series of events that would lead in a few short years to the end of slavery and the grant of votes to all males twenty-one or older of either race and without regard to the payment of taxes. In 1861 the General Assembly called a constitutional convention,[91] as authorized under the 1835 amendments. Delegates to this convention, unlike those twenty-six years earlier, were not limited in any way in the matters they could consider. Drawing their power directly from the people, they regarded themselves as superior to the General Assembly, which continued in session, and even defied an order by the latter to disband.[92] In addition to seceding from the federal Union and ratifying the Constitution of the Confederate States of America, the convention—like that at Fayetteville in 1789—also amended the state constitution.[93] (Under the provision adopted in 1835 there was no requirement that it submit amendments to the voters.)

Most of the 1861–62 amendments concerned adjustments required by secession and the ensuing war, but a few involved other changes. Of greatest significance, perhaps, was an amendment providing for a tax on land and slaves based on their assessed value (*ad valorem*);[94] previously, they had been taxed at a flat rate. Long desired by western North Carolinians, this change had been blocked during more settled times by eastern interests.[95] By another amendment the convention altered the religious test for office, deleting the words requiring belief in the "truth of the Christian religion" and amending the biblical test to exclude only those who denied "the divine authority of both the Old and New Testaments,"[96] thereby formally admitting Jews.

After defeat in the Civil War, the provisional governor, William W. Holden, who had been named by the president of the United States,[97] called a convention that ratified two ordinances, one nullifying secession and the other abolishing slavery.[98] The same convention later proposed a new organic law, largely a restatement of the 1776 Constitution and its 1835 amendments. Black men were not to be enfranchised, and political apportionment in the General Assembly was to be based on the number of whites,[99] defined (in keeping with the 1835 amendment) as those having "less than one-sixteenth of Negro blood"[100]—the purpose apparently being to reduce the representation of the eastern counties, where the black population was largely concentrated, even below that accorded by the three-fifths rule. Property qualifications for office holding were to be retained.[101] Among the white electorate the more liberal element favored black enfranchisement, while conservatives were opposed to disturbing the sectional balance, so the constitution proposed in 1866 was rejected at the polls.[102]

THE CONSTITUTION OF 1868

In 1868, perhaps even more than in 1776, North Carolinians were "a set of people shipwrecked." As in the struggle for independence from Great Britain, so in the Civil War, the state severed itself from a source of constitutional legitimacy. But this time the center did manage, however bloodily, to hold. While not quite bereft, strictly speaking, of laws, magistrates, or government, the legal authority after the war was that of the victorious army. Just as defeat in the earlier revolutionary struggle would have led to the displacement of an important segment of the colonial elite and a significant diminution of local control, so actual surrender in 1865 caused an upheaval in political leadership and a dramatic shift of power toward the federal government.

The North Carolina Constitutional Convention of 1868 was called on the initiative of Congress,[103] then in the hands of the Radical Republicans, although it was approved in a state election.[104] Reconstruction legislation required the selection of delegates by the state's male citizens, black as well as white, except those disfranchised for rebellion or felony, despite the fact that the 1776 Constitution (as amended), which restricted voting to white taxpayers, was still legally in force. Federal legislation stipulated further that the resulting state constitution must extend the suffrage on the same basis. Of the 120 delegates that assembled in Raleigh in January 1868, 15 were black and 18 were carpetbaggers.[105] One of the most influential among the latter was a twenty-nine-year-old native of Ohio, Albion W. Tourgée, a lawyer and Union veteran who had moved to Greensboro in 1865 and established a newspaper; he left his mark on many parts of the convention's work, including the judiciary, local government, and public welfare. The constitution they drafted was approved at a special election in April 1868.[106]

The new constitution, North Carolina's second, marked a sharp break with what went before, a break as sharp, if not more so, than that marked by the Independence Constitution itself. Just as the 1776 Constitution had carried over the best elements of the past, so the Reconstruction Constitution continued some aspects of its predecessor—the declaration of rights largely reappeared as Article I—but changes were more numerous than continuities. For one thing, the new constitution was much more detailed than the old. While the 1776 organic law had been comprised of a declaration of rights of 25 sections and a constitutional text of 46 sections, the 1868 Constitution was divided into 14 articles (of which the first was the declaration of rights), with 197 sections in all. The old constitution could be printed in eight pages; the new covered twenty-three.[107]

A few of the changes introduced in 1868 related directly to the outcome of the Civil War. A preamble was added, piously thanking Almighty God "for the preservation of the American Union,"[108] a piety that must have been wormwood to many Confederate veterans, and a new section was prefixed to Article I, the Declaration of Rights, drawn from the American Declaration of Independence, declaring it to be "self-evident that all men are created equal."[109] At the decree of Congress, secession was rejected,[110] allegiance to the U.S. Constitution proclaimed,[111] and the Confederate war debt repudiated.[112] Slavery was "forever prohibited."[113] Otherwise, ancient rights were restated and perhaps refined. For the first time, the "privilege of the writ of habeas corpus" was expressly guaranteed;[114] the men of 1776 may have thought the precaution unnecessary in light of the state's reception of basic English statutes, including the Habeas Corpus Act.[115]

Only one new principle was formulated: "As political rights and privileges are not dependent upon, or modified by property, therefore no property qualification ought to affect the right to vote or hold office."[116] Implementing this principle, later articles changed the plan of representation in the senate from one based on taxes paid into the state treasury, as provided in 1835, to one based on population.[117] The 1835 apportionment plan was retained for the lower house, renamed in conformity with American usage the house of representatives, although, of course, the "federal population" plan of counting slaves as three-fifths persons for purposes of representation was deleted.[118]

Elective offices were multiplied. While North Carolina voters since 1835 had chosen representatives and governors (and senators, if they met the property qualification in effect until 1857), the new constitution provided for the direct election of all significant executive officers: governor, secretary of state, auditor, treasurer, superintendent of public works, superintendent of public instruction, and attorney general.[119] The office of lieutenant governor (also elective) was created, replacing the former speaker of the senate as presiding officer of that chamber[120] and further complicating the principle of separation of powers. Legislative terms remained two years, as set in 1835, although annual legislative sessions were required, while executive officers enjoyed four-year terms. The procedure for impeachment was spelled out[121]—just in time for the trial of Governor William W. Holden, the first American governor to be removed from office.[122] The supreme court was enlarged from three members as provided by statute in 1818[123] to five members,[124] and all judges were to be elected for eight-year terms.[125] Local government was to be based on the township,[126] a unit new to North Carolina, and its officers, a clerk and two justices of the peace, were to be elected biennially.[127]

As decreed by Congress, universal manhood suffrage was provided,[128] although in practice it would be some years before all ex-Confederates could vote. With the elimination of property qualifications and the end of slavery—all persons now were legally free—no foundation remained for a republic based on status and wealth such as that created in 1776. A republic erected on race and property was also, for the time being, excluded; a Reconstruction convention dominated by Union loyalists, carpetbaggers, and blacks could hardly be expected to do otherwise. Despite the stirrings of a national women's movement, no serious consideration was given to ending the sexual qualification. A mention of votes for women (and for those under the age of twenty-one) came in the minority report of the committee on suffrage, protesting the end of the racial qualification: "We do not regard the right to vote as natural or inherent, but conventional merely—to be regulated in such way as will best promote the welfare of the whole community. Upon this principle, women and minors have been excluded. Is there any reason why the negro should be advanced to a higher position?"[129] In fact, there was to be considerable backsliding on the principle of universal manhood suffrage, at least insofar as black men were concerned, before further extensions of the franchise were considered, and in the cases of race, sex, and age, national developments would be required before North Carolina would enlarge the basis of representation.

State government was modeled anew, catching up and leaping ahead at the same time. The judicial system was overhauled, and the ancient distinction between actions at law and suits in equity was abolished.[130] A commission of three (including Albion W. Tourgée) was appointed by the convention to prepare enlightened codes of civil and criminal procedure for consideration at the next session of the General Assembly[131]; the commissioners were also to work on a comprehensive code of substantive law.[132] Capital punishment was permitted by the constitution for only four crimes: murder, arson, burglary, and rape; Tourgée would have limited it to murder alone.[133] The object of punishment was proclaimed to include "reform of the offender" as well as satisfaction of justice.[134] Dueling, part of the antebellum elite's atavistic code of honor, now would disqualify a person from holding public office.[135] The religious test for office holding was shrunken to its first clause only, excluding those "who shall deny the being of Almighty God";[136] even this would have gone but for the belief that "no oath would bind a man who denied the existence of a higher power."[137]

The new constitution detailed a system of taxation, based on a capitation (poll) tax and taxes on property;[138] the secession convention's mandate for *ad valorem* rates on property was reaffirmed. For the first time, the constitution included a limitation on state borrowing,[139] as well as an explicit guarantee of repayment of the state debt[140] (except, of course, for the Confederate war debt). In a novel provision, an equation linked and limited the rates of taxation on property and persons.[141] As explained by a leading member of the convention:

> The Constitution admitted to the suffrage a class of persons who had never been entitled to it before, equal in numbers to about one-half of the former voting population, and this class was at that time almost universally destitute of property. It was foreseen as at least possible in the somewhat unnatural condition of things then existing, that whichever of these two powers should obtain a majority in the Legislature might attempt to put on the other an undue portion of the public burdens through taxation; to prevent the confiscation of property by numbers, a proportion was established; to prevent the oppression of numbers of property, the poll tax was limited.[142]

Innovations, pioneered in other states, were adopted. Counties were required to provide free public schools at least four months a year,[143] and the state was required to care for deaf mutes, the blind, and the insane.[144] Married women secured control over their own property,[145] a right the common law had denied them. Laborers' and mechanics' liens were secured.[146] In contrast to advances elsewhere, however, the cumbersome amendment procedure devised in 1835 was simply carried over: A convention could be called by a two-thirds vote of each house, or a specific amendment could be proposed by the General Assembly if adopted by two successive sessions, with an intervening election, by majorities of three-fifths and two-thirds, respectively.[147]

Ratification of the 1868 Constitution and of the Fourteenth Amendment to the U.S. Constitution earned North Carolina readmission to representation in Congress and the end of Reconstruction.[148] When prewar political forces reemerged in 1870 in the form of the Conservative party and won control of the General Assembly, they immediately proposed a convention to replace the hated Carpetbagger Constitution.[149] Although not required to submit the issue to the voters, they did so—and suffered an embarrassing defeat.[150] The assemblymen were then forced to resort to the process for individual amendments.

In 1873 eight amendments were submitted to the voters[151] and approved by wide margins.[152] Despite the preceding political furor, some of the changes were relatively minor, such as eliminating the state census[153] and amending the dual-office-holding provision.[154] Retrenching the commitments of 1868, other amendments abolished the office of superintendent of public works[155] and terminated the code commission,[156] leaving unfulfilled the promise of an up-to-date law code for the state. In addition, the amendments restored some familiar arrangements obliterated in 1868: biennial legislative sessions,[157] authorized in 1835, and legislative control over the University of North Carolina,[158] secured by statute in the wake of the judicial decision in Trustees of the University of North Carolina

v. Foy (1805). Finally, the General Assembly gained enhanced authority to exempt personal property from taxation,[159] and the prohibition against repudiation of the state debt was repealed.[160] Indeed, Henry G. Connor, prominent politician and jurist of the next generation, remembered the 1873 amendments as primarily economic, dealing "chiefly with the question of taxation which, by reason of the immense debt which had been created by the Convention and the Legislature (1868–9), would without such amendments have been a grievous burden to the people."[161]

In 1875 the General Assembly called a constitutional convention,[162] this time not risking defeat by submitting the question to the voters. The convention, the last in the state's history, was supposedly limited by legislation in the topics it could consider, being forbidden, for example, to alter the section providing for *ad valorem* taxation of property. As in 1835, an oath was required to secure compliance, and, again as in 1835, after a protest[163] the oath was finally taken and its terms observed, so the question of the validity of such limitations remains unanswered. The strength of the state Republican party was still such that it elected as many delegates as the Conservatives (shortly to be renamed Democrats), leaving the deciding votes to a few independents.[164] The convention proposed and the voters in 1876 ratified a set of thirty amendments affecting no less than thirty-six sections of the 1868 Constitution.[165]

Given the sheer number of changes and perhaps as well the desire on the part of the elite to signal the end of Reconstruction, the practice arose of referring to the amended 1868 Constitution as the "Constitution of 1876,"[166] but in legal circles it was always recognized that the amendments did not result, juridically speaking, in an altogether new instrument. The terminology does indicate, however, the new practice of incorporating amendments into the text of the constitution, rather than merely appending them, as had been done earlier. The effect has been to make the constitution appear to be a sort of super-statute, alterable only by extraordinary means, rather than a repository of fundamental principles and an outline of institutional structures. The excessive detail of some provisions, such as the minimum length of the public school term, has contributed to the impression.

The principal aim of the 1876 amendments was to restore to the General Assembly more of the power it had lost. The elective offices created in 1868 had lessened legislative control over the executive and judicial branches; the General Assembly now reclaimed the power to provide for legislative appointments to executive offices created by statute.[167] Although direct election of judges was retained, the amendments reduced the number of supreme court justices from five to three[168] and restored to the legislature the power to create new courts and to determine the jurisdiction of all lower courts,[169] a power that resulted over time in an unduly complicated judicial system.

In addition, the General Assembly regained its former power over local government. By simple legislative enactment it could resume the power to appoint township and county officers.[170] The purpose of this amendment, as was well understood, was to block control of local government in the eastern counties by blacks who were in the majority there.[171] William S. Powell, North Carolina historian, has tartly observed: " 'Home rule' was restored, Democrats said. Nevertheless, under acts of the 1877 General Assembly, elected county govern-ment was abolished and local power was concentrated in appointed officials."[172]

The unsettled conditions in the aftermath of the Civil War and Reconstruction were reflected in amendments to Article I, the Declaration of Rights, denouncing "secret political societies" and the practice of carrying concealed weapons.[173] The enlightened article on penal institutions was hopelessly compromised by an amendment authorizing "convict labor on public works, or highways, or other labor for public benefit"[174]—that is, the notorious "chain gangs" that became a sinister feature of the Southern landscape. Still worse, the same amendment authorized "farming out," the system by which convicts were rented out for industrial as well as agricultural labor, a practice referred to years later in *Gone with the Wind* by Margaret Mitchell: After the Civil War Scarlett O'Hara eagerly hired convicts to work in her sawmill because she could get them, as she said, "for next to nothing and feed them dirt cheap."[175] Race had been an explicit part of North Carolina's constitution from 1835 to 1868. After a brief eclipse it reappeared in 1876 in two amendments, the first providing for racially segregated schooling[176] ("separate but equal"), the second banning interracial marriages.[177]

In other amendments the process of constitutional change was simplified, perhaps in response to the Conservatives' unhappy experience with the old system. In place of the cumbersome machinery of 1835, carried over in 1868, an amendment provided that the General Assembly by a three-fifths vote of each house could submit an amendment to the voters at the next election.[178] This became the preferred means of constitutional change for the next century and was eventually used for the adoption of the 1971 Constitution.

Another amendment fixed in the constitution for the first time the rate of legislative compensation: four dollars a day for a sixty-day session (thereafter without pay).[179] Over the years voters faced frequent proposals to authorize increases, and amendments were approved in 1927,[180] 1949,[181] and 1955.[182] Only in 1967 were the members of the General Assembly once again trusted with authority to set their own compensation,[183] a sensible provision carried over into the 1971 Constitution.[184]

The amendments of 1876 brought a certain quietude to North Carolina con-stitutional history. As constitutional scholar John L. Sanders has observed: "With the passage of time and amendments, the attitude towards the Constitution of 1868 had changed from resentment to a reverence so great that until the second third of the twentieth century, amendments were very difficult to obtain."[185] In the last quarter of the nineteenth century only four amendments were submitted to the voters, and one of these failed to be ratified.[186] Retreating still further from Tourgée's humanitarian program, voters in 1880 amended the constitutional command that the General Assembly "shall provide" for the care of deaf mutes, the blind, and the insane[187] to read that the General Assembly *may* so provide.[188]

As part of the state's ongoing struggle with its creditors, the constitution was also amended in 1880 to prohibit payment of the debt contracted by the Reconstruction regime and to reduce payments on the balance of the state debt.[189] By this amendment, state bonds with a face value of more than $12 million and accrued interest of $7 million were repudiated.[190] In 1888 the overworked state supreme court was again enlarged to five members.[191]

During the first third of the twentieth century North Carolinians became even more reluctant to tamper with the state's basic law, ratifying only fifteen of thirty-five proposed amendments.[192] Undoubtedly, the most important to succeed in those years was the first: the suffrage amendment of 1900 which added a literacy test and a poll tax requirement for voting.[193] (The poll tax requirement was subsequently abolished in 1920,[194] something not required by the U.S. Constitution until the ratification of the Twenty-Fourth Amendment in 1964; the literacy test remains in the constitution to this day,[195] although it is of no practical effect because of federal civil rights legislation.[196]) Copied from an earlier scheme developed in Louisiana, the literacy test included a "grandfather clause" to protect illiterate white male voters: Whether one was literate or not, he was entitled to vote if he or a lineal ancestor—the amendment did not actually specify a "grandfather"—had been qualified to vote on January 1, 1867, a date artfully chosen. As we have seen, an 1835 amendment still in effect on that date had provided that "No free Negro, free mulatto, or free person of mixed blood, descended from Negro ancestors to the fourth generation inclusive (though one ancestor of each generation may have been a white person) shall vote for members of the Senate or House of Commons."[197]

To take advantage of the grandfather clause, illiterate white men had to register by December 1, 1908; white males coming of age thereafter would have to pass the literacy test to qualify to vote. It has often been observed that state politicians' enthusiasm for "universal education" (sometimes creating an oxymoron when explicitly qualified by "of the white children") dates to this era.[198] Although in 1915 the U.S. Supreme Court ruled grandfather clauses unconstitutional,[199] North Carolina's had by then safely accomplished its mission. As later described by Henry G. Connor, one of the architects of the suffrage amendment:[200] "With the qualification imposed by this amendment the political power of the State practically passed to the white voters—certainly for the present generation."[201] The racial republic expressly avowed in 1835 was thus recreated by other means.

Ironically at the very moment of this retreat from democratic principles, the state Democratic party began to select nominees for U.S. senator by primary election, the winners being then formally chosen by the General Assembly.[202] When the Seventeenth Amendment to the U.S. Constitution provided for the direct election of senators in 1913, the process was made official. Just as in 1835, white males gained political power as black males were shut out.

Votes for women came with the ratification of the Nineteenth Amendment to the U.S. Constitution in 1920, with no thanks to the North Carolina General Assembly. In the 1868 convention, as we have seen, it was taken for granted that women and those under age could not vote, and the minority had argued from this premise against votes for black men. In 1897 a women's suffrage bill was introduced in the General Assembly, but was derisively referred to the committee on insane asylums.[203] The legislature even refused the opportunity provided by a special session in 1920 to add the last necessary vote in favor of the Nineteenth Amendment. Instead, assemblymen joined in a cowardly "round robin" petition—signed in a circle so that no one would know whose name was put down first—urging the Tennessee General Assembly, also considering the amendment, not to ratify it.[204]

Without its membership in the federal Union, North Carolina would apparently have long delayed advancing beyond universal (white) adult manhood suffrage. In 1946 the state constitution belatedly registered the new reality when an amendment deleted the superseded sexual qualification for voting, part of a thoroughgoing editorial revision replacing masculine with neuter nouns, designed in general to make the constitution "equally applicable to men and women" and in particular to admit women to jury service.[205] In 1971, long after the triumph of the democratic principle, the General Assembly added its token support to the Nineteenth Amendment.[206]

As the large issues of constitutionalism shifted to the national level, North Carolina constitutional development became increasingly preoccupied with details. In 1916, in an effort to concentrate the minds of legislators on statewide concerns, the General Assembly was prohibited from enacting special legislation on a long list of subjects, mostly matters of local government.[207] The finance article was revised in 1920, eliminating the mandatory equation between poll and property taxes and replacing it with maximum rates on each.[208] The mandatory minimum school term was lengthened from four to six months in 1918,[209] a change that had been rejected only four years earlier.[210]

In the second third of the twentieth century North Carolinians displayed a far greater willingness to accept constitutional change. Between 1933 and 1968 only seven of forty-nine proposed amendments were rejected by the voters.[211] Again, the changes were matters of detail, rather than of broad constitutional principle: They authorized the classification of property for taxation[212] and strengthened limitations on the state debt[213]; authorized the General Assembly to enlarge the supreme court from five to seven justices[214] and to create a Department of Justice[215]; enlarged the Council of State to include the commissioners of agriculture, labor, and insurance;[216] created an appointive State Board of Education;[217] and transferred the governor's power to assign judges to the chief justice[218] and his parole power to a Board of Paroles (now the Parole Commission).[219] In 1962 an amendment completely rewrote the judiciary article,[220] an early installment of thoroughgoing constitutional revision.

Two amendments were adopted in this period in response to U.S. Supreme Court decisions, further indications of the reactive mode that characterized the state's relationship with the federal government. Responding to the ruling in 1954 in Brown v. Board of Education which required the desegregation of public

schools, the voters authorized the closing of schools on a local option basis and
the payment of educational expense grants,[221] an option that was in fact never
exercised[222] and was later, in a further Supreme Court decision concerning a
similar law in another state, declared unconstitutional.[223] In the next decade, in
response to the 1962 decision in Baker v. Carr, requiring one person–one vote,
the apportionment provisions of the state constitution were rewritten to reflect
the new federal requirements,[224] a change that particularly affected apportionment
of the state house of representatives.

Merely as a matter of housekeeping, redrawing the state constitution in order
to consolidate the changes and eliminate anachronisms became politically at-
tractive. As early as 1933 a new constitution had been drafted,[225] although it
never reached the voters because of a technicality;[226] a comprehensive reform
effort in 1959 came to grief in the General Assembly.[227] By the late 1960s the
time seemed ripe for another try, and the North Carolina state bar, acting on the
suggestion of the governor, formed a commission to draft a new constitution.

THE CONSTITUTION OF 1971

Some of the changes are substantive, but none is calculated to impair any present right
of the individual citizen or to bring about any fundamental change in the power of state
and local government or the distribution of that power.[228]

In 1971 North Carolina was not a "shipwrecked" society, either from revolution or civil war; quite the opposite, the state was experiencing an era of
prosperity. Many of its social problems, even the grievous one of race, looked
more likely to be resolved than ever before. The 1971 Constitution, the state's
third, was not therefore a product of haste and social turmoil. It was instead a
good-government measure, long matured and carefully crafted by the state's
lawyers and politicians, designed to consolidate and conserve the best features
of the past, not to break with it. The State Constitution Study Commission,
whose report is quoted above, clearly avowed its non-revolutionary character.
Unlike its two predecessors, the latest constitution was not drafted by elected
representatives; prepared by experts, it was referred to the General Assembly,
which then presented it to the voters.[229] Although an entirely new instrument,
it was routed through the process normally used for piecemeal change.

The text of the new frame of government was that of the 1868 Constitution
as amended, subjected to rigorous editorial revision. The organization into four-
teen articles was retained, although the total number of sections was significantly
reduced. A number of non-controversial changes were introduced; the minimum
school term, for example, was lengthened from six months (set in 1918) to nine
months,[230] where it had in fact been fixed by statute since 1943.[231] The section
on amendment by constitutional convention was clarified by authorizing the
General Assembly to propose limitations on the convention which, if adopted

by the voters, would be binding;[232] no longer would the legislature have to rely on the oaths of the delegates as in 1835 and 1875.

Fundamental reforms were left to the ordinary amendment process; indeed, five amendments were approved by the voters at the same election that ratified the new constitution.[233] Of these, the most important was an amendment concerning state finance, of particular significance for local government.[234] A further amendment assigned the income from escheats to a special fund providing scholarships for state university students.[235] For two centuries, ever since a 1794 statute accompanying the charter of the University of North Carolina, escheats had provided a source of revenue for the university; now that the university received regular appropriations from the state, the income from escheats was less needed, and, of course, giving the money to needy students was, so to speak, "keeping it in the family."

Since 1971, amendments have continued to accumulate. During the period from 1972 to 1992, twenty-eight amendments have been proposed to the voters, of which twenty-two have been adopted[236]—a sign that the state's constitutional conservatism, from which the first two constitutions benefited, is wearing thin. On the very day the new constitution became effective, its provision limiting the franchise to persons twenty-one years of age or older[237] was rendered obsolete by the ratification of the Twenty-Sixth Amendment to the U.S. Constitution, enfranchising those eighteen and over. In short order the state constitution caught up with the Twenty-Sixth Amendment,[238] as it had earlier, but more slowly, caught up with the Nineteenth. In 1977 a popular politician secured an amendment permitting the governor to serve two consecutive terms[239]—a privilege of which he promptly took advantage. The ultimate prize, the gubernatorial veto, continued, however, to elude the state's chief executive. In 1977, too, the legislature's power of the purse was curtailed: The state's longstanding commitment to a balanced budget was reinforced by a constitutional amendment empowering the governor to effect "necessary economies" in order to prevent expenditures from exceeding revenues.[240]

Like its two predecessors, the 1971 Constitution includes the bold declaration that "all political power is vested in and derived from the people,"[241] yet we have seen the changing realities of popular sovereignty over two centuries: from tax-paying freemen (1776), to white male taxpayers (1835), to all males twenty-one and older (1868), to all males twenty-one or older who passed a literacy test or were enfranchised by the grandfather clause (1900), to all persons twenty-one or older (1920), and finally to all persons eighteen and over (1971). The fundamental principle remains the same, but its application has changed dramatically over time. It is now hard to imagine any retreat from universal suffrage; the racial disfranchisements of 1835 and 1900 would doubtless today fall foul of the U.S. Constitution. Yet it is equally difficult to foresee further advances of the democratic principle.

From 1776 until the present, North Carolina constitutions have also unequivocally declared the principle of separation of powers: "The legislative, executive, and supreme judicial powers shall be forever separate and distinct from each other."[242] As with popular sovereignty, this principle, too, has had its changing applications. If the legislative branch was separate from the other two branches in the first constitution, it was only in the Orwellian sense of being "more separate" than the others. As we have seen, the General Assembly elected all executive and judicial officers; the first and for long the only exception came in 1835 when the governor became popularly elected. In 1868 appeared the long ballot and clouds of elective officials, executive, judicial, and local. The governor gained in constitutional power and benefited politically from a lengthened term. In the years following Reconstruction, however, the General Assembly regained the initiative and recovered parts of its lost power. Over the years the lines have wavered, but the legislative power continues to preponderate.

What the effects of the long ballot have been and whether it actually increased popular sovereignty and strengthened separation of powers are difficult questions. One effect, at least, was soon apparent. Speaking in 1889 on the history of the state supreme court, Kemp P. Battle, president of the University of North Carolina, observed: "All the judges as a rule belong to the same political party, whereas the old Court had generally representatives of the two leading parties."[243] The same could be said of the other newly elected officers, as could Battle's candid recognition that the effect had been to transfer the choice from the General Assembly to the party nominating conventions. What was still new when Battle spoke became settled practice in later years: The suffrage amendment in 1900 clinched one-party rule in the state for most of the twentieth century.[244] Although the short ballot has been commended by experts for reasons of efficiency and accountability,[245] it is the recent prospect of partisan judicial elections that has prompted calls for a return to the practice of having judges chosen by another branch—this time, significantly, by the governor with the "advice and consent" of the General Assembly.[246] Such a change, if made, would raise in most minds no serious questions of constitutional conflict with the fundamental principles of popular sovereignty and separation of powers, just as the gubernatorial veto, if conceded, would doubtless be immune from challenge on that score. The reality is that these fundamental principles are general guidelines only and not detailed blueprints.

Just as North Carolina lost power to the federal government as a result of the defeat in the Civil War and the ratification of the Reconstruction amendments, so the General Assembly lost power, not just to the other branches of state government, but also to the people. In his 1889 address Battle observed from close range the sea change that had occurred in 1868. The state's first constitution, he said, had been founded on the assumption that the General Assembly could be entrusted with powers "almost unlimited." Antebellum legislators "could tax any subject to any amount, and exempt any subject from any tax at all. They had boundless right to pledge the State credit." They had, in addition, "vast powers in the control of the other departments of government" and "full discretion as to nearly all subjects of legislation." By contrast, the 1868 Constitution was founded on the assumption that "the representatives may be untrustworthy." This explains, Battle pointed out, "the limitations on the taxing power, and on the power of pledging the State credit," as well as the many provisions declaring "what the General Assembly must do, what it may do, and what it may or may not do," provisions that "seem properly to belong to the statute books, to be modified or amended whenever the interests of the people require."[247] States other than North Carolina had lost their revolutionary confidence in the legislature by the mid-nineteenth century, but in Southern states such as North Carolina the displacement of the elite was more dramatic.

Patterns established more than a century ago continue to be discernible in the 1971 Constitution. Although the legislators have regained some of their discretionary power—they recovered, as we have seen, the power to set their own wages in 1968—they remain far from the "almost unlimited" powers of their predecessors under the state's first constitution. The taste for repeated constitutional amendment acquired during the middle of the twentieth century shows little sign of abating: The 1776 Constitution was amended only three times in eighty-five years; its modern successor has more than once equaled or exceeded that in a single year, although admittedly not all the amendments together have rivaled the extensive changes adopted in 1835. Government has certainly become far more complex than it was in the eighteenth century, and the pace of change has greatly quickened, but that alone does not explain the modern fondness for constitutional amendment. In fact, the process has become a complicated version of the initiative or referendum, a means by which democracy occasionally becomes direct, rather than representative—with the people legislating for themselves, rather than through delegates.

Over the centuries, by far the most stable provisions of North Carolina's organic law have been those safeguards of due process expressed in the declaration of rights, now Article I. Gleaned from English tradition, they have (among other things) prohibited excessive bail or fines and cruel or unusual punishments; they have specifically guaranteed trial by jury and have generally proclaimed the rule of law ("law of the land"). Unlike the sweeping fundamental principles of popular sovereignty and separation of powers, these provisions have over the years been given specific content by the courts; indeed, they empower the state courts to provide protections going even beyond those secured by the U.S. Constitution.[248] Such clauses have become the hallmark of American constitutionalism. Perhaps they suggested the idea of giving other policy statements constitutional status, such as the sections in the 1776 Constitution calling for public schools and the regulation of entails or the section in the 1868 Constitution calling for the codification of state law. Of course, the nearer such sections came to outright legislation, the more frequent became the need for amendments, as political and social realities changed. The minimum public school term, set at four months in the 1868 Constitution, was lengthened to six months by amendment in 1918 and finally reached nine months in the 1971 Constitution. Provisions such as this one are undoubtedly benign; others such as the constitutional determination of legislative compensation from 1876 to 1968 are mere nuisances.

There is reason for concern, however, if too frequent amendments so habituate voters to constitutional change that they someday, in the grip of temporary passion or fear, tamper with the fundamental guarantees of due process. Of course, the U.S. Constitution, far more immune to change, would continue to provide protection, but only to the extent recognized by the justices of the U.S. Supreme Court. The best guarantee of North Carolinians' basic rights must ever be what it has always been: not only a balanced institutional arrangement of government subject to wise restraints enforced when necessary by fearless judges, but above all a thoughtful and informed citizenry, conscious of its constitutional history and zealous to preserve the best for posterity.

NOTES

1. William L. Saunders, ed., *The Colonial Records of North Carolina* (Raleigh: Josephus Daniels, 1890), vol. 10, 918 (hereafter cited as *Colonial Records*).

2. *Ibid.*, 870a–870h.

3. Letter from William Hooper to Fifth Provincial Congress (October 26, 1776), reprinted in *ibid.*, 862–70. For a tabular comparison of the North Carolina Declaration of Rights with the earlier declarations of Maryland, Pennsylvania, and Virginia, see John V. Orth, "North Carolina Constitutional History," *North Carolina Law Review* 70 (1992): 1797–1802.

4. Letter from John Adams to William Hooper (*ante* March 27, 1776), reprinted in Robert J. Taylor, ed., *Papers of John Adams* (Cambridge: Harvard University Press, 1979), vol. 4, 73–78; letter from John Adams to John Penn (*ante* March 27, 1776), reprinted in *ibid.*, 78–84. The letters formed the basis for Adams's later pamphlet, "Thoughts on Government: Applicable to the Present State of the American Colonies. In a Letter from a Gentleman to His Friend," reprinted in *ibid.*, 86–93.

5. *Colonial Records* 10: 973. The text may be found in Walter Clark, ed., *The State Records of North Carolina* (Goldsboro: Nash Brothers, 1904), vol. 23, 977 (hereafter cited as *State Records*).

6. *Colonial Records* 10: 974; *State Records* 23: 980.

7. N.C. Const. of 1776, § 44.

8. *Colonial Records* 10: 696 (misnumbered 996). For a political analysis of this election, see Robert L. Ganyard, "Radicals and Conservatives in Revolutionary North Carolina: A Point at Issue, The October Election, 1776," *William and Mary Quarterly* 24 (1967): 585.

9. N.C. Const. of 1776, Declaration of Rights, § 1.

10. N.C. Const. of 1776, § 7.

11. *Id.* § 8.

12. *Id.* § 5.

13. *Id.* § 6.

14. *Id.* § 15. The pound sterling, the British medium of exchange, remained in circulation in North Carolina for many years after the Revolution. From time to time the legislature set an exchange rate for dollars and pounds. See William S. Powell, *North*

Carolina Through Four Centuries (Chapel Hill: University of North Carolina Press, 1989), 178.

15. N.C. Const. of 1776, Declaration of Rights, § 4.

16. N.C. Const. of 1776, § 15.

17. *Id.* § 16.

18. *Id.* § 22.

19. *Id.* § 24 (three-year term).

20. *Id.* § 13 (good behavior tenure). The attorney general enjoyed the same tenure as the judges, apparently on the theory that he was an officer of the court.

21. *Id.* (good behavior tenure).

22. *Id.* § 14.

23. *The Federalist*, No. 47 (James Madison), ed. Benjamin Fletcher Wright (Cambridge: Harvard University Press, 1966), 339, 342.

24. N.C. Const. of 1776, § 15.

25. *Id.* § 33.

26. *Id.* §§ 18 (calling out the militia), 19 (imposing embargoes), 20 (filling vacancies).

27. *Id.* § 11.

28. N.C. Const. of 1776, Declaration of Rights, § 19.

29. N.C. Const. of 1776, § 34. On the institution disestablished by this section, see Paul Conkin, "The Church Establishment in North Carolina, 1765–1776," *North Carolina Historical Review* 32 (1955): 1–30.

30. N.C. Const. of 1776, § 31.

31. *Id.* § 32.

32. Henry G. Connor, Introduction to *The Constitution of the State of North Carolina Annotated* by Henry G. Connor and Joseph B. Cheshire, Jr. (Raleigh: Edwards & Broughton, 1911), xxvii.

33. N.C. Const. of 1776, § 10.

34. See Leon Huhner, "Religious Liberty in North Carolina with Special Reference to the Jews," in *Publications of the American Jewish Historical Society*, no. 16 (1907): 37–71.

35. See John Bartlett, ed., *Familiar Quotations*, 13th ed. (Boston: Little, Brown & Co., 1955), 703 (attributed to Timothy J. Campbell).

36. Amend. 1835, art. IV, § 2.

37. N.C. Const. of 1776, Declaration of Rights, § 1.

38. Va. Const. of 1776, Declaration of Rights, § 2.

39. Md. Const. of 1776, Declaration of Rights, § 6.

40. Pa. Const. of 1776, Declaration of Rights, § 2.

41. N.C. Const. of 1776, Declaration of Rights, § 10.

42. Va. Const. of 1776, Declaration of Rights, § 9.

43. Md. Const. of 1776, Declaration of Rights, § 22.

44. 1 W. & M., st. 2, ch. 2, § I, cl. 10 (1689).

45. N.C. Const. of 1776, Declaration of Rights, § 12.

46. Md. Const. of 1776, Declaration of Rights, § 21.

47. Magna Carta, § 39 (1215).

48. N.C. Const. of 1776, § 41. Compare Pa. Const. of 1776, § 44.

49. Powell, *North Carolina*, 216.

50. Act of January 8, 1839, ch. 8, 1838–39 N.C. Pub. Laws 12.

51. Act of 1789, ch. 20, reprinted in *State Records* 25: 21.

52. Act of 1789, ch. 21, § 2, reprinted in *State Records* 25: 25. See also Act of 1794, ch. 405, § 1, reprinted in Henry Potter, ed., *Laws of North Carolina* (Raleigh: J. Gales, 1821), vol. 1, 738.

The *State Records* cease reprinting state statutes with the laws of 1790. Thereafter reference is made to Henry Potter's edition of the laws in force from 1715 to 1820, commissioned by the General Assembly and known to generations of North Carolina lawyers as Potter's Revisal. The chapter numbers in the *State Records* differ from those in Potter's Revisal because the former, following modern practice, assigns numbers beginning anew with the first act of each session, while the latter assigns numbers in sequence beginning with the first act of the 1715 session.

53. N.C. Const. of 1776, § 43. Compare Pa. Const. of 1776, § 37. See also N.C. Const. of 1776, Declaration of Rights, § 23 ("Perpetuities . . . ought not to be allowed").

54. See John V. Orth, "Does the Fee Tail Exist in North Carolina?" *Wake Forest Law Review* 23 (1988): 767–95.

55. Act of 1784, ch. 22, § 5, reprinted in *State Records* 24: 574.

56. Connor, Introduction, xxxviii.

57. N.C. Const. of 1776, Declaration of Rights, § 14.

58. Act of December 29, 1785, ch. 7, reprinted in *State Records* 24: 730.

59. Act of 1805, ch. 678, reprinted in Potter, ed., *Laws* 2: 1041.

60. Amend. 1873, VI. See Act of January 19, 1872, ch. 53, 1871–72 N.C. Pub. Laws 81; Act of February 24, 1873, ch. 86, 1872–73 N.C. Pub. Laws 116. See also Act of March 3, 1873, ch. 153, 1872–73 N.C. Pub. Laws 249.

61. N.C. Const. of 1776, § 2.

62. *Id.* § 3.

63. See Mary P. Smith, "Borough Representation in North Carolina," *North Carolina Historical Review* 7 (1930): 177–91.

64. N.C. Const. of 1776, § 3.

65. *State Records* 22: 47–49. See Louise I. Trenholme, *The Ratification of the Federal Constitution in North Carolina* (New York: Columbia University Press, 1932); Albert Ray Newsome, "North Carolina's Ratification of the Federal Constitution," *North Carolina Historical Review* 17 (1940): 287–301. More recent views may be found in Walter F. Pratt, Jr., "Law and the Experience of Politics in Late Eighteenth-Century North Carolina: North Carolina Considers the Constitution," *Wake Forest Law Review* 22 (1987): 577–605; John C. Cavanagh, *Decision at Fayetteville: The North Carolina Ratification Convention and General Assembly of 1789* (Raleigh: North Carolina Department of Cultural Resources, 1989).

66. Amend. 1789, reprinted in *State Records* 22: 50–53.

67. Act of January 6, 1835, ch. 1, 1834–35 N.C. Pub. Laws 3; Act of January 9, 1835, ch. 2, 1834–35 N.C. Pub. Laws 6.

68. *Proceedings and Debates of the Convention of North-Carolina, Called to Amend the Constitution of the State, Which Assembled at Raleigh, June 4, 1835* (Raleigh: Joseph Gales & Son, 1836), 4–8 (hereafter cited as *Proceedings and Debates, 1835*). The amendments are reprinted in an appendix, pp. 418–24.

69. Amend. 1835, art. I, § 1, cl. 1.

70. *Id.* cl. 2.

71. Compare *id.* with U.S. Const. art. I, § 2, cl. 3.

72. Amend. 1835, art. I, § 4, cl. 7.

73. E.g., Act of 1715, ch. 10, § 5 (repealed by His Majesty's Order), reprinted in *State Records* 23: 12.

74. *Proceedings and Debates, 1835*, 65, 70, 80. See John Hope Franklin, *The Free Negro in North Carolina, 1790–1860* (Chapel Hill: University of North Carolina Press, 1943), 105–20.

75. *Proceedings and Debates, 1835*, 80.

76. Amend. 1835, art. I, § 3, cl. 3.

77. *Id.* cl. 2.

78. *Id.* cl. 1.

79. See Harold J. Counihan, "The North Carolina Constitutional Convention of 1835: A Study in Jacksonian Democracy," *North Carolina Historical Review* 46 (1969): 348.

80. Amend. 1835, art. II, cl. 1.

81. *Id.* cl. 2. In addition to lengthening the governor's term, the 1835 amendments altered the terms of two other executive officers: The secretary of state's term was reduced from three years to two, *id.* art. I, § 4, cl. 7; the attorney general's tenure was changed from "good behavior" to a four-year term, *id.* art. III, § 4.

82. *Proceedings and Debates, 1835*, 335.

83. Amend. 1835, art. IV, § 1, cl. 1.

84. *Id.* cl. 2.

85. *Id.* § 2.

86. The election returns in *Proceedings and Debates, 1835*, facing page 424, are analyzed in Counihan, "The North Carolina Constitutional Convention of 1835," 361.

87. See Thomas E. Jeffrey, " 'Free Suffrage' Revisited: Party Politics and Constitutional Reform in Antebellum North Carolina," *North Carolina Historical Review* 59 (1982): 24–48.

88. Amend. 1857. See Act of February 3, 1855, ch. 7, 1854–55 N.C. Pub. Laws 22; Act of December 11, 1856, ch. 12, 1856–57 N.C. Pub. Laws 12. See also Act of January 8, 1857, ch. 13, 1856–57 N.C. Pub. Laws 13. Election returns are in R.D.W. Connor, ed., *A Manual of North Carolina, 1913* (Raleigh: E. M. Uzzell & Co., 1913), 1010–12 (hereafter cited as *North Carolina Manual, 1913*).

89. Jeffrey, " 'Free Suffrage,' " 24.

90. Reprinted in MariJo Buhle and Paul Buhle, eds., *The Concise History of Woman Suffrage* (Urbana: University of Illinois Press, 1978), 91–98.

91. Act of May 1, 1861, ch. 9, 1860–61 N.C. Pub. Laws (1st Extra Sess.), 100.

92. Powell, *North Carolina*, 348.

93. See *Ordinances and Resolutions Passed by the State Convention of North Carolina at Its Several Sessions in 1861–62* (Raleigh: John W. Syme, 1862), 174–75 (hereafter sited as *Ordinances, 1861–62*).

94. Ord. 1861–62, VI, in *ibid.*, 32–33.

95. Powell, *North Carolina*, 252, 339.

96. Ord. 1861–62, IX, in *Ordinances, 1861–62*, 56.

97. Proclamation of President Andrew Johnson (May 29, 1865), in *Messages and Papers of the Presidents, 1789–1897*, ed. James D. Richardson (Washington, D.C.: Government Printing Office, 1896–99), vol. 6, 312.

98. *Executive Documents. Convention, Session 1865. Constitution of North-Carolina, with Amendments, and Ordinances and Resolutions Passed by the Convention, Session, 1865* (Raleigh: Cannon & Holden, 1865), 39–40 (pagination begins anew with each document).

99. "N.C. Const. of 1866, art. II, § 3." See *Ordinances and Resolutions Passed by the North Carolina State Convention, Second Session, 1866* (Raleigh: W. W. Holden & Son, 1866).

100. *Id.* "art. V, § 10."

101. *Id.* "art. II, § 7" (senators shall possess "not less than three hundred acres of land in fee; or a freehold of not less value than one thousand dollars"); *id.* "§ 8" (representative in house of commons shall possess "a freehold of one hundred acres of land, or the value of three hundred dollars"); *id.* "art. III, § 2" (governor shall possess "a freehold in lands and tenements of the value of two thousand dollars").

102. Election returns are in Connor, ed., *North Carolina Manual, 1913*, 1016–18.

103. Act of March 2, 1867, ch. 153, 14 Stat. 428; Act of March 23, 1867, ch. 6, 15 Stat. 2; Act of July 19, 1867, ch. 30, 15 Stat. 14; Act of March 11, 1868, ch. 25, 15 Stat. 41.

104. Election returns are in *Journal of the Constitutional Convention of the State of North-Carolina, at Its Session 1868* (Raleigh: Joseph W. Holden, 1868), 114–18 (hereafter cited as *Journal of the Constitutional Convention, 1868*). The text of the 1868 Constitution is in *ibid.*, 3–39.

105. Powell, *North Carolina*, 392.

106. Election returns are in Connor, ed., *North Carolina Manual, 1913*, 1016–18.

107. See Francis Newton Thorpe, ed., *The Federal and State Constitutions* (Washington, D.C.: Government Printing Office, 1909), vol. 5, 2787–94 (1776 Const.), 2800–22 (1868 Const.).

108. N.C. Const. of 1868, preamble.

109. *Id.* art. I, § 1.

110. *Id.* § 4.

111. *Id.* § 5.

112. *Id.* § 6.

113. *Id.* § 33.

114. *Id.* § 21.

115. 31 Car. 2, ch. 2 (1679). See "Report of the Commissioners Appointed by an Act of the Legislature of 1817, To Revise the Laws of North-Carolina," in Potter, ed., *Laws* 1: v–vi.

116. N.C. Const. of 1868, art. I, § 22.

117. *Id.* art. II, § 5.

118. *Id.* § 7.

119. *Id.* art. III, § 1.

120. *Id.* art. II, § 21; art. III, § 11.

121. *Id.* art. IV, §§ 5–6.

122. Powell, *North Carolina*, 400. See *Trial of William W. Holden* (Raleigh: Sentinel Printing Office, 1871), 3 vols.

123. Acts of 1818, ch. 962–63, in Potter, ed., *Laws* 2: 1433.

124. N.C. Const. of 1868, art. IV, § 8.

125. *Id.* § 26. For an edited transcript of the debate concerning judicial selection, see John V. Orth, "Tuesday, February 11, 1868: The Day North Carolina Chose Direct Election of Judges," *North Carolina Law Review* 70 (1992): 1825–51.

126. N.C. Const. of 1868, art. VII, §§ 3–4.

127. *Id.* § 5.

128. *Id.* art. VI, § 1.

129. *Journal of the Constitutional Convention, 1868*, 236.

130. N.C. Const. of 1868, art. IV, § 1.

131. *Id.* § 2; Ordinance of March 13, 1868, ch. 41, in *Journal of the Constitutional Convention, 1868*, 79.

132. N.C. Const. of 1868, art. IV, § 3.

133. Otto H. Olsen, *Carpetbagger's Crusade: The Life of Albion Winegar Tourgée* (Baltimore: Johns Hopkins University Press, 1965).

134. N.C. Const. of 1868, art. XI, § 2.

135. *Id.* art. XIV, § 2.

136. *Id.* art. VI, § 5.

137. Proceedings and Debates of the 1868 Constitutional Convention (February 18, 1868), reported in *North Carolina Standard*, February 26, 1868.

138. N.C. Const. of 1868, art. V, §§ 1 and 3.

139. *Id.* §§ 4–5.

140. *Id.* art. I, § 6; art. V, § 4.

141. *Id.* art. V, §§ 1 and 7.

142. University Railroad v. Holden, 63 N.C. 410, 427 (1869) (Rodman, J.).

143. N.C. Const. of 1868, art. IX, § 2.

144. *Id.* art. XI, § 10.

145. *Id.* art. X, § 6.

146. *Id.* art. XIV, § 4.

147. *Id.* art. XIII.

148. Act of June 25, 1868, ch. 70, 15 Stat. 73.

149. Act of February 8, 1870, ch. 63, 1870–71 N.C. Pub. Laws 119; Act of April 3, 1870, ch. 211, 1870–71 N.C. Pub. Laws 326.

150. For election totals, see John L. Sanders, "A Brief History of the Constitutions of North Carolina," in *North Carolina Government, 1585–1979: A Narrative and Statistical History*, ed. John L. Cheney, Jr. (Raleigh: North Carolina Department of the Secretary of State, 1981), 797.

151. Amend. 1873. See Act of January 19, 1872, ch. 53, 1871–72 N.C. Pub. Laws 81; (I) Act of February 24, 1873, ch. 81, 1872–73 N.C. Pub. Laws 111; (II) Act of February 24, 1873, ch. 82, 1872–73 N.C. Pub. Laws 112; (III) Act of February 24, 1873, ch. 83, 1872–73 N.C. Pub. Laws 113; (IV) Act of February 24, 1873, ch. 84, 1872–73 N.C. Pub. Laws 114; (V) Act of February 24, 1873, ch. 85, 1872–73 N.C. Pub. Laws 115; (VI) Act of February 24, 1873, ch. 86, 1872–73 N.C. Pub. Laws 116; (VII) Act of February 24, 1873, ch. 87, 1872–73 N.C. Pub. Laws 117; (VIII) Act of February 24, 1873, ch. 88, 1872–73 N.C. Pub. Laws 118. See also Act of March 3, 1873, ch. 153, 1872–73 N.C. Pub. Laws 249.

152. For election totals, see John L. Sanders and John F. Lomax, Jr., *Amendments to the Constitution of North Carolina, 1776–1989* (Chapel Hill, N.C.: Institute of Government, 1990), 2.

153. Amend. 1873, I.

154. *Id.* VIII.

155. *Id.* IV.

156. *Id.* VII.

157. *Id.* II.

158. *Id.* VI.

159. *Id.* III.

160. *Id.* V.

161. Connor, Introduction, xxxvi.

162. Act of March 19, 1875, ch. 222, 1874–75 N.C. Pub. Laws 303.

163. See *Journal of the Constitutional Convention of the State of North Carolina, Held in 1875* (Raleigh: Josiah Turner, 1875), 3–4.

164. Powell, *North Carolina*, 404.

165. See *Amendments to the Constitution of North Carolina, Proposed by the Constitutional Convention of 1875* (Raleigh: Josiah Turner, 1875), 5–27. For voting totals, see Sanders, "Brief History," 798.

166. See, e.g., Thorpe, ed., *Federal and State Constitutions* 5: 2822–43 ("Constitution of North Carolina—1876"); William F. Swindler, ed., *Sources and Documents of United States Constitutions* (Dobbs Ferry, N.Y.: Oceana Publications Inc., 1978), vol. 7, 443–48 ("Constitution of 1876").

167. Amend. 1875, IX (deleting phrase "and no such [executive] officer shall be appointed or elected by the General Assembly").

168. *Id.* XII.

169. *Id.* XI, XVII.

170. *Id.* XXV.

171. See Connor, Introduction, xxxvii.

172. Powell, *North Carolina*, 406 (referring to Act of February 27, 1877, ch. 141, 1876–77 N.C. Pub. Laws 226, providing for election of county commissioners by county justices of the peace who were appointed by the General Assembly).

173. Amend. 1875, I–II.

174. *Id.* XXVIII.

175. Margaret Mitchell, *Gone wth the Wind* (New York: Avon Books, 1936), 734. See generally Edward L. Ayers, *Vengeance and Justice: Crime and Punishment in the Nineteenth Century American South* (1984).

176. Amend. 1875, XXVI. See Frenise A. Logan, "Legal Status of Public School Education for Negroes in North Carolina, 1877–1894," *North Carolina Historical Review* 32 (1955): 346–57.

177. Amend. 1875, XXX.

178. *Id.* XXIX.

179. *Id.* VIII.

180. Amend. 1927, II (members $600; presiding officers $700). See Act of March 9, 1927, ch. 203, 1927 N.C. Pub. Laws 549. This amendment was ratified by the narrowest of margins: 147,946 votes for; 147,734 votes against. Election returns are in A. R. Newsome, ed., *A Manual of North Carolina, 1929* (Raleigh: N.C. Historical Commission, 1929), 413–14.

181. Amend. 1949, V (members $15 a day; presiding officers $20 a day—both up to ninety days). See Act of April 23, 1949, ch. 1267, 1949 N.C. Sess. Laws 1661. Election returns are in *A Manual of North Carolina, 1951* (Raleigh: Secretary of State, 1951), 244–47 (hereafter cited as *North Carolina Manual, 1951*).

182. Amend. 1955, I (compensated sessions extended to 120 days). See Act of May 20, 1955, ch. 1169, 1955 N.C. Sess. Laws 1163. Election returns are in *A Manual of North Carolina, 1957* (Raleigh: Secretary of State, 1957), 255–58 (hereafter cited as *North Carolina Manual, 1957*).

183. Amend. 1967, I. See Act of May 10, 1967, ch. 391, 1967 N.C. Sess. Laws 406.

Election returns are in *A Manual of North Carolina, 1969* (Raleigh: Secretary of State, 1969), 336–37 (hereafter cited as *North Carolina Manual, 1969*).

184. N.C. Const. of 1971, art. II, § 16.

185. Sanders, "Brief History," 798.

186. *Ibid.*

187. N.C. Const. of 1868, art. XI, § 10.

188. Amend. 1879, I. See Act of March 14, 1879, ch. 314, 1879 N.C. Pub. Laws 489. See also Act of March 14, 1879, ch. 254, 1879 N.C. Pub. Laws 421. For voting totals, see Sanders and Lomax, *Amendments*, 2.

189. Amend. 1879, II. See Act of March 14, 1879, ch. 268, 1879 N.C. Pub. Laws 436. For voting totals, see Sanders and Lomax, *Amendments*, 2.

190. Benjamin U. Ratchford, "The Adjustment of the North Carolina Public Debt, 1879–1883," *North Carolina Historical Review* 10 (1933): 166. See John V. Orth, "The Eleventh Amendment and the North Carolina State Debt," *North Carolina Law Review* 59 (1981): 747–66.

191. Amend. 1887. See Act of March 7, 1887, ch. 212, 1887 N.C. Pub. Laws 449. For voting totals, see Sanders and Lomax, *Amendments*, 2.

192. Sanders, "Brief History," 798. For a study of ten proposed amendments that were rejected by the voters in 1914, see Joseph F. Steelman, "Origins of the Campaign for Constitutional Reform in North Carolina, 1912–1913," *North Carolina Historical Review* 56 (1979): 396–418.

193. Amends. 1899–1900. See Act of February 21, 1899, ch. 218, 1899 N.C. Pub. Laws 341. See also Act of June 13, 1900, ch. 2, 1900 N.C. Pub. Laws 54. Election returns are in Connor, ed., *North Carolina Manual, 1913*, 1016–18.

194. Amend. 1919, V. See Act of March 5, 1919, ch. 129, 1919 N.C. Pub. Laws 305; Act of Aug. 26, 1920, ch. 93, 1920 Pub. Laws (Extra Sess.) 119. Election returns are in R.D.W. Connor, ed., *A Manual of North Carolina, 1921* (Raleigh: Edwards & Broughton Printing, 1921), 327–28 (hereafter cited as *North Carolina Manual, 1921*).

195. N.C. Const. of 1971, art. VI, § 4.

196. See Gaston County, N.C. v. United States, 395 U.S. 285 (1969) (upholding application of federal Voting Rights Act of 1965).

197. Amend. 1835, art. I, § 3, cl. 3.

198. Powell, *North Carolina*, 443.

199. Guinn v. United States, 238 U.S. 347 (1915) (Okla. Const.).

200. See William A. Mabry, " 'White Supremacy' and the North Carolina Suffrage Amendment," *North Carolina Historical Review* 13 (1936): 2–4.

201. Connor, Introduction, xxxvii.

202. Powell, *North Carolina*, 439 n. 1.

203. 1877 *N.C. Senate Journal* 295.

204. See A. Elizabeth Taylor, "The Woman Suffrage Movement in North Carolina," *North Carolina Historical Review* 38 (1961): 186.

205. Amend. 1945, I. See Act of March 15, 1945, ch. 634, 1945 N.C. Sess. Laws 875. Election returns are in *A Manual of North Carolina, 1947* (Raleigh: Secretary of State, 1947), 231–32.

206. Act of May 6, 1971, ch. 327, 1971 N.C. Sess. Laws 258.

207. Amend. 1915, III. See Act of March 9, 1915, ch. 99, 1915 N.C. Pub. Laws 148. Election returns are in R.D.W. Connor, ed., *A Manual of North Carolina, 1917*, (Raleigh: Edwards & Broughton Printing, 1917), 294.

208. Amends. 1919, I, II, and III. See Act of March 5, 1919, ch. 129, 1919 N.C. Pub. Laws 305; Act of August 26, 1920, ch. 93, 1920 N.C. Pub. Laws (Extra Sess.) 119. Election returns are in Connor, ed., *North Carolina Manual, 1921*, 327–28.

209. Amend. 1917, II. See Act of March 6, 1917, ch. 192, 1917 N.C. Pub. Laws 343. Election returns are in R.D.W. Connor, ed., *A Manual of North Carolina, 1919*, (Raleigh: Edwards & Broughton Printing, 1919), 300–301.

210. "Amend. 1913, X." See Act of October 13, 1913, ch. 81, 1913 N.C. Pub. Laws (Extra Sess.) 95. Election returns are in R.D.W. Connor, ed., *A Manual of North Carolina, 1915* (Raleigh: Edwards & Broughton Printing, 1915), 222–23.

211. Sanders, "Brief History," 801.

212. Amend. 1935, I, § 1. See Act of April 29, 1935, ch. 248, 1935 N.C. Pub. Laws 270. Election returns are in H. M. London, ed., *A Manual of North Carolina, 1937* (Raleigh: Legislative Reference Library, 1937), 152–53 (hereafter cited as *North Carolina Manual, 1937*).

213. Amend. 1935, I, § 3. Election returns are in *North Carolina Manual, 1937*, 152–53.

214. Amend. 1935, II, § 1. See Act of May 11, 1935, ch. 444, 1935 N.C. Pub. Laws 745. Election returns are in *North Carolina Manual, 1937*, 154–55. The General Assembly promptly exercised its newfound power. Act of February 3, 1937, ch. 16, 1937 N.C. Pub. Laws 47. The increased size was incorporated in the 1971 Constitution, art. IV, § 6 (1).

In 1930 the voters had refused to ratify a proposed amendment that would have made the change directly. "Amend. 1929, III." See Act of March 13, 1929, ch. 142, 1929 N.C. Pub. Laws 166. Election returns are in H. M. London, ed., *A Manual of North Carolina, 1931* (Raleigh: N.C. Historical Commission, 1931), 116–17.

215. Amend. 1937, II. See Act of March 23, 1937, ch. 447, 1937 N.C. Pub. Laws 908. Election returns are in H. M. London, ed., *A Manual of North Carolina, 1939* (Raleigh: Legislative Reference Library, 1939), 131–32.

216. Amend. 1943, I. See Act of February 10, 1943, ch. 57, 1943 N.C. Sess. Laws 50. Election returns are in *A Manual of North Carolina, 1945* (Raleigh: Secretary of State, 1945), 234–36 (hereafter cited as *North Carolina Manual, 1945*).

217. Amend. 1941, I. See Act of March 14, 1941, ch. 151, 1941 N.C. Pub. Laws 240. Election returns are in *A Manual of North Carolina, 1943* (Raleigh: Secretary of State, 1943), 241–42. Amend. 1943, III. See Act of March 5, 1943, ch. 468, 1943 N.C. Sess. Laws 527. Election returns are in *North Carolina Manual, 1945*, 234–36.

218. Amend. 1949, III. See Act of April 4, 1949, ch. 775, 1949 N.C. Sess. Laws 882; Act of April 23, 1949, ch. 1194, 1949 N.C. Sess. Laws 1523. Election returns are in *North Carolina Manual, 1951* (Raleigh: Secretary of State, 1951), 245–47.

219. Amend. 1953, II. See Act of April 2, 1953, ch. 621, 1953 N.C. Sess. Laws 465. Election returns are in *A Mamual of North Carolina, 1955* (Raleigh: Secretary of State, 1955), 255–58.

220. Amend. 1961, I. See Act of May 2, 1961, ch. 313, 1961 N.C. Sess. Laws 436. Election returns are in *A Manual of North Carolina, 1963* (Raleigh: Secretary of State, 1963), 305–308.

221. Amend. 1956. See Act of July 27, 1956, ch. 1, 1956 N.C. Sess. Laws (Extra Sess.) 1. Election returns are in *North Carolina Manual, 1957*, 255–56.

222. Powell, *North Carolina*, 524.

223. Griffin v. County School Board of Prince Edward County, 377 U.S. 218 (1964) (Va. law).

224. Amend. 1967, II. See Act of May 31, 1967, ch. 640, 1967 N.C. Sess. Laws 704. Election returns are in *North Carolina Manual, 1969* (Raleigh: Secretary of State, 1969), 336–37.

225. *Report of the North Carolina Constitutional Commission to the Governor and General Assembly, 1932* (summarized in *North Carolina Law Review* 11 (1934): 5–11). See Dillard S. Gardner, "The Proposed Constitution for North Carolina: A Comparative Study," *Popular Government* 1 (1934) and M. T. Van Hecke, "A New Constitution for North Carolina," *North Carolina Law Review* 12 (1934): 193–212.

226. Opinions of the Justices in the Matter of Whether the Election Held on Tuesday After the First Monday in November, 1933, Was the Next General Election Following the Adjournment of the 1933 Session of the General Assembly, 207 N.C. 879, 181 S.E. 557 (1934) (answering in the affirmative and thereby indicating that the proposed 1933 Constitution could not be submitted to the voters at the 1934 election).

The judges of only a small minority of American states give advisory opinions such as the one cited. Of those that do, most are acting pursuant to authorization in the state constitution or a state statute. Perhaps alone, the justices of the North Carolina Supreme Court have rendered advisory opinions without either. See Preston W. Edsall, "The Advisory Opinion in North Carolina," *North Carolina Law Review* 27 (1949): 297–343.

There has recently been an indication that the North Carolina justices will no longer issue advisory opinions. See State ex rel. Martin v. Preston, 325 N.C. 438, 454, 385 S.E.2d 473, 481 (1989) (referring to "advisory opinions *formerly* issued on occasion by this Court") (emphasis added).

227. See John L. Sanders, *Constitutional Revision and Court Reform: A Legislative History, 1959* (Chapel Hill, N.C.: Institute of Government, 1959).

228. *Report of the North Carolina State Constitution Study Commission to the North Carolina State Bar and the North Carolina Bar Association* (Raleigh, 1968), 4.

229. Act of July 2, 1969, ch. 1258, 1969 N.C. Sess. Laws 1461. Election returns are in *A Manual of North Carolina, 1971* (Raleigh: Secretary of State, 1971), 359–67 (hereafter cited as *North Carolina Manual, 1971*).

230. N.C. Const. of 1971, art. IX, § 2(1).

231. Act of February 26, 1943, ch. 255, 1943 N.C. Sess. Laws 244.

232. N.C. Const. of 1971, art. XIII, § 1.

233. Amend. 1969. See (I) Act of June 13, 1969, ch. 827, 1969 N.C. Sess. Laws 920; (II) Act of June 16, 1969, ch. 872, 1969 N.C. Sess. Laws 976; (III) Act of June 20, 1969, ch. 932, 1969 N.C. Sess. Laws 1074; (IV) Act of June 23, 1969, ch. 1004, 1969 N.C. Sess. Laws 1149; (V) Act of July 2, 1969, ch. 1200, 1969 N.C. Sess. Laws 1385; (VI) Act of July 2, 1969, ch. 1270, 1969 N.C. Sess. Laws 1492. Election returns are in *North Carolina Manual, 1971*, 359–67. "Amend. 1969, IV," which would have eliminated the literacy test for voting, was defeated.

234. Amend. 1969, V.

235. Amend. 1969, I.

236. See Sanders and Lomax, *Amendments*, 23.

237. N.C. Const. of 1971, art. VI, § 1.

238. Amend. 1971, I. See Act of April 16, 1971, ch. 201, 1971 N.C. Sess. Laws 150. Election returns are in *A Manual of North Carolina, 1973* (Raleigh: Secretary of

State, 1973), 434–37. This change had first been called for in North Carolina by Governor W. Kerr Scott (1949–53). See Powell, *North Carolina*, 514.

239. Amend. 1977, III. See Act of May 11, 1977, ch. 363, 1977 N.C. Sess. Laws 369. Election totals are in Sanders and Lomax, *Amendments*, 17.

240. Amend. 1977, V. See Act of June 23, 1977, ch. 690, 1977 N.C. Sess. Laws 837. Election totals are in Sanders and Lomax, *Amendments*, 18.

241. N.C. Const. of 1971, art. I, § 2. Compare N.C. Const. of 1868, art. I, § 2; N.C. Const. of 1776, Declaration of Rights, § 1.

242. N.C. Const. of 1971, art. I, § 6. Compare N.C. Const. of 1868, art. I, § 8; N.C. Const. of 1776, Declaration of Rights, § 4.

243. Kemp P. Battle, "An Address on the History of the Supreme Court" (Feb. 4, 1889), reprinted in 103 N.C. 363 (1889).

244. See Powell, *North Carolina*, 443.

245. See Brookings Institution, *Report on a Survey of the Organization and Administration of the State Government of North Carolina Submitted to Governor O. Max Gardner* (Washington, D.C.: Brookings Institution, 1930).

246. *Report of the Judicial Selection Study Commission* (Raleigh: State of North Carolina, 1989). See Comment, "Changing North Carolina's Method of Judicial Selection," *Wake Forest Law Review* 25 (1990): 253–85.

247. Battle, "An Address," 103 N.C. 366–67.

248. E.g., State v. Carter, 322 N.C. 709, 370 S.E.2d 553 (1988) (finding no good faith exception to the exclusionary rule under the North Carolina Constitution, in contrast to the U.S. Constitution).

Part II

North Carolina Constitution and Commentary

> Since multiplicity of comments, as well as of laws, have great inconveniences, and serve only to obscure and perplex, all manner of comments and expositions on any part of these fundamental constitutions, or on any part of the common or statute laws of Carolina, are absolutely prohibited.
>
> Fundamental Constitutions of Carolina (1669, abrogated 1693)

The Constitution of North Carolina appears as amended through January 1, 1993. A few internal inconsistencies in matters such as punctuation and capitalization are reproduced exactly as they appear in the text proposed by the General Assembly and ratified by the voters.

Preamble

We, the people of the State of North Carolina, grateful to Almighty God, the Sovereign Ruler of Nations, for the preservation of the American Union and the existence of our civil, political and religious liberties, and acknowledging our dependence upon Him for the continuance of those blessings to us and our posterity, do, for the more certain security thereof and for the better government of this State, ordain and establish this Constitution.

Copied verbatim from the 1868 Constitution, the Preamble strikes a solemn religious tone, in contrast to the Preamble to the state's Revolutionary Constitution adopted in 1776 which concentrated on political grievances against Great Britain and which lacked any reference to the deity. Despite its prayerful language, the current Preamble conveys a powerful political message, more obvious in 1868 than in 1971, concerning the paramount importance of the "American Union." God is thanked first for the preservation of the federal system and thereafter for "our civil, political and religious liberties." Without a strong central government, it seems to say, these blessings would be insecure.

In its general form the Preamble follows that in the U.S. Constitution, emphasizing the people as the source of political power. The vigorous phrasing "We, the people of the State of North Carolina" is in sharp contrast to the Preamble to the 1776 Constitution in which, after several "whereases," the adopting authority was described as "We, the Representatives of the Freemen of North Carolina." The present language accurately reflects reality: The state's eligible voters ratified the 1971 Constitution as well as its 1868 predecessor, while elected representatives adopted the 1776 Constitution on behalf of the people.

Article I

Declaration of Rights

That the great, general, and essential principles of liberty and free government may be recognized and established, and that the relations of this State
to the Union and government of the United States and those of the people
of this State to the rest of the American people may be defined and affirmed,
we do declare that:

Most sections of Article I may be traced back through the 1868 Constitution to
the Revolutionary Constitution. Originally a separate document, the declaration
of rights was first incorporated as Article I in 1868, when the present introduction
was added. The twofold statement of purpose reveals the development of the
rights enumerated: The majority date back to independence and concern "the
great, general, and essential principles of liberty and free government," while
the additions made in the Reconstruction Constitution adopted in 1868 mainly
concern "the relations of this State to the Union and government of the United
States and those of the people of this State to the rest of the American people."
The drafters cautiously refer to the rights being "defined and affirmed," rather
than created or conferred; the constitution, in other words, safeguards preexisting
human rights, traceable (as suggested in the Preamble and explicitly affirmed in
the following section) to the divinely ordained order of things.

The idea of beginning with a declaration of rights was widespread in the newly
independent states after the Revolution. The constitutions of Virginia, Maryland,
and Pennsylvania, copies of which were available to the drafters of North Carolina's declaration and from which sections were freely borrowed, all began that
way. The reasoned statement of principles, arranged as a series of propositions,
was part of the Anglo-American tradition of political expression. The colonists
had used the form to register their complaints in 1765 about the Stamp Act and

again in 1774 concerning trade and representation, but the grandfather of all
such documents was undoubtedly the 1689 English Declaration (or Bill) of
Rights, which placed limitations on royal power in the aftermath of the Glorious
Revolution. Like the Bill of Rights added to the U.S. Constitution, North Carolina's Declaration of rights proclaims certain basic ''principles of liberty,'' such
as freedom of religion, free speech and press, and the right of assembly; but,
unlike its federal counterpart, the declaration begins by detailing the ideological
premises that underlie the structure of government. Fundamental principles, such
as popular sovereignty and separation of powers, are first set out in general
terms, to be given specific application in later articles.

SECTION 1

> **The equality and rights of persons.** We hold it to be self-evident that
> all persons are created equal; that they are endowed by their Creator with
> certain inalienable rights; that among these are life, liberty, the enjoyment
> of the fruits of their own labor, and the pursuit of happiness.

Added in 1868, this section echoes the most famous lines of the Declaration of
Independence; only a few years earlier in the Gettysburg Address President
Abraham Lincoln had associated the words with Northern war aims in the Civil
War. In the context of North Carolina's Reconstruction Constitution, the section,
proclaiming the equal rights of all, was intended to lay the foundation for a
racially integrated society. To Thomas Jefferson's original wording two noticeable changes have been made. In 1946, as part of a thoroughgoing editorial
revision that made the constitution ''equally applicable to men and women'' (as
the ballot issue put it), the famous phrase ''all men are created equal'' became
''all persons are created equal,'' a change that was carried forward in 1971. And
in 1868 Jefferson's cadenced trinity of ''life, liberty, and the pursuit of happiness'' was expanded to include ''the enjoyment of the fruits of their own labor,''
an addition that may have been intended to strike an ideological blow at the
slave labor system, specifically prohibited by a later section.

The rights to life, liberty, and the pursuit of happiness have not given rise to
much litigation, presumably because of more detailed provisions elsewhere in
the constitution, but the guarantee of the right to the fruits of one's own labor,
although perhaps aimed originally at slavery, has been the basis for many constitutional challenges to various occupational regulations. Licensing of the
learned professions such as law and medicine has long been taken for granted,
and the exclusion from practice of those failing to pass qualifying examinations
has never been questioned. Yet as licensing spread to more and more occupations
in the twentieth century, the state supreme court was called on to scrutinize the
justifications for limiting access to many other means of livelihood. Although
the U.S. Supreme Court forswore in 1938 the close examination of economic
regulations (U.S. v. Carolene Products Co., 1938), the North Carolina court,

because of this text, has maintained a form of economic due process. In State v. Harris (1940), the court distinguished between, on the one hand, professions requiring special knowledge or involving a fiduciary relationship with the public and, on the other, "ordinary trades and occupations, harmless in themselves." The former are presumptively suitable for licensing, while the latter are not. By this test certain licensing regimes—for example, those involving photography and contracting to install ceramic tile—were declared invalid (Roller v. Allen, 1957; State v. Ballance, 1949).

More generally, by repeating the exalted language of the Declaration of Independence, the present section explicitly recognizes the existence of "inalienable rights," today better known as human rights. Although the Declaration of Independence has itself never been a source of justiciable rights in federal court, in North Carolina this section does extend constitutional protection. The list of enumerated rights—"life, liberty, the enjoyment of the fruits of their own labor, and the pursuit of happiness"—is exemplary, not exhaustive; the text makes it clear that they are only "among" the protected rights. Section 13 of this article itemizes another "natural and inalienable right": religious liberty, also mentioned in the Preamble.

SECTION 2

Sovereignty of the people. All political power is vested in and derived from the people; all government of right originates from the people, is founded upon their will only, and is instituted solely for the good of the whole.

See the commentary following Section 3.

SECTION 3

Internal government of the State. The people of this State have the inherent, sole, and exclusive right of regulating the internal government and police thereof, and of altering or abolishing their Constitution and form of government whenever it may be necessary to their safety and happiness; but every such right shall be exercised in pursuance of law and consistently with the Constitution of the United States.

Popular sovereignty is the basis of American democracy. After the thirteen colonies declared their independence from Great Britain in 1776, political authority could no longer be derived from the British Crown, so American revolutionaries located the ultimate source of sovereignty in the people themselves. These two sections, which are substantially the same as the first and second sections of North Carolina's original declaration of rights, contain both a general and a specific assertion of democratic theory. Section 2, the key phrases of which were copied from a section of the Virginia Declaration of Rights, is an abstract statement of principle: "All political power is vested in and derived from the people." This revolutionary truism is not limited, but pertains by its terms to "all government." Section 3, based on a section of the Maryland Declaration of Rights, follows with a specific local application of the general rule: "The people of this State have the inherent, sole, and exclusive right of regulating the internal government and police thereof." In other words, all people everywhere are vested with original political power, but that power is now being exercised within the boundaries of the state. The American Revolution, while it dissolved the tie with Great Britain, did not dissolve the political society of North Carolina. As all democratic politicians know, power comes from the people, but the results of an election often depend on how the boundaries are drawn.

Since the state's first constitution lacked a preamble proclaiming the constituting authority as "We, the people," these sections originally served to declare the revolutionary faith in popular sovereignty. Displaced in 1868, when a conventional preamble was added, they now serve as a fuller theoretical statement of that principle. Because of their abstractness, they do not give rise to justiciable rights; the details of democracy—which officials are elected, for what terms, and by whom—are reserved for later articles of the constitution. The mechanics of constitutional amendment are set out in Article XIII. Over the years the application has changed dramatically, but the principle has remained the same.

By 1868 one limit on North Carolinians' right of regulating their state's internal government was painfully apparent: Nothing could be done in violation of the U.S. Constitution. For an obvious reason the state's first declaration of rights contained no analog to the clause added to Section 3—"every such right shall be exercised in pursuance of law and consistently with the Constitution of the United States": In 1776 there was no Constitution of the United States. When North Carolina joined the federal Union in 1789, the supremacy clause established the limit not expressly set out in the state constitution until 1868. In its present placement the addition to Section 3 serves as an effective link between the revolutionary faith in popular sovereignty and the Civil War's stern lesson of the indestructible Union. Just as the beginning of Section 2 now connects with the first words of the Preamble, so the last clause of Section 3 introduces the distinctive Reconstruction sections that follow.

SECTION 4

> **Secession prohibited.** This State shall ever remain a member of the American Union; the people thereof are part of the American Nation; there is no right on the part of this State to secede; and all attempts, from whatever source or upon whatever pretext, to dissolve this Union or to sever this Nation, shall be resisted with the whole power of the State.

See the commentary following Section 5.

SECTION 5

Allegiance to the United States. Every citizen of this State owes paramount allegiance to the Constitution and government of the United States, and no law or ordinance of the State in contravention or subversion thereof can have any binding force.

Added in 1868, this pair of sections neatly complements the preceding pair, dating largely from 1776. The obvious point of the addition is succinctly stated in Section 4: "there is no right on the part of this State to secede." Of course, a solemn ordinance of secession had been adopted by a North Carolina constitutional convention on May 20, 1861.[1] The inutility of that ordinance had been finally established on the great battlefields of the Civil War, and the result had been expressed in another ordinance, ratified at the polls in 1865, declaring that the "supposed ordinance is now and at all times hath been null and void."[2] In 1868 the rationale of the indestructible Union was spelled out: The American people—all of them, in all states—form one "American Nation." Just as the sovereignty of the people of North Carolina is expressed in their regulation of the internal government of the state (see Article I, Section 3), so, too, the sovereignty of the American people is expressed in the "American Union," already mentioned in the Preamble. The political society of North Carolina may have survived the Revolution, but it did not remain unchanged when it joined the federal Union. The Union derives its power not from the states, but directly from their people. The new reality is expressed in language redolent of feudalism: Whatever duties they owe their state, the citizens of North Carolina owe "paramount allegiance" to the United States.

Secession, too, had had its logic. The people of North Carolina had debated long and hard before joining the American Union. At the Hillsborough convention in 1788 the ordinance of ratification had been rejected, a decision reversed a year later at the Fayetteville convention. What was attempted in 1861 was the repeal of the ratification ordinance. The legal argument of the victor in the Civil War was that secession was, and always had been, an utter impossibility; in other words, while the Hillsborough decision (not to join the Union) had been reversible, the Fayetteville decision (to join) was irrevocable. For that reason in 1865 the secession ordinance did not technically need to be repealed; only a "supposed ordinance" in the first place, it was subsequently declared never to have been effective. Sections 4 and 5 are intended to preclude the possibility of future attempts at secession.

SECTION 6

Separation of powers. The legislative, executive, and supreme judicial powers of the State government shall be forever separate and distinct from each other.

Along with popular sovereignty, separation of powers is one of the fundamental principles on which state government is constructed. In the exercise of their right to regulate the state's internal government, North Carolinians separated political power into its constituent parts: legislative, executive, and judicial. The language of the original provision in the state's first constitution was copied almost verbatim from a section of the Maryland Declaration of Rights and reflected contemporary analysis of the functions of government. The order in which this trinity of powers is listed was not accidental. Experience with the British parliament had convinced Americans of the primacy of the lawmaking power; the executive carried out laws made elsewhere, while the judiciary resolved legal disputes brought to it by litigants.

Separated powers naturally suggested separate branches of government. Although the institutional lines were not sharply drawn in 1776, American experience during the first century of independence greatly clarified matters. The U.S. Constitution in 1787, without specific mention of the principle, had provided a suggestive blueprint: Legislative, executive, and judicial powers were neatly distributed in Articles I, II, and III. Once the declaration of rights was prefaced to the state constitution as Article I in 1868, it was almost inevitable that the following three articles would constitute the state's three branches of government.

Nowhere was it stated that the three powers or branches had to be equal. In fact, although the balance occasionally shifted, the preponderant power has always rested with the legislature. Even the separateness of the powers could be questioned. Writing in *The Federalist* (No. 47) in 1788, James Madison observed:

The constitution of North Carolina, which declares "that the legislative, executive, and supreme judicial powers of government ought to be forever separate and distinct from each other," refers, at the same time, to the legislative department, the appointment not only of the executive chief, but all the principal officers within both that and the judiciary department.[3]

In 1835 the governor became directly elected, and in 1868 direct election of other executive officers and of the judiciary was instituted; over the years still more executive officers were made directly elected. As with popular sovereignty, so with separation of powers: The principle has remained the same, only the application has changed.

Unlike popular sovereignty, separation of powers has given rise to repeated judicial controversy. In cases dating back to the early nineteenth century, the state supreme court has invoked the principle to protect its prerogatives from legislative interference. For example, a statute purporting to alter the effect of a prior law as to one deed made under it was declared unconstitutional in Robinson v. Barfield (1818). The court viewed the statute as an invasion of the judicial function of deciding what the law was; today the court would more likely view it as an attempt to take the property vested by the deed contrary to the "law of the land,'' a violation of Article I, Section 19. So zealous has the court been to preserve its separateness that it rejected an attempt by the legislature to prescribe rules of practice, although in a conciliatory gesture it adopted on its own motion an almost identical code (Herndon v. Imperial Fire Insurance Co., 1892). The supreme court's ''exclusive authority'' to make rules of appellate procedure is now recognized by Article IV, Section 13, Subsection 2.

In the twentieth century the most frequently litigated issues concerning separation of powers have involved the delegation of legislative power and the creation of administrative agencies that combine the constitutionally separated powers. Administrative agencies, bodies in the executive branch empowered to make and enforce rules in designated areas, were pioneered on the federal level, beginning with the Interstate Commerce Commission in 1887. At first, federal judges were hostile to the attempted regulations and greatly restricted the powers of the agencies, but in time the judicial attitude changed. Delegation of legislative power was eventually accepted so long as adequate standards were prescribed to guide administrative discretion.

North Carolina began to create administrative agencies only after the federal struggle was over, and state courts readily accepted the by-then-benevolent federal judicial position. Standards are required (North Carolina Turnpike Authority v. Pine Island, Inc., 1965), although it may be questioned whether these are really detailed enough in all cases to limit the agency's discretion in practice. For instance, the elimination of ''unethical conduct'' has been upheld as a sufficiently definite standard for an occupational regulatory agency (Farlow v. North Carolina State Board of Chiropractic Examiners, 1985). Conferring judicial powers on an administrative agency is a different matter: The constitution expressly permits it so long as ''reasonably necessary'' to the accomplishment of the agency's purpose (Article IV, Section 3).

The appointment of members of administrative agencies may also raise problems under the present section. A statute authorizing the appointment of legislators to serve simultaneously on administrative agencies has been held to violate the principle of separation of powers (State ex rel. Wallace v. Bone, 1982), although it seemed to pass muster under the constitution's dual-office-holding provision (Article VI, Section 9). On the other hand, a statute authorizing the chief justice of the North Carolina Supreme Court to appoint the director of the Office of Administrative Hearings has been upheld, a divided court ruling either that the legislature is empowered to provide for all appointments not spelled out in the constitution (see Article III, Section 5, Subsection 8) or that the agency in question is within the judicial branch (State ex rel. Martin v. Melott, 1987).

Curiously, one time-hallowed judicial practice in North Carolina itself raises questions concerning separation of powers. In response to questions from either of the other branches, the justices of the state supreme court have from time to time given advisory opinions—that is, answers about the law or constitution not required to resolve pending legal disputes. Although always carefully labeled as the individual opinions of the justices and not final judgments, advisory opinions indicate the likely outcome of any subsequent litigation. Federal judges early refused to issue such opinions, pointing to the language in the U.S. Constitution limiting the judicial power to the decision of "cases or controversies" (art. III, § 2, cl. 1). The theoretical underpinning of the federal judicial position has always been understood to be respect for the principle of separation of powers: The characteristic business of the judiciary is resolving disputes; giving opinions would draw the judges unnecessarily into the business of other branches.

Although the North Carolina Constitution lacks a case-or-controversy requirement, it contains the present declaration in favor of separation of powers. In light of the above, it was especially ironic in 1982 when the state supreme court justices issued the officially captioned Advisory Opinion in re Separation of Powers (1982), opining that statutes authorizing a joint legislative commission to make budgetary decisions would exceed legislative power and interfere with the governor's duty to administer the budget under Article III, Section 5, Subsection 3.

SECTION 7

> **Suspending laws.** All power of suspending laws or the execution of laws
> by any authority, without the consent of the representatives of the people,
> is injurious to their rights and shall not be exercised.

Some political problems, vexatious enough in their own days, do eventually reach final solution. This section stands in the North Carolina Constitution of 1971 as the final monument to the defeat of royal pretensions in the seventeenth and eighteenth centuries. England's Stuart monarchs, particularly King James II, had claimed the power to suspend laws that had been validly adopted, and royal governors in England's colonies had also interfered with local legislation. North Carolina took its emphatic rejection of the practice almost word for word from a section of the Virginia Declaration of Rights, but the progenitor of both was the English Declaration of Rights in 1689, which began with these words: "the pretended power of suspending of laws, or the execution of laws, by regal authority, without consent of parliament, is illegal." Immediately after declaring their political independence, the colonists claimed for their legislatures the right asserted a century earlier by the Mother of Parliaments. Monarchy is no more in America, but to prevent a renewed threat from another quarter the present section roundly declares that a suspending power may not be exercised without legislative consent "by *any* authority" (emphasis added).

In general, this section is designed to safeguard the lawmaking power of the legislature; to that extent, it is merely a specific application of the principle of separation of powers. Although the executive may not suspend a law in the sense of refusing to enforce it, the governor in the exercise of the power of clemency may reduce or eliminate the punishment imposed on an individual lawbreaker (Article III, Section 5, Subsection 6). Also, in the exercise of the customary power of prosecutorial discretion, district attorneys may refrain from charging an individual despite evidence of lawbreaking. So long as decisions not to prosecute for crime or to pardon convicts are applied on a case-by-case basis, they do not amount to an unconstitutional suspension of the laws.

SECTION 8

> **Representation and taxation.** The people of this State shall not be taxed or made subject to the payment of any impost or duty without the consent of themselves or their representatives in the General Assembly, freely given.

Consent is the basis of lawful government, and taxation is government's most sensitive function. No taxes of any sort may be levied without the consent of the people, which may be given either directly by themselves or indirectly by their elected representatives. As a practical matter, the necessary consent is usually expressed through the legislature, here referred to for the first time by its proper name, the General Assembly (Article II, Section 1). Even the legislature cannot pass tax laws with retroactive effect, a form of ex post facto law expressly prohibited by Article I, Section 16. Revenue bills require special formalities (Article II, Section 23), and public finance is the subject of an entire article, Article V. Public borrowing secured by a pledge of the taxing power requires in most cases approval by the voters, an instance in which direct democracy supplants the representative variety.

"No taxation without representation" was the most famous slogan of the American Revolution, and this section translates it into constitutional language. Taken almost verbatim from the 1776 Constitution, Section 8 is in a sense the converse of Section 7. While the earlier section rejects the idea of any independent power to suspend validly adopted laws, thus derogating from the power of the legislature, the present section rejects the idea that taxes could originate anywhere else. The power to tax is the exclusive prerogative of the legislative branch; as such, of course, it is only one aspect of the General Assembly's monopoly of lawmaking power, which is, in turn, only another specific application of the general principle of separation of powers. On joining the federal Union in 1789, North Carolina surrendered to the federal government a modicum of its power to tax. Pursuant to the U.S. Constitution, "Imposts or Duties on Imports or Exports" may be levied only with the consent of Congress, and then only for the benefit of the U.S. Treasury (art. I, § 10, cl. 2). Congressional consent is also required for levying a "Duty of Tonnage," a tax on ships based on their cargo capacity (art. I, § 10, cl. 3).

People need not actually vote or even have a right to vote as a precondition for validly taxing them. In upholding a statute empowering a town to tax non-residents who carry on their ordinary business there, the North Carolina Supreme Court commented: "The maxim invoked in aid of the argument that taxation and representation go together has no application to individuals, but to political communities as such" (Moore v. Mayor and Commissioners of Fayetteville, 1879). Transposed to the time of the American Revolution, this observation means that the British response to the colonists' slogan (i.e., that they already had "virtual representation" in Parliament) was wrong because their "political community" was not represented there. In the final analysis, the dispute between Mother Country and colonies concerned just how extensive that community actually was. Democracy is fair, by and large, even to those without the vote, because there usually are enough voters with similar interests.

SECTION 9

> **Frequent elections.** For redress of grievances and for amending and strengthening the laws, elections shall be often held.

See the commentary following Section 10.

SECTION 10

> **Free elections.** All elections shall be free.

Just as Sections 7 and 8 are specific applications of the principle of separation of powers, so this pair of sections concerns the application of the principle of popular sovereignty, first stated in Section 2. The further development of the idea of "people power" was postponed, first for constitutional formulations of the results of the Civil War, and then for elaborations of the three types of government power. In Sections 9 and 10 the theme of popular sovereignty is sounded once again, and elections, the principal means of translating it into reality, are mentioned for the first time. To be effective elections must be frequent and free.

Section 9 was based on a section of the Maryland Declaration of Rights, but both derive ultimately from the English Declaration of Rights in 1689: "for redress of all grievances, and for the amending, strengthening and preserving of the laws, parliaments ought to be held frequently." In their first constitution North Carolinians settled on annual elections for the General Assembly; in 1835 biennial elections were substituted, and the governor was made directly elected. Responding to opponents of change who quoted the Founders in favor of annual elections, one delegate to the 1835 convention voiced the sensible view: "An election is sufficiently frequent in its occurrence, when it comes often enough for the redress of monstrous grievances."[4] In the second constitution more offices were made elective. The constitutional convention in 1868 recommended four-year terms for executive officers and eight-year terms for judges, as well as a reaffirmation of the requirement that elections "be often held," and the people approved of both. Details of suffrage and eligibility for office are set out in Article VI.

According to the laconic Section 10, shortest in the constitution, elections shall be "free." The word originally derives, by way of a section of the Virginia Declaration of Rights, from the English Declaration of Rights (1689): "election of members of parliament ought to be free." In 1776 North Carolinians adapted the idea to their new institutions: "Elections of Members to serve as Representatives in General Assembly ought to be free." In 1868, as elective offices proliferated, the section attained substantially its modern form: "All elections ought to be free." The meaning is plain: free from interference or intimidation. Sadly it must be said that North Carolina's black voters have not always found them so.

The purpose of holding frequent and free elections is spelled out in the first clause of Section 9: "For redress of grievances and for amending and strengthening the laws." The phrase "redress of grievances" appears again in Section 12 of this article as one of the objects of political assembly and figures in the same context in the First Amendment in the U.S. Bill of Rights. To the modern reader it is perhaps surprising that elections are not specifically said to be for the purpose of making new laws as well as for "amending and strengthening" the old ones. This conservative phrasing is, however, in keeping with much of so-called "revolutionary" theory, both English and American: To a large extent it looked back to the common law and the "ancient constitution" in its defiance of encroaching power. Consequently, it seemed natural to emphasize the role of elected representatives in improving and enforcing already existing laws.

SECTION 11

> **Property qualifications.** As political rights and privileges are not dependent upon or modified by property, no property qualification shall affect the right to vote or hold office.

Added in 1868, this section represents a milestone on the road to modern democracy. Although it is confidently declared that politics and property are not related to one another, the fact was not self-evident to the generation that made the Revolution. On the contrary, the state's 1776 Constitution excluded paupers from the franchise: Those without property had, it was thought, no stake in society. To vote for members of the lower house, one had at least to be a taxpayer; voters for members of the upper chamber had to be landowners. Likewise, to hold office, landownership was required; the higher the office, the more land was required. Senators needed more than representatives, and the governor needed more than anybody else. Eventually restrictions on voting were reduced, and what was called "universal manhood suffrage" (excluding paupers and all non-whites) was attained in 1857, but property qualifications for office holding were retained until the Civil War. Even in 1868 a determined Conservative minority, representing the defeated Confederates, argued that property should remain a precondition for office, but democratic theory had triumphed with the Union Army, and the Republican delegates in 1868 insisted that popular sovereignty not be limited by property. From 1900 until 1920, however, payment of the poll tax was a prerequisite to voting, a requirement that along with the literacy test for registration (see Article VI, Section 4) was designed to exclude black voters.

SECTION 12

> **Right of assembly and petition.** The people have a right to assemble together to consult for their common good, to instruct their representatives, and to apply to the General Assembly for redress of grievances; but secret political societies are dangerous to the liberties of a free people and shall not be tolerated.

Popular sovereignty means elections, and for elections to express the popular will, the right to assemble and consult for the common good must be guaranteed. Between elections the sovereign people may want to instruct their representatives or petition for "redress of grievances." Although sometimes described as a general "right of association," freedom of assembly was originally placed in an exclusively political context, as an adjunct to elections and representation. In the U.S. Bill of Rights the comparable provision, guaranteeing "the right of the people peaceably to assemble and to petition the Government for a redress of grievances," appears at the end of the First Amendment, after the guarantees of freedom of religion, speech, and the press. By contrast, in the North Carolina Declaration of Rights, freedom of assembly precedes the others, not because it is more important, but because of its connection with the mechanics of popular sovereignty. This section forms an effective transition from the political sections that begin Article I to the enumeration of civil liberties that follows.

The notion that the people may "instruct their representatives"—not repeated in the U.S. Bill of Rights—raises a sensitive issue in democratic theory: whether elected representatives are bound by their constituents' opinions or whether they should "vote their own consciences." Some of the delegates to the provincial congress that drafted the state's first constitution came equipped with instructions that they were "required to follow in every particular with the strictest regard."[5] The declaration of rights in 1776 presupposed this widespread view—the exact language was copied from the Pennsylvania Declaration of Rights—but Edmund Burke had already formulated the classic response to it in his speech to the electors of Bristol (November 3, 1774). The notion of "*authoritative* instructions . . . which the member is bound blindly and implicitly to obey" is based, he said, on a fundamental misconception of representative government: The legislature is not an assembly of "ambassadors from different and hostile interests," but rather "a *deliberative* assembly" (emphasis in original). In consequence,

Burke argued, "[y]our representative owes you, not his industry only, but his judgment; and he betrays, instead of serving you, if he sacrifices it to your opinion."[6] As a practical matter, instructions may be issued, but there is no way to see that they are obeyed. Representatives willing to risk defeat at the next election are free to vote as they see fit.

The people's right to assemble is, of course, subject to regulation as to time, manner, and place. Municipal ordinances may constitutionally require those planning a parade to apply for a permit and penalize those who gather without one. In times of mass demonstrations and protest marches, the denial of a permit or the arrest of a person parading without one will be scrutinized for possible violation of the present section. So long as the ordinance is not discriminatory and does not restrain free speech, protected by Section 14 of the present article, it will be upheld (State v. Frinks, 1974).

The clause concerning "secret political societies" was added on the recommendation of the 1875 constitutional convention, aimed at the Ku Klux Klan which had flourished in the aftermath of Reconstruction.

SECTION 13

> **Religious liberty.** All persons have a natural and inalienable right to worship Almighty God according to the dictates of their own consciences, and no human authority shall, in any case whatever, control or interfere with the rights of conscience.

Section 1 of this article, based on the Declaration of Independence, affirms the existence of "certain inalienable rights" and lists four of them: "life, liberty, the enjoyment of the fruits of their own labor, and the pursuit of happiness." In language drawn from a section of the Pennsylvania Declaration of Rights, the present section itemizes another: freedom of religion. In North Carolina's first constitution this freedom was given concrete effect by a later section disestablishing the Church of England. Since that section was dropped in 1868, having long since had its intended effect, North Carolina today lacks a specific prohibition of "an establishment of religion," such as in the First Amendment in the U.S. Bill of Rights; nonetheless, the state supreme court has construed this section along with the First Amendment to require "secular neutrality toward religion" (Heritage Village Church and Missionary Fellowship, Inc. v. State, 1980).

The present section seems to take the existence of God for granted; how the Almighty is worshipped is left to the individual conscience. Nor is this the only reference to the deity or religion in the constitution. Thanks are returned to the "Sovereign Ruler of Nations" in the Preamble, and the "Creator" is declared in Section 1 to be the source of all human rights. Elsewhere in the constitution state officers are required to swear a solemn oath, concluding "so help me God" (Article VI, Section 7). Because oaths not backed by religious belief were thought to be worthless, the drafters of the 1868 Constitution disqualified atheists from office, a disqualification that was carried over in the 1971 Constitution (Article VI, Section 8), although it is almost certainly unenforceable under the U.S. Constitution. The practical value of religion is affirmed in the first section of Article IX on education, quoting the Northwest Ordinance: "religion, morality, and knowledge being necessary to good government and the happiness of mankind." Finally, in providing for the creation of a board of public welfare, the constitution declares: "Beneficent provision for the poor, the unfortunate, and the orphan is one of the first duties of a civilized and a Christian state" (Article XI, Section 4), the necessary implication being that North Carolina is (or ought to be) such a state.

A Christian state might well regulate what may be done on Sunday, but it was decided in 1860 by the state supreme court that North Carolina could not prohibit labor on the sabbath that is done in private and does not offend public decency or disturb the religious devotions of others (Melvin v. Easley, 1860). Entering a once lively debate about whether Christianity is part of the common law, a proposition that Sir William Blackstone affirmed and Thomas Jefferson denied, the state supreme court asserted the negative. "Sunday laws" were upheld only as police regulations. In the words of Chief Justice Walter Clark, "if . . . the cessation of labor or the prohibition or performance of any act were provided by statute for religious reasons, the statute could not be maintained" (Rodman v. Robinson, 1904).

Secular reasons can be found not only for the Sunday laws, but also for the laws prohibiting drug use, notwithstanding the user's asserted belief that it is required by divine law (State v. Bullard, 1966). Likewise, a municipal ordinance can prohibit the handling of poisonous snakes, despite the handler's use as part of a religious ritual based on New Testament sayings (Mark 16:18) (State v. Massey, 1949).

Although church and state are separate, state courts may be called on to adjudicate disputes concerning church property. The most troublesome of these arise out of struggles among the faithful for control of the parsonage and sanctuary. In such cases the judges must scrupulously refrain from basing their decisions on any determination of controversies about religious doctrines. In hierarchical churches with authoritative teaching bodies, the courts may determine whether there has been a departure from official doctrine, but in fully congregational churches they must respect the decision of the majority (Atkins v. Walker, 1973). In a few cases, drawing the line may require the wisdom of Solomon.

SECTION 14

> **Freedom of speech and press.** Freedom of speech and of the press are two of the great bulwarks of liberty and therefore shall never be restrained, but every person shall be held responsible for their abuse.

It is curious, but true, that North Carolina's first two constitutions contained no specific provision protecting freedom of speech; the present safeguard was inserted only in 1971. Perhaps the earlier lapse is best explained by the fact that the section of the Virginia Declaration of Rights on which the original free press section was modeled had also been silent on the subject. The ban on restraint of the press thus dates back to 1776, but the monitory clause, threatening those who abuse the right, was added in 1868 when the Reconstruction authorities were concerned about their treatment by the opposition press. In the end, the provision on the press approximates Sir William Blackstone's summary a century earlier: "The liberty of the press . . . consists in laying no *previous* restraints upon publications, and not in freedom from censure for criminal matter when published."[7]

As with freedom of assembly so with free speech, reasonable restrictions are permitted. The legislature may outlaw profane language that is a disturbance of the peace (State v. Warren, 1893), and a county may enforce an ordinance regulating the posting of signs (County of Cumberland v. Eastern Federal Corporation, 1980). Trespass laws may be invoked by owners of private property to which the public is admitted, such as shopping malls, to enforce policies against solicitation or distribution of handbills (State v. Felmet, 1981). Because some press coverage of criminal trials might interfere with constitutional guarantees of fair procedures, it is even possible to consider prior restraints on expression, although one seeking a "gag rule" must carry a heavy burden of showing the necessary justification (State v. Williams, 1981). The guarantee of free speech, although not expressly so limited, has been held to protect only against state (as opposed to individual) restraints. Ordinarily, well-established remedies are available to one whose rights have been infringed, but in their absence a direct action against the state is available under the present section. As Justice Harry C. Martin put it on behalf of the state supreme court, "the provision of our Constitution which protects the right of freedom of speech is self-executing" (Corum v. University of North Carolina, 1992).

Once an expression has been made, the question of "abuse" can be considered. So great is the value of free speech and press in matters of public interest that recovery of damages in case of claimed defamation is permitted only when the plaintiff can show that the words were uttered maliciously. The falsity of the statement is not alone sufficient to establish malice (Johnston v. Time, Inc., 1971).

SECTION 15

> **Education.** The people have a right to the privilege of education, and it
> is the duty of the State to guard and maintain that right.

Like many other sections in Article I, the Declaration of Rights, this section states a general proposition that is given concrete realization elsewhere in the constitution. The people's right to education correlates with the state's duty "to guard and maintain that right." The details are spelled out in Article IX, wholly devoted to the subject. Added to the declaration of rights in 1868, the right to education was intended to mark a new and more positive role for state government. Not a restriction on what the state may do, it requires a commitment to social betterment.

SECTION 16

> **Ex post facto laws.** Retrospective laws, punishing acts committed before the existence of such laws and by them only declared criminal, are oppressive, unjust, and incompatible with liberty, and therefore no ex post facto law shall be enacted. No law taxing retrospectively sales, purchases, or other acts previously done shall be enacted.

Following sections on the political organization of the state and basic human rights (freedom of religion, speech, and the press), the present section begins a series of sections dealing with the administration of justice, especially law enforcement. Eighteenth-century thinkers who applied rational analysis to criminal law had emphasized its deterrent function. A law made after the fact (ex post facto) could not logically have deterred the crime; to punish a person for an act not contrary to law when committed was therefore unjust. More than individual injustice was involved; the whole social basis of republican government was jeopardized if the people did not know exactly what was prohibited.

The first sentence of the North Carolina section was originally copied from a section of the Maryland Declaration of Rights; the U.S. Constitution later included a prohibition without explanation: "No . . . ex post facto Law shall be passed" (art. I, § 9, cl. 3). Although the first sentence of the state constitutional provision is clearly applicable only to criminal laws, the federal clause is not expressly so limited, and some of the Framers of the U.S. Constitution may have believed it would rule out all retroactive legislation. In the early case of Calder v. Bull (1798), however, the U.S. Supreme Court confined the prohibition to retrospective penal laws, relying in part on the more explicit language of the Maryland and North Carolina constitutions.

As interpreted, ex post facto laws include, in addition to those "punishing acts committed before the existence of such laws," laws that punish those acts more severely than they would have been punished at the time they were committed. For example, where the punishment at the time of the offense was death *or* life imprisonment at the discretion of the jury, a change by the legislature to death alone would be an ex post facto law (State v. Waddell, 1973). On the other hand, a law that changes, but does not increase, the punishment is constitutional. For example, when the common law punishment for larceny—whipping *and* imprisonment—was changed to imprisonment only, there was no constitutional violation (State v. Kent, 1871).

Although civil (as opposed to criminal) laws are not generally covered by the present section, the final sentence, added in 1868, does extend the prohibition to one category of civil legislation: tax laws. Taxes may be imposed only prospectively. The rationale would seem to be similar to that for the ban on retrospective criminal laws. To the extent one could have avoided the event that is taxed, it is unjust not to give the taxpayer the chance. Revenue bills generally are the subject of Article II, Section 23, and public finance is the subject of Article V.

SECTION 17

Slavery and involuntary servitude. Slavery is forever prohibited. Involuntary servitude, except as a punishment for crime whereof the parties have been adjudged guilty, is forever prohibited.

One of the handful of sections added to the declaration of rights in 1868, the present section constitutionalized the principal social consequence of the Civil War. Section 1, also added at that time, affirms the legal equality of all persons; this section is the complementary negative, prohibiting slavery as well as any other arrangement that approximates it. As a practical matter it was redundant to abolish slavery; the Thirteenth Amendment to the U.S. Constitution, using phrases on which this section was based, had already consigned it to the legal dustbin.

Slavery did not need to be defined for North Carolinians in 1868; the state's slave code had been refined over many years. Involuntary servitude, by contrast, was a phrase of broad and indeterminate content—deliberately so. After the Civil War many Southern states including North Carolina had adopted "black codes" designed to reproduce features of slavery; this section is intended to prohibit legislation creating new forms of peonage. Legislation is not the only object of the prohibition; all enforceable arrangements, including private contracts, are also barred.

Racial discrimination, one of the "badges of slavery," has proved harder to eliminate. In 1971, a century after the end of Reconstruction, two new provisions were added to the declaration of rights addressing this continuing social problem: a general non-discrimination clause in Section 19 and a specific prohibition of discrimination in the selection of juries in Section 26.

SECTION 18

Courts shall be open. All courts shall be open; every person for an injury done him in his lands, goods, person, or reputation shall have remedy by due course of law; and right and justice shall be administered without favor, denial, or delay.

Although added to the North Carolina Declaration of Rights only in 1868, this section traces its pedigree to the oldest and most honorable source in Anglo-American jurisprudence: the Magna Carta. In 1215 a reluctant King John made a promise to his rebellious barons: "*Nulli vendemus nulli negabimus aut differemus rectum vel justitiam.*" ("To no one will we sell, to no one will we deny or delay right or justice.") Disputes would be resolved, in other words, impartially. The institutional realization of this promise was a system of courts, staffed by professional judges. Justice would be available to all who were injured; to this end, the courts would be "open." The word meant not that the judges would sit round-the-clock or that every spectator would always be welcome, but that legal remedies would not be withheld. Dr. Samuel Johnson's famous *Dictionary*, published in 1755, listed, among other meanings of the word, "not restrained; not denied" and illustrated this usage with an apt quotation from the King James version of the Bible: "If Demetrius and the Craftsmen have a matter against any man, the law is *open* and there are deputies; let them implead one another" (Acts 19:38). In other words, the core meaning of this section is that properly qualified courts shall be regularly in session. (Under Article IV, Section 9, Subsection 2, superior courts are required to be "open at all times for the transaction of all business.")

The guarantee of a legal remedy for every injury is traceable not to the Magna Carta directly, but rather to Sir Edward Coke's influential seventeenth-century commentary on it. Open courts were not enough, Coke pointed out; they had to be righting wrongs and doing justice. "And therefore every Subject of the Realm, for injury done to him in *bonis, terris, vel persona* [goods, lands, or person] . . . may take his remedy by the course of the Law. . . . "[8] "Goods" and "lands" have been interpreted broadly to include all rights of property (Wilson v. Board of Aldermen of the City of Charlotte, 1876). The right a person has in his or her reputation, which was added to Coke's original list, is protected by laws against libel and slander. Section 14 of this article, guaranteeing freedom of speech and the press, expressly authorizes remedies for their "abuse." The present section's guarantee of a remedy for every wrong has been held to mean that although the legislature may eliminate punitive damages, it cannot deprive a person of the right to recover actual damages (Osborn v. Leach, 1904). The wording of the whole section applies to civil disputes, those between one person and another, not to criminal prosecutions. For the latter, the next section is obviously suited.

Like other constitutional rights, the right to open courts is subject to reasonable restrictions. Statutes of limitations, for example, may bar stale claims. More controversial are statutes of repose, which set a gross period of years within which an action must be commenced regardless of the date of actual injury; these, too, have been upheld (Tetterton v. Long Manufacturing Co., 1985). The present section does not operate to freeze the law as it was when the constitution was adopted: The legislature retains the power to abolish causes of action and to alter the remedies available. As the North Carolina Supreme Court once put it, "No person has a vested right in a continuance of the common or statute law" (Pinkham v. Unborn Children of Jather Pinkham, 1946).

Although originally aimed at ensuring that courts were open to civil plaintiffs, this section has been interpreted by the state supreme court to mean that their proceedings must be open to the public generally. "Open" can also mean "unclosed; not shut," so the guarantee of open courts has become a guarantee of public trials (In re Edens, 1976). Having once created this right, the court has then had to confine it within reasonable limits. Trial courts may be constitutionally closed to the public, for example, during the testimony of a child rape victim (State v. Burney, 1981), and trial judges may constitutionally restrict access by spectators who would be distracting to juries (State v. Clark, 1989).

Just as the open courts provision has by interpretation become a guarantee of public trials, so, too, it has become a guarantee of speedy criminal trials. "Every person formally accused of crime," the North Carolina Supreme Court has held, "is guaranteed a speedy and impartial trial by Article I, Section 18 of the Constitution of this State and the Sixth and Fourteenth Amendments of the federal Constitution" (State v. Tindall, 1978). Insofar as the U.S. Constitution is concerned, this is unexceptionable. The Sixth Amendment expressly guarantees that "in all criminal prosecutions the accused shall enjoy the right to a speedy and public trial by an impartial jury . . . ," and the Fourteenth Amendment has been interpreted to extend this federal guarantee to state proceedings (Klopfer v. North Carolina, 1967). While Section 18 does mention the "delay" of justice, it is doubtful that it should be equated with the Sixth Amendment.

SECTION 19

Law of the land; equal protection of the laws. No person shall be taken, imprisoned, or disseized of his freehold, liberties, or privileges, or outlawed, or exiled, or in any manner deprived of his life, liberty, or property, but by the law of the land. No person shall be denied the equal protection of the laws; nor shall any person be subjected to discrimination by the State because of race, color, religion, or national origin.

Certainly the most important section of Article I, the Declaration of Rights, this section is comparable to the Fourteenth Amendment to the U.S. Constitution in the amount of judicial commentary it has spawned. Like the preceding section, the first sentence of the present section, concerning the law of the land, traces its antecedents back to the Magna Carta, although unlike the prior section, it has been part of the state's constitution ever since 1776, when it was modeled on a section of the Maryland Declaration of Rights. The second sentence was added only in 1971, the equal protection clause being drawn from the Fourteenth Amendment, and the non-discrimination clause, which complements the abolition of slavery, being based on federal civil rights legislation.

The Law of the Land

The archaic phrasing of the first sentence of this section should not distract attention from the sweeping constitutional guarantee at its heart. Parsing the sentence discloses six forbidden acts: "No person shall be [1] taken, [2] imprisoned, or [3] disseized of his freehold, liberties, or privileges, or [4] outlawed, or [5] exiled, or [6] in any manner deprived of his life, liberty, or property, but by the law of the land." The converse, of course, would seem to be that all these things may be done, if carried out according to the law of the land. To take a person is to seize him or her, while imprisonment is any restraint on individual liberty. "Disseized" is an ancient word, showing the section's origin in medieval England. Roughly equal to "dispossessed," it refers most often to the taking of property. Since rights ("liberties" and "privileges") were once thought of as tangible things, it was as natural to speak of their loss as a dispossession as it was to refer to being dispossessed (disseized) of a freehold, an estate in land. Outlawry is now the state of being a criminal, but once—at the time of the Magna Carta—it actually meant the punishment solemnly declared by a court of being put outside the protection of the law; to kill such a person was not then a legal offense, any more than to kill a wild animal. Today, of course, the law of the land does not provide for the medieval form of outlawry. Exile, too, was once a legally recognized punishment. In English law it survived the Middle Ages in the form of the transportation (as it was called) of criminals to the colonies. Exile in any form is today unknown to the law of the land. The final clause, "No person shall be . . . deprived of his life, liberty, or property, but by the law of the land," is the still-beating heart of this ancient section. In large measure it repeats in more familiar terms all that went before. Depriving a person of his liberty occurs when he is taken or imprisoned and is just another way of saying "disseized of his . . . liberties, or privileges." So, too, being deprived of one's property is being "disseized of his freehold." For all practical purposes, the first sentence of Section 19 could be confined to its final clause; all the cases that have arisen under it could have been decided the same way without the other clauses.

In many of its aspects the first sentence of Section 19 echoes other provisions in Article I, the Declaration of Rights. The guarantee of the famous trinity of life, liberty, and property, for instance, is reminiscent of Section 1's declaration of the God-given and inalienable rights to "life, liberty, the enjoyment of the fruits of their own labor, and the pursuit of happiness." And many of the rights safeguarded in general terms by this sentence are given more detailed treatment elsewhere. "No person shall be taken . . . but by the law of the land." Section 20, banning general warrants, prohibits arrest warrants that do not name the person and describe the offense with particularity. "No person shall be . . . imprisoned . . . but by the law of the land." Section 21 provides for speedy inquiries into the lawfulness of any restraints on liberty. Much that has been decided under the more specific language of other sections could have been decided under the general language of Section 19, and vice versa.

The guarantee that no person shall be unlawfully deprived of life, liberty, or property is familiar from the U.S. Constitution. The Fifth Amendment in the Bill of Rights protects against violations by the federal government, while the Fourteenth Amendment extends the same protection against state violations; in neither case can there be a deprivation of protected rights "without due process of law."

Less familiar is the comparable phrase in the North Carolina Declaration of Rights, "but by the law of the land." This key phrase is mentioned once in the U.S. Constitution, in the supremacy clause (art. VI, § 2): "This Constitution, and the Laws of the United States which shall be made in Pursuance thereof, and all Treaties made, or which shall be made, under the Authority of the United States, shall be the supreme *Law of the Land.* . . ." In this context, the law of the land means simply the law. The phrase in Section 19 certainly encompasses that meaning. "An act of the Legislature, which speaks for the people in making its laws, is 'the law of the land,' " Chief Justice Walter Clark wrote, although he added the necessary qualifier, "unless there is a provision of the Constitution which forbids it to enact such a law" (Daniels v. Homer, 1905). In other words, the North Carolina Constitution is itself the supreme law of the land. If it meant nothing else, the first sentence of Section 19 would be a small, but important, safeguard against unauthorized or unregulated actions. Notice that its protections, unlike those of the second sentence, are not expressly limited to actions by the state.

From the earliest days of North Carolina's independence, the law of the land has had in addition a substantive content. In 1794 the state's attorney general contended that it meant "according to the course of the common law" (State v. Anonymous, 1794). That meant, in turn, that since the constitution was superior to acts of the legislature, the judges could test legislation against the norms of the common law. In a leading case in 1834 Chief Justice Thomas Ruffin explained the consequence: "[S]uch legislative acts, as profess in them-selves directly to punish persons or to deprive the citizen of his property, without trial before the judicial tribunals, and a decision upon the matter of right, as determined by the laws under which it vested, according to the course, mode and usages of the common law as derived from our forefathers, are not effectually 'laws of the land' for those purposes" (Hoke v. Henderson, 1834). Legislative acts that purport to impose criminal punishment, known as bills of attainder, are placed by the U.S. Constitution beyond the power of Congress (art. I, § 9, cl. 3). Under the North Carolina Declaration of Rights they would seem to violate the principle of separation of powers (Section 6), as well as the guarantee of criminal proceedings initiated by the grand jury (Section 22), the right to confront one's accusers (Section 23), and the right to trial by jury (Section 24). Legislative acts that purport to deprive a person of his property without trial would also seem violative of separation of powers (Section 6) and the right to jury trial in civil cases respecting property (Section 25). Or one could say simply with Chief Justice Ruffin that they are "not effectually 'laws of the land' for those purposes" and therefore violate Section 19.

The law of the land has become the focus for judicial thinking concerning fundamental fairness. Confronting a difficult problem in 1874, Justice William B. Rodman turned naturally to this section: "Notwithstanding there is no clause in the Constitution of North Carolina which expressly prohibits private property from being taken for public use without compensation . . . , yet the principle is so grounded in natural equity that it has never been denied to be a part of the law of North Carolina" (Johnston v. Rankin, 1874). In the exercise of its power of eminent domain the state can indeed deprive a person of his or her property, but only "by the law of the land," meaning in this case with just compensation because that is demanded by "natural equity."

In later days, as zoning and other governmental regulations occasionally reduce the value of property, the state supreme court has struggled to determine whether a taking has occurred; in general it has found no taking (and therefore no right to compensation) if the interference with the use of the property is deemed to be reasonable (Responsible Citizens v. City of Asheville, 1983). When legislation closes the market to a would-be competitor, the court has scrutinized the public policy justifying the act and has not hesitated to strike down a statute it finds inadequately supported, a modern instance of substantive due process (In re Aston Park Hospital, 1973). As federal court decisions made famous the phrase "due process of law," North Carolina courts increasingly associated the law of the land with federal due process. While the state courts are always careful to reserve their right to an independent determination, they readily admit that federal interpretations are "highly persuasive" (Bulova Watch Co. v. Brand Distributors of North Wilkesboro, Inc., 1974).

In appropriate cases the law of the land protects corporations, artificial persons, as well as natural ones. In an 1805 decision involving the rights of the University of North Carolina the state supreme court justified this coverage by pointing to the old-fashioned language of one of the earlier clauses: The word "liberties," if found, "peculiarly signifies those privileges and rights which corporations have by virtue of the instruments which incorporate them" (Trustees of the University of North Carolina v. Foy, 1805). Years later in construing the Fourteenth Amendment, which lacks this peculiar phrasing, the U.S. Supreme Court nonetheless found this inclusive meaning too obvious for argument (Santa Clara County v. Southern Pacific Railroad Co., 1886). In recent years the debate over abortion has again focused attention on the definition of "person." In a challenge to public funding of elective abortions the state supreme court found a human fetus not to be a person within this section (Stam v. State, 1981).

The greatest development of the law of the land has concerned proper criminal procedure. In some cases this is because the state constitution failed to provide explicit protection to all the rights required by fundamental fairness or made familiar by express provisions of the U.S. Bill of Rights. For instance, the notion that one is innocent until proven guilty is nowhere spelled out, but can be found in the requirements of the law of the land (State v. Divine, 1887). Likewise with the protection against double jeopardy secured against federal action by the Fifth Amendment: "It is a fundamental and sacred principle of the common law, deeply imbedded in our criminal jurisprudence, that no person can be twice put in jeopardy of life or limb for the same offense. . . . While the principle is not stated in express terms in the North Carolina Constitution, it has been regarded as an integral part of the 'law of the land' " (State v. Crocker, 1954). Because it was supposedly always implicit in the law of the land, the North Carolina Supreme Court could maintain that the decision of the U.S. Supreme Court in Benton v. Maryland (1969), making the double jeopardy clause of the Fifth Amendment applicable to the states through the Fourteenth Amendment, "added nothing to our law" (State v. Battle, 1971).

So susceptible to an expansive interpretation has the law of the land proved to be that there has developed a tendency to subsume under it topics that are explicitly dealt with elsewhere in Article I, the Declaration of Rights. For instance, the right to counsel and the privilege against self-incrimination have been found implied in the law of the land despite their express guarantee in Section 23. This, too, is the case with the ban on racial discrimination in the selection of juries spelled out in Section 26 and the prohibition of cruel or unusual punishments in Section 27. In this commentary, if not in the cases themselves, these topics are discussed under the specific sections.

Equal Protection; Non-discrimination

Unlike the first sentence of Section 19, the second sentence guaranteeing "the equal protection of the laws" and forbidding "discrimination by the State" is limited to state action. The characteristics protected against discrimination are listed: race, color, religion, or national origin. In marked contrast to Section 26, which prohibits discrimination in the selection of juries, this list does not include sex. While the equal protection clause extends to corporate "persons" as well as natural ones, the non-discrimination clause seems to be limited to the latter. In a famous phrase Sir Edward Coke once asserted that corporations, unlike human beings, have "no souls" (Sutton's Hospital Case, 1613). Although they may be composed of persons all of the same race, color, religion, or national origin, corporations as such would seem to lack the physical, moral, or historical characteristics referred to.

While again reserving the final say on state law to itself, the North Carolina court has tended to follow federal interpretations of the requirements of equal protection: Any legislative classification that interferes with the exercise of a fundamental right is subject to "strict scrutiny" and is permissible only if necessary to promote a "compelling governmental interest" (Northampton County Drainage District Number One v. Bailey, 1990); when a classification does not burden the exercise of a fundamental right, it is permissible if based on differences that are reasonably related to a conceivable legitimate interest of the government (White v. Pate, 1983). Not only must a law be fair on its face, but also it must be fairly applied. Quoting with approval a famous sentence by U.S. Supreme Court Justice Stanley Matthews, the state supreme court observed: "If it is applied and administered by public authority with an evil eye and an unequal hand, so as to make unjust and illegal discriminations between persons in similar circumstances, material to their rights, the denial of equal justice is still within the prohibition of the Constitution" (S.S. Kresge Co. v. Davis, 1971). It should be noted that these standards of equal protection seem to cover classification based on sex, so that despite its absence from the list of protected classes in the nondiscrimination clause, it may be equally protected.

SECTION 20

> **General warrants.** General warrants, whereby any officer or other person may be commanded to search suspected places without evidence of the act committed, or to seize any person or persons not named, whose offense is not particularly described and supported by evidence, are dangerous to liberty and shall not be granted.

Following the bold declaration in the preceding section in favor of the "law of the land," the present section begins a series of constitutional guarantees of the rights of those suspected or accused of crime. Based on their study of English constitutional history and on their own experiences during the colonial era, Americans knew of the potential for abuse of the criminal law. The defense of law and order could be perverted by the powers that be into the oppression of their political opponents. Law enforcement is therefore subjected to step-by-step analysis, and safeguards are imposed at every stage from search and arrest through detention, prosecution, trial, and final punishment.

Drawn originally from a section of the Virginia Declaration of Rights, the ban on general warrants reflects colonial experience with abuses of the procedures of criminal investigation by the authorities. The government may, indeed should, search for evidence of crime and arrest suspected criminals, but indiscriminate searches and arrests disturb the routines of ordinary life and instill fear of the forces of law and order. They are, in the words of this section, "dangerous to liberty"; the Fourth Amendment in the U.S. Bill of Rights particularizes them as violations of the "right of the people to be secure in their persons, houses, papers and effects." Both the state and the U.S. constitutions prohibit general warrants, but only the state constitution defines them as such: warrants that are not supported by evidence and that do not name names. Two types of warrants are referred to in this section: warrants to search suspected places and warrants to arrest ("to seize") a person or persons. Although not expressly mentioned, warrants to seize things are included by implication.

Since general warrants are prohibited, the kinds of warrants to be used must be specific; in the words of the Fourth Amendment, they may be issued only on a showing of "probable cause" and must include a particular description of "the place to be searched, and the person or things to be seized." The emphasis is on justifying the search and seizure in advance. An unlawful search does not become lawful by the discoveries made during the search (State v. Hall, 1965), and evidence obtained as a result of an unlawful search may not be admitted in a subsequent trial (State v. Small, 1977). Such evidence is excluded not because it is unreliable, but rather because the criminal justice system must be preserved from the taint of illegal procedures. So strong is the perceived public policy in this area that the state supreme court has refused to recognize an exception to the exclusionary rule in cases in which the officer conducting the search acted in a good faith, but mistaken, belief that it was lawful (State v. Carter, 1988)— an exception to the Fourth Amendment recognized by the U.S. Supreme Court (United States v. Leon, 1984).

Warrants are required only to conduct searches that are not voluntarily permitted; in other words, a person can waive the requirement of a warrant by consenting to a search (State v. Little, 1967). What need not be searched for may be seized without prior authorization; that is, items in plain view may be seized by law enforcement officers without a warrant (State v. Colson, 1968). Finally, exigent circumstances may justify search and seizure: Lacking the time and opportunity to secure a warrant, an officer may conduct a lawful search in its absence. This principle applies in any case in which the evidence may be destroyed or removed. The most common example is a search of a motor vehicle; its mobility justifies immediate search (State v. Simmons, 1971).

The needs of modern administrative agencies have led to a relaxation of the rules that developed in the context of traditional criminal investigation. Charged with the enforcement of complex regulations, often in industrial settings, agencies require access to work places and records. Warrants to conduct administrative inspections that are permitted by state law on a lesser showing of cause have been upheld because sufficient safeguards are required to avoid the abuses associated with general warrants (Brooks v. Taylor Tobacco Enterprises, Inc., 1979).

SECTION 21

Inquiry into restraints on liberty. Every person restrained of his liberty is entitled to a remedy to inquire into the lawfulness thereof, and to remove the restraint if unlawful, and that remedy shall not be denied or delayed. The privilege of the writ of habeas corpus shall not be suspended.

The first sentence of this section dates from 1776 and was aimed at abuse of the power of imprisonment. The word chosen, "restraint," is intentionally comprehensive and includes all sorts of confinement, not limited to jails and prisons.

Nor is it limited to abuse by the state; false imprisonment by anyone is covered. The remedy to which everyone is entitled, although somewhat obscured by the punctuation, is twofold: to inquire into the lawfulness of the restraint and to remove it if unlawful. Perhaps because of the inclusion of this section, there was no separate guarantee in the state's first constitution of the writ of habeas corpus, the historic means by which the lawfulness of confinement was determined. The absence of a specific reference was of no practical import since England's Habeas Corpus Act (1679) was accepted as part of the state's common law. In the aftermath of the Civil War, an express prohibition of suspending the "great writ" was added, copied from the U.S. Constitution (art. I, § 9, cl. 2), although noticeably without the federal proviso "unless when in Cases of Rebellion or Invasion the public Safety may require it."

Relatively few cases have been decided on this section because the North Carolina courts have adopted a restrictive—and historically accurate—interpretation of its scope. In an early case the state supreme court refused to issue the writ of habeas corpus to a prisoner in the state penitentiary whose sentence may have been erroneous because that sentence was issued by a court of competent jurisdiction (In re Schenck, 1876). In other words, the writ may be used to challenge the authority that imposed the restraint, not its fairness; if properly authorized, the restraint is lawful for purposes of this section. The usual remedy for error committed by a lawful authority is an appeal in due course.

SECTION 22

> **Modes of prosecution.** Except in misdemeanor cases initiated in the District Court Division, no person shall be put to answer any criminal charge but by indictment, presentment, or impeachment. But any person, when represented by counsel, may, under such regulations as the General Assembly shall prescribe, waive indictment in non-capital cases.

The kernel of this section, "no person shall be put to answer any criminal charge but by indictment, presentment, or impeachment," first appeared in 1776; the rest was added later. The section lists all the means of initiating a criminal action, defined elsewhere in the constitution as one "prosecuted by the people of the State as a party against a person charged with a public offense, for the punishment thereof" (Article IV, Section 13, Subsection 1). Presentment and indictment both involve the grand jury, a body that at common law consisted of not less than twelve and not more than twenty-three persons; in North Carolina it is made up of eighteen. To charge a person at least twelve must concur. A presentment is returned upon the initiative of the grand jury; an indictment, the usual method, is returned upon evidence presented by the district attorney. Impeachment, an allegation of malfeasance in public office, begins the process of disciplining an officeholder. Punishment is limited to removal from office and disqualification from future office holding, but further criminal prosecution remains possible. The mechanics of impeachment are detailed in Article IV, Section 4.

The additions to this section provide for exceptions to proceeding by indictment. The opening clause, added in 1971, concerns misdemeanors, lesser offenses, that may be tried in the District Court Division of the General Court of Justice (Article IV, Section 10) upon an accusation other than the traditional one, usually an "information" brought directly by the district attorney without the interposition of a grand jury. This exception correlates with another in Section 24 of this article, guaranteeing trial by jury, but permitting non-jury trials for misdemeanors covered by statutes. The effect of the two exceptions taken together is to provide a cheaper and more efficient means of trying those accused of minor crimes. A problem in harmonizing these sections is encountered when a person convicted of a misdemeanor without indictment or trial by jury in district court exercises the right also guaranteed by Section 24 to appeal and demand a jury trial. In such a case, the defendant may be tried in superior court on the original accusation without an indictment (State v. Thomas, 1952).

The second sentence of the present section, which was added to the 1868 Constitution by amendment in 1950 and carried over in the 1971 Constitution, permits the informed waiver of the constitutional right to proceedings initiated by the grand jury in cases of felonies, except those punishable by death. For capital offenses the public interest in all the traditional safeguards precludes a waiver. By limiting the right to waive indictment to those represented by counsel, the section seeks to guarantee that no procedural advantage is lost without proper advice.

SECTION 23

> **Rights of accused.** In all criminal prosecutions, every person charged with crime has the right to be informed of the accusation and to confront the accusers and witnesses with other testimony, and to have counsel for defense, and not be compelled to give self-incriminating evidence, or to pay costs, jail fees, or necessary witness fees of the defense, unless found guilty.

A compendium of the requisites of a fair trial, this section largely dates from 1776; the right to counsel and the last clause concerning costs and fees were added in 1868.

1. "Informed of the accusation." The accused has a right not to be kept "in the dark" concerning the crime of which he or she is charged. This is primarily to enable the accused to prepare a defense, but it also gives meaning to the guarantee implied in Section 19 of this article against being twice put in jeopardy for the same offense. The judge also benefits from the provision since in case of conviction he or she must pronounce sentence according to law. Usually the indictment contains the necessary information; to be valid, it must allege "lucidly

and accurately all the essential elements of the offense endeavored to be charged''
(State v. Greer, 1953).

2. "Confront the accusers and witnesses with other testimony." The accused
has a right to respond to the charges against him or her. This clause and the
preceding one are the primary safeguards against the abuses of criminal procedure
described in Franz Kafka's nightmarish novel *The Trial*, which begins with the
chilling sentence: "Someone must have been telling lies about Joseph K., for
without having done anything wrong he was arrested one fine morning." The
accused not only may present testimony in his or her own behalf, but also is
entitled to "confront" his or her accusers, which excludes vague charges brought
by an anonymous "somebody." Confrontation includes the right to cross-ex-
amine opposing witnesses (State v. Perry, 1936). In case of trial by jury all must
occur in the presence of the jury.

The right to confront the accusers and witnesses necessarily means the defendant has a right to be present in the courtroom. Indeed, in capital cases the
accused must be present; in other words, the accused cannot waive this right
(State v. Kelly, 1887). The purpose, of course, is to prevent trials of such serious
crimes *in absentia*. In other than capital cases, the accused may waive the right
of confrontation by express consent, by failure to assert it, or by conduct inconsistent with a purpose to insist on it (State v. Mitchell, 1896). In no case is
it essential under this clause that the accused be present in an appellate court
hearing his or her appeal (State v. Jacobs, 1890). By that stage, the facts have
been determined, and the only issues are questions of law.

Although the confrontation clause generally requires the presence of the accusers and witnesses in court, it has always been subject to a number of exceptions. These include the testimony of a witness examined at a former trial who
has since become unavailable, the dying declarations of a person now dead, and
facts contained in official records (State v. Behrman, 1894). The right of the
accused to present his or her own witnesses includes the right to compulsory
process—that is, to the same instruments of state power available to the prosecution—but the state may require that a defendant requesting such process at
state expense establish at least a colorable need for the person to be summoned
(State v. House, 1978).

3. "Counsel for defense." The right to counsel in criminal trials was not
recognized at common law and was not mentioned in North Carolina's first
constitution. It was guaranteed in federal court by the Sixth Amendment in the
Bill of Rights and was added to the state's declaration of rights in 1868. At a
minimum the accused's right to counsel means the right to retain a lawyer to
conduct his or her defense. This right applies not just at trial, but also at every
critical stage leading to trial (State v. Hill, 1971). The courts have read into the
clause the word "effective," making it a guarantee of lawyerly competence as
well (State v. Vickers, 1982). The accused may waive the right to counsel and
conduct his or her own defense unaided (State v. Morris, 1969), although the
preceding section prohibits an unrepresented person from waiving indictment.

The North Carolina Supreme Court early recognized a duty of the trial court to appoint a lawyer for an accused who is unable to afford one (State v. Collins, 1874). Like the more affluent defendent, the indigent defendant has a right to counsel at every critical stage in the proceedings and to effective representation; also like one better off, the indigent has a right to refuse counsel and to represent himself or herself (State v. Mems, 1972), although all defendants would do well to remember the old adage that "he who acts as his own lawyer has a fool for a client."

4. "Not be compelled to give self-incriminating evidence." The horror of torture and coerced confessions, particularly the abuses in the sixteenth century by the English Court of High Commission, led to a common law ban on compulsory self-incrimination that was enshrined in the 1776 Constitution. The accused has a right to remain silent, and this silence may not be considered an admission of guilt (State v. Castor, 1974). The protection is not limited to testimony, but includes other "self-incriminating evidence" as well, so the accused may not be compelled to produce papers or effects that could be used against him or her (State v. Hollingsworth, 1926). On the other hand, an accused may not refuse to be looked at by those who might identify him or her as a criminal. By extension, other objective characteristics may also be examined despite the accused's objection. "Handwriting samples, blood samples, fingerprints, clothing, hair, voice demonstrations, even the body itself, are identifying physical characteristics and are outside the privilege against self-incrimination" (State v. Greene, 1971).

It may be confidently asserted that the accused is not the only one covered by this clause; so, too, is every witness—despite a literal reading: "[E]very person *charged with crime* has the right . . . not [to] be compelled to give self-incriminating evidence" (emphases added). The state supreme court, interpreting earlier wording—"every man has the right . . . not to be compelled to give evidence against himself"—held that "the fair interpretation of this clause seems to be to secure one who is *or may be* accused of crime from making any compulsory revelations which may be given in evidence against him on his trial for the offense" (La Fontaine v. Southern Underwriters Association, 1880) (emphasis added). In 1946 the present phrasing was adopted; it was carried over unchanged in the 1971 Constitution. The purpose of that amendment was, as the ballot issue put it, to make the constitution "equally applicable to men and women." In the process of substituting "person" for "man" in this section, the amendment added the words "charged with crime," but there is no reason to believe that any change was intended in the right against self-incrimination.

In the same case concerning the constitutional rights of witnesses, the state court adopted U.S. Chief Justice John Marshall's description of the proper roles of judge and witness in this area:

It is the province of the court to judge whether any direct answer to the question that may be proposed will furnish evidence against the witness. If such answer may disclose a fact which forms a necessary and essential link in the chain of testimony which would be sufficient to convict him of any crime, he is not bound to answer it, so as to furnish matter for that conviction. In such case the witness must himself judge what his answer will be, and if he says on his oath he cannot answer without accusing himself, he cannot be compelled to answer. (La Fontaine v. Southern Underwriters Association, 1880)

The right not to be compelled to give self-incriminating evidence does not extend beyond its terms. Without compulsion there is no violation, so a voluntary confession is admissible. (In cases of treason against the state it must under Section 29 of this article be "in open court.") By the same token, an accused may agree to testify in his or her own defense, but if the accused does so, he or she must also submit to cross-examination. Restated in terms of waiver, this means that an accused may waive his or her right to remain silent. Just as a person may give self-incriminating evidence if not compelled, so a person may be compelled to give evidence that is not incriminating. "[W]hen, as in our State, the statute provides that the witness in such case shall have absolute immunity from punishment in regard to his participation in the offense as to which he has been required to testify, the rule is universal that he may be compelled to testify" (In re Briggs, 1904). The grant of immunity eliminates not the compulsion, but the criminality.

5. "Not be compelled . . . to pay costs, jail fees, or necessary witness fees of the defense, unless found guilty." This clause, added in 1868, is designed to spare an accused some of the costs of proving his or her innocence. Before its addition, criminal defendants in North Carolina were obliged to pay costs even if acquitted (State v. Hodson, 1876).

SECTION 24

> **Right of jury trial in criminal cases.** No person shall be convicted of any crime but by the unanimous verdict of a jury in open court. The General Assembly may, however, provide for other means of trial for misdemeanors, with the right of appeal for trial de novo.

Continuing the emphasis on fair trial procedures begun in the preceding section, the present section is the first of three devoted to the jury. The first sentence dates from 1776, the second from 1868. Originating in the customary law of the Middle Ages, the jury had become by the time of the American Revolution a prized protection against tyranny. Even the Tory legal scholar Sir William Blackstone hailed it as "the grand bulwark" of English liberty.[9] Traditionally a group of twelve—in the 1776 and 1868 constitutions they were referred to by the time-hallowed phrase "good and lawful men"—the jury could act only with the agreement of all; this section makes unanimity a constitutional requirement. The legal act of the jury is its verdict (from Latin meaning "truth telling"), and this section also requires that it be rendered "in open court"—the openness here referred to being not the open-to-suitors of Section 18's open-courts requirement, but the ordinary sense of out in the open. Guilt or innocence is too important to be pronounced in secret. (Compare the requirement in Section 29 that any confession in a prosecution for treason be made "in open court.")

Although the number of persons constituting a jury is not specified in the constitution, the state supreme court has held that the term "jury" must be interpreted to mean what it meant at common law—that is, a body of twelve. So integral is this to proper procedure that a defendant cannot consent to trial by a jury composed of fewer (State v. Rogers, 1913). Since a jury was not used in contempt proceedings, this section does not require one (State v. Woodfin, 1844). Likewise, certain modern proceedings not known to the common law, such as delinquency proceedings in juvenile court, are not covered (In re Burrus, 1971). If the proceeding is a civil action as opposed to a criminal one, this section is obviously inapplicable; an action to revoke a driver's license, for example, although prosecuted by the state and resulting in the loss of a valuable privilege, is not a prosecution for crime and therefore not covered (State v. Carlisle, 1974). Juries in civil cases are guaranteed by the following section "[i]n all controversies at law respecting property." Despite the unqualified words "No person shall be convicted of any crime but by the unanimous verdict of a jury in open court," a conviction may nonetheless be entered on a defendant's plea of guilty without a trial by jury.

Before 1868 the legislature had no explicit authority to provide for the trial of minor offenses without a jury. The last sentence of the present section dates (with insignificant variations) to an addition made in the state's second constitution in 1868. The purpose is to avoid the expense and delay of jury trials for all misdemeanors. Nonetheless, the regard for this ancient bulwark of liberty is so great that it remains available at the defendant's demand on appeal, in which case the charge must be proved *de novo* (anew) without regard to the earlier juryless proceeding. While the General Assembly has the power to define misdemeanors, it could not constitutionally classify as a misdemeanor a crime whose punishment is "clearly not of that class of offenses" (State v. Lytle, 1905).

SECTION 25

Right of jury trial in civil cases. In all controversies at law respecting property, the ancient mode of trial by jury is one of the best securities of the rights of the people, and shall remain sacred and inviolable.

Dating to 1776 when it was modeled on a section in the Virginia Declaration of Rights, the guarantee of trial by jury in civil cases was the basis of one of the most famous decisions in North Carolina's legal history, Bayard v. Singleton (1787). Notwithstanding the constitutional guarantee, the General Assembly had adopted a statute concerning the confiscation and sale of land belonging to Tories in the Revolutionary War that directed judges to dismiss challenges to titles to confiscated estates on a showing that the defendant had purchased from a state commissioner. To obey the statute would have been to deny trial by jury, so the judges refused, setting an early precedent for judicial review.

Although this section, unlike the preceding one, does not specify a unanimous verdict, one is held to be required. That certainly was the "ancient mode"; for the same reason a jury of no less than twelve is also required (Rhyne v. Lipscombe, 1898). In the state's first constitution the reference to controversies *at law* operated to exclude from the constitutional guarantee those *in equity*. In the second constitution, law and equity were merged (see Article IV, Section 13, Subsection 1), and the guarantee of trial by jury was subsequently held to apply to all cases in which juries were used at common law or in which they were provided by statute at the time the 1868 Constitution was adopted (Groves v. Ware, 1921). Despite the adoption of the third constitution in 1970, the justices of the state supreme court have refused to update the requirement: The determinative date for purposes of the guarantee remains 1868. The rationale is that the latest constitution was not intended to change substantive rights (North Carolina State Bar v. DuMont, 1982).

"Property," as used in this section, is defined expansively and includes "everything which a man may have exclusive dominion over" (Wilson v. Board of Aldermen of the City of Charlotte, 1876). By necessary implication it excludes controversies not concerning such things as, for example, removal from office of a district attorney (Hyatt v. Hamme, 1920), revocation of a driver's license (State v. Carlisle, 1974), and child custody (In re Clark, 1981). Proceedings for the taking of property by eminent domain are not included (Kaperonis v. State Highway Commission, 1963); nor are proceedings for the equitable distribution of marital property upon divorce included (Kiser v. Kiser, 1989), not because no property is at issue—it obviously is—but because jury trials were not available in such cases in 1868.

For the guarantee of trial by jury to become applicable there must be a genuine controversy concerning the facts; that is, a judge must make a preliminary determination that there exists an issue of fact to be resolved by a jury. Otherwise, none is required (North Carolina National Bank v. Burnette, 1979). Even when there is such an issue, the right to a jury trial may be waived and the facts determined by the judge (Article IV, Section 14).

SECTION 26

Jury service. No person shall be excluded from jury service on account of sex, race, color, religion, or national origin.

Although in the spirit of much that was done in 1868, this section does not in fact date from Reconstruction. North Carolina women gained the right to vote in 1920 when the Nineteenth Amendment to the U.S. Constitution was ratified, but they had remained ineligible for jury service. In 1944 the state supreme court held that the phrase "good and lawful men," then in the constitutional guarantee of jury trial in criminal cases, had to be taken literally (State v. Emery, 1944). In 1946 state voters ratified a series of amendments presented as "making the Constitution equally applicable to men and women." Chief among them was a sentence added to the section on jury trials in civil cases that prohibited the exclusion of women as jurors; the historical reference to "good and lawful men" in the guarantee of jury trials in criminal cases was also altered. At the same time, the famous phrase in Section 1, "all men are created equal," became "all persons are created equal," and the rights of the accused in Section 23 were reworded to apply not just to "every man," but to "every person charged with crime." In 1971 the provision on jury service became a separate section, and exclusion on account of race, color, religion, or national origin was also banned, a prohibition that repeats the non-discrimination clause of Section 19.

Perhaps the main reason for the non-discriminatory selection of jurors is the increased likelihood of doing justice to all individuals, but it is also true that the judicial system has its own interest in non-exclusivity. The composition of juries now approximates that of the state's population as a whole, giving a democratic reality to the age-old notion of trial by a jury of one's peers. For this reason the state supreme court has proscribed all challenges to jurors based on race; challenges for cause are obviously prohibited by this section, while peremptory challenges, which need not ordinarily be explained, have been held also to be prohibited if based on race. When all (or most) of those challenged are of the same race, the prosecutor must offer convincing non-discriminatory explanations (Jackson v. Housing Authority of High Point, 1988).

This section applies to the grand jury as well as to the trial (or petit) jury and also prohibits racial discrimination in the selection of the foreman of the grand jury. A defendant may prove racial discrimination in the selection of a foreman by showing that "for a substantial period in the past, relatively few blacks have served in the position of foreman even though a substantial number have been selected to serve as members of grand juries" (State v. Cofield, 1987). In a later stage of the same case it was held that the state can overcome the statistical evidence only by showing "both a racially neutral selection process and a racially neutral reason for the grand jury foreman's selection" (State v. Cofield, 1989).

A special problem arises under this section when a juror is excused from service in a case involving a crime punishable by death because of a conscientious objection to the death penalty. Although the juror's opposition to capital punishment may in fact be based on religion, the state supreme court has not found this to violate the present section. The juror is excused primarily because of an inability to follow the law regarding jury service, not because of religious affiliation (State v. Davis, 1989).

SECTION 27

Bail, fines, and punishments. Excessive bail shall not be required, nor excessive fines imposed, nor cruel or unusual punishments inflicted.

Bail, security for a later appearance, comes before trial for a criminal offense or while awaiting the decision of an appeal for a criminal conviction; fines and punishments come after conviction of a criminal offense. With the exception of pretrial bail, the subjects of this section are the rights not of the accused, but of convicted criminals. The three are linked by a common concern with how the power of the state is applied to individuals. They are also linked by a common history. The North Carolina drafters may have borrowed the provision in 1776 from either the Virginia or the Maryland Declaration of Rights, although they changed the wording slightly to "cruel *nor* unusual punishments" (since 1868 it has read "cruel *or* unusual punishments")—a change that may conceivably have practical consequences (Medley v. Department of Correction, 1992). In any event, the ultimate source of the guarantee was the English Declaration of Rights of 1689 which the U.S. Bill of Rights repeats almost verbatim in the Eighth Amendment. Although no right to bail is spelled out, it is widely assumed.

What is "excessive" or "cruel or unusual" is difficult to define. Perhaps the most usable touchstone was indicated as long ago as 1911 in Henry G. Connor and Joseph B. Cheshire's annotations to the state constitution: "[W]hatever is greater than has ever been prescribed, or known, or inflicted, must be excessive, cruel and unusual."[10] There is plentiful and eminent authority, dating back to Justice William Gaston's opinion in State v. Manuel (1838), that the constitutional prohibition applies mainly to judges and then "only in those cases where they have a discretion in the amount of bail, the quantum of fine, and the nature of the punishment." The argument is that the General Assembly must have discretion to regulate criminal procedure and to prescribe the punishment of crimes and that the judges should not interfere except in cases "so enormous that there can be no doubt but that all discretion has been thrown aside." It is certainly true that the legislature must not be shackled by history, limited by what has been done before; it must be free to respond to new social threats and to reflect changing perceptions of relative degrees of seriousness in criminal offenses. Nonetheless, it would be going too far to affirm that the legislature is exempt from this section, and a number of cases (e.g., State v. Rogers, 1969; State v. Smith, 1917) have seemed to recognize that a statute's provisions for punishment must also pass constitutional muster.

SECTION 28

Imprisonment for debt. There shall be no imprisonment for debt in this State, except in cases of fraud.

Although the prohibition of imprisonment for debt did not enter the declaration of rights until 1868, something like it, modeled on a section of the Pennsylvania Constitution, had earlier appeared in the body of the 1776 Constitution: "[T]he Person of a Debtor, where there is not a strong Presumption of Fraud, shall not be continued in Prison after delivering up, *bona fide*, all his Estate, real and personal, for the Use of his Creditors, in such Manner as shall hereafter be regulated by Law.'' It should be noted that this early provision did not prevent debtors from going to prison in the first place, only from staying there after they had complied with the statute.

Imprisonment for debt was part of the common law. Its essence was that a person who failed to pay as required by an enforceable promise could be ordered by a court to perform or suffer imprisonment. As a practical matter, imprisonment could cause a debtor to disgorge concealed assets or friends of a debtor to ''ransom'' the unfortunate one. The effect, however, was to impose a criminal punishment for a civil ''offense,'' breach of contract. In time, this lapse of legal logic made imprisonment for debt vulnerable to critics; it had always been cruel in the case of the impecunious and friendless, as the novels of Charles Dickens amply illustrated. In England, the original home of the practice, it was ended by the Debtor's Act in 1869.

The present section has been held to apply only to causes of action based on contract—that is, debt voluntarily assumed. Justice William B. Rodman, who had been a leader of the 1868 Constitutional Convention, pointed out that if the Framers had meant to forbid imprisonment in every civil action, they would have said so (Moore v. Green, 1875). Specifically that means that the section has no application to actions based on tort (Long v. McLean, 1883). It is also inapplicable to actions to collect back taxes (State v. Locklear, 1974).

Criminal penalties are covered by the preceding section, prohibiting ''excessive fines,'' so they are not covered by this section, and the costs of prosecution, which may be assessed on those found guilty (see Section 23), do not constitute a contract debt, so a person may be imprisoned for their nonpayment as well (State v. Wallin, 1883). Likewise, failure to perform judicial decrees, even those requiring the payment of money, may be enforced by imprisonment for contempt of court (Wilson v. Wilson, 1964). Conditioning a suspended sentence on a requirement that the convicted criminal pay restitution to the victim is also permitted (State v. Caudle, 1970).

Even with contract debts, imprisonment is allowed ''in cases of fraud.'' In Melvin v. Melvin (1875), the court held that these words ''comprehend not only fraud in attempting to hinder, delay and defeat the collection of a debt by concealing property and other fraudulent devices, but embrace, also, fraud in making the contract—false representations, for instance, and fraud in incurring the liability. . . . ''

SECTION 29

Treason against the State. Treason against the State shall consist only of levying war against it or adhering to its enemies by giving them aid and comfort. No person shall be convicted of treason unless on the testimony

of two witnesses to the same overt act, or on confession in open court. No
conviction of treason or attainder shall work corruption of blood or forfeiture.

Loyalty is a duty owed the sovereign; treason is the crime committed by one
actively disloyal. By declaring their independence and taking up arms against
Great Britain, Americans rejected the sovereignty of the British monarch; in
their state constitutions they proclaimed instead the sovereignty of the people.
Of course, the American Revolution began with a treasonable act, but military
victory led to legal recognition of American independence. "Treason doth never
prosper: what's the reason?" asked the Elizabethan rhymer Sir John Harington,
"For if it prosper, none dare call it treason."

By adopting the U.S. Constitution, Americans created a system with two
sovereigns; hence, they owe two duties of loyalty, and two distinct treasons are
possible: against the state and against the United States. Of course, in case of
conflict, the national claim is superior; in the old-fashioned language of Section
5 of this article, "paramount allegiance" is owed to the Constitution and government of the United States. After the Civil War, in which the cause of the
Confederacy did not "prosper," treason was on everyone's mind, and the crime
of treason against the state was first added to the North Carolina Constitution in
1868 in a section modeled on the provisions of the U.S. Constitution (art. III,
§ 3). Although originally located in Article IV on the judiciary, that section was
moved in 1962, when that article was rewritten, to Article I, the Declaration of
Rights, where it remains in the 1971 Constitution.

Treason is the only crime created directly by the constitution. The three
sentences of the present section deal respectively with the definition of the crime,
the evidence necessary for conviction, and the punishment to be meted out. The
description of the two substantive acts—"levying war" against the state and
"adhering to its enemies by giving them aid and comfort"—are ultimately
traceable to the English Statute of Treasons (1351). In modern North Carolina,
as in medieval England, a restrictive definition of this most serious crime is
desirable to avoid expansive common law constructions. For the same reason
restrictive rules of evidence are necessary. The prosecution must prove an "overt
act"—that is, an outward act done in actual preparation for the crime; mere
inward intention to commit it is not enough. Requiring two witnesses to the
same act is a substantial hurdle: No comparable requirement existed at common
law for any crime except perjury, and English statutes required two witnesses
only for treason. To lessen the risk of coerced confessions, it is required that
any such self-incrimination be—like jury verdicts in criminal cases (see Section
24 of this article)—"in open court." Finally, a limit is placed on the punishment
for treason: On conviction or "attainder," which in this context is the same
thing, there shall be no "corruption of blood" (i.e., disability to inherit land or
to pass it on to anyone by descent) or "forfeiture" (i.e., escheat or loss of lands
presently held).

SECTION 30

Militia and the right to bear arms. A well regulated militia being necessary to the security of a free State, the right of the people to keep and bear arms shall not be infringed; and, as standing armies in time of peace are dangerous to liberty, they shall not be maintained, and the military shall be kept under strict subordination to, and governed by, the civil power. Nothing herein shall justify the practice of carrying concealed weapons, or prevent the General Assembly from enacting penal statutes against that practice.

The first clause of this section, as it appeared in 1776, provided: "the People have a right to bear Arms, for the Defense of the State." It was copied from a section of the Pennsylvania Declaration of Rights with one significant omission: The Pennsylvania instrument recognized the people's "right to bear arms for the defence *of themselves* and the state" (emphasis added). The current phrasing, which was adopted in 1868, conforms the clause to the Second Amendment in the U.S. Bill of Rights. The other clause, prohibiting "standing armies in time of peace," also copied from the same section of the Pennsylvania Declaration of Rights, is noticeably lacking in the U.S. Constitution. The final sentence, like the phrase in Section 12 of this article banning secret political societies, was added on the recommendation of the constitutional convention in 1875. Both are designed to prevent constitutional safeguards—freedom of assembly and the right to bear arms, respectively—being used as shields by those bent on undermining the constitution.

As both the present wording and the original wording of this section make plain, the right to bear arms in North Carolina is intimately connected with the defense of the state; as befits a republic, the people will defend it themselves. But the right has also been extended by the state supreme court to include the right to possess a weapon to exercise the "common-law right of self-defense," in effect reinserting the phrase deleted in 1776; like other constitutional rights, this one, too, is subject to reasonable regulation (State v. Dawson, 1968). Peacetime armies, known in England in the seventeenth century when Stuart monarchs had maintained them, could be misused by the executive. Particularly in the premodern era, officer corps could foster aristocratic traditions, and soldiers could develop loyalties to the army rather than to the state. Standing armies are therefore prohibited, and to minimize the risks when military force is required, a civilian is placed in ultimate control. Elsewhere, the governor is designated the state's commander in chief (Article III, Section 5, Subsection 5 and Article XII, Section 1).

SECTION 31

Quartering of soldiers. No soldier shall in time of peace be quartered in any house without the consent of the owner, nor in time of war but in a manner prescribed by law.

War and peace are again the concern in this section, added to the constitution
in 1868 when the Civil War was still fresh in men's minds. Having conformed
the guarantee of North Carolinians' right to bear arms in the preceding section
to the wording of the Second Amendment to the U.S. Constitution, the delegates
to the Reconstruction convention may have decided to remedy the failure in the
state's original declaration of rights to provide against abuses in the quartering
of troops as in the Third Amendment. The earlier lapse is probably explained
by the state's experience during the American Revolution: What British forces
there were in North Carolina were mostly passing through, engaged in actual
combat, so the problem of long-term quarters never became the grievance it did
elsewhere.

The present section repeats the Third Amendment, and the preceding one the
Second—with additions carried over from 1776. It is the older material that
causes a certain logical difficulty: How can there be soldiers to be quartered "in
time of peace" under Section 31 when "standing armies in time of peace" are
banned by Section 30? In wartime, of course, there would be scope for the
present section—no quartering of troops in private houses except as prescribed
by law—but it is hard to imagine a modern military establishment dispersing its
soldiers, rather than building barracks.

SECTION 32

> **Exclusive emoluments.** No person or set of persons is entitled to exclusive
> or separate emoluments or privileges from the community but in
> consideration of public services.

See the commentary following Section 33.

SECTION 33

> **Hereditary emoluments and honors.** No hereditary emoluments,
> privileges, or honors shall be granted or conferred in this State.

Sections 32 and 33 concerning emoluments both date from 1776, although in
the state's first and second declarations of rights they were widely separated; the
former derives originally from a section of the Virginia Declaration of Rights.
Section 33, prohibiting the creation of inheritable interests in offices or titles,
has never generated significant legal controversy. By contrast, Section 32 has,
on the state supreme court's own reckoning, been "frequently invoked" to strike
down legislation (Brumley v. Baxter, 1945). Attention has focused not so much
on emoluments—that is, payments for public services—as on privileges conferred
by the state. Whenever a "person or set of persons," including, of course,
entities endowed by law with legal personality such as corporations, is granted

special rights or exemptions, a question is raised under this section. Unless the public welfare is served, the privilege is invalid; it has been held, for example, that legislation burdening businesses operating in only a certain portion of the state violates Section 32 when similar businesses elsewhere in the state operate freely (State v. Harris, 1940). Today the problem might also be considered under the equal protection clause of Article I, Section 19, added in 1971.

Although many laws have been struck down, many others have survived challenge under Section 32. The state may constitutionally grant exclusive franchises to corporations to operate railroads, ferries, or utilities. Grants to public service corporations are, the court has said, "directly within the words and meaning of the exception" (Reid v. Norfolk & Southern Railroad, 1913). The problem, as ever, is in drawing the line in the right place. It is often said that the legislative intention is determinative. For example, a statute restricting traffic, but conferring an exemption in favor of a certain set of persons, was upheld because it passed two tests: "(1) [T]he exemption is intended to promote the general welfare rather than the benefit of the individual, and (2) there is a reasonable basis for the legislature to conclude the granting of the exemption serves the public interest" (Town of Emerald Isle ex rel. Smith v. State, 1987).

SECTION 34

Perpetuities and monopolies. Perpetuities and monopolies are contrary to the genius of a free state and shall not be allowed.

The "security of a free State" is safeguarded in Section 30 by guaranteeing the right to bear arms; now the "genius [or special character] of a free state" is invoked to prohibit certain economic practices. In 1776 when this section was first adopted, perpetuities meant legal arrangements involving entails that tied up land in one family for all future generations—the legal basis, in other words, of a landed aristocracy. Monopolies, too, had at that time political overtones. English monarchs had used grants of monopolies to reward their political favorites, provoking the Statute of Monopolies in 1624, which made all monopolies illegal except those authorized by parliament or those granted to protect inventions, an exception reflected today in federal patent law (see U.S. Const. art. I, § 8, cl. 8). In the state's first declaration of rights the present section had correlated with a constitutional provision that directed the legislature to "regulate Entails in such a manner as to prevent Perpetuities." Discharging its duty in 1784, the General Assembly spelled out the connection with political freedom: "[E]ntails of estates tend only to raise the wealth and importance of particular families and individuals, giving them an unequal and undue influence in a republic, and prove in manifold instances the source of great contention and injustice."[11]

The 1784 legislation regulating entails eliminated the possibility of perpetuities strictly so called. There exists in addition a complicated common law rule known as the Rule Against Perpetuities that bars other long-lasting arrangements. Although the North Carolina Court of Appeals has mentioned in passing that the application of this rule has the "continuing sanction" of this section (North Carolina National Bank v. Norris, 1974), it should not be taken to mean that the Rule Against Perpetuities in its present formulation is beyond the reach of the legislature.

Although to the revolutionary generation the evil of monopolies lay in their political consequences, in modern minds the economic ill effects are uppermost. Since a legal monopoly would be the grant of an exclusive right to trade in a certain area or to deal in certain goods, it is indistinguishable from the "exclusive . . . privileges" referred to in Section 32. The problem is that Section 32 permits such arrangements when "in consideration of public services," and on this basis public utility companies have been created. By and large, such companies are functioning monopolies, although the state retains the legal right to create competing companies (Durham v. North Carolina, 1968).

SECTION 35

> **Recurrence to fundamental principles.** A frequent recurrence to fundamental principles is absolutely necessary to preserve the blessings of liberty.

Based on a section of the Pennsylvania Declaration of Rights, this section has been included in all three state constitutions. It is a salutary reminder that commentaries of all sorts, whether in judicial opinions or in academic treatises, no matter how helpful in explicating particular texts, are no substitute for the originals. All generations are solemnly enjoined to return *ad fontes* (to the sources) and rethink for themselves the implications of the fundamental principles of self-government that animated the revolutionary generation. In interpreting the constitution, the admonition may offer a clue in difficult cases. In a leading Virginia case from 1794 the respected Judge Spencer Roane, mindful of the cognate provision in the Virginia Declaration of Rights, defined "fundamental principles" as "those great principles growing out of the Constitution, by the aid of which, in dubious cases, the Constitution may be explained and preserved inviolate; those landmarks, which it may be necessary to resort to, on account of the impossibility to foresee or provide for cases within the spirit, but without the letter of the Constitution" (Kamper v. Hawkins, 1794).

SECTION 36

> **Other rights of the people.** The enumeration of rights in this Article shall not be construed to impair or deny others retained by the people.

This section was added in 1868, modeled on the Ninth Amendment in the U.S. Bill of Rights. Lists have a way of seeming exclusive: It may be argued that what was not included was intentionally excluded. *Inclusio unius est exclusio alterius* (the inclusion of one thing is the exclusion of another) is an old legal maxim. Section 36 effectively counters that argument. Although the people of North Carolina have expressly declared many rights in Article I, they have not attempted a complete enumeration. This concluding section may have been rendered necessary by the introduction to the declaration of rights, also added in 1868, describing its purpose as the recognition and establishment of *"the* great, general, and essential principles of liberty and free government" (emphasis added). The fact that the definite article was used is not to be taken to mean that the list is definitive. This last section harks back to Section 1 which recognizes "inalienable rights" and then lists four "among these." Section 36 reminds us that the whole declaration of rights, despite its great importance, is no more than that: a selection only, not a complete catalog.

The drafters of the 1971 Constitution took care to prune some potentially troublesome language from the 1868 original. The comparable section in the prior constitution had concluded with "and all powers, not herein delegated, remain with the people." The implication might have been that the state government, like the federal, is one of delegated powers only. On the contrary, the North Carolina General Assembly has long been recognized to possess all legislative powers not specifically denied it, and the curtailed phrasing of the present section is consistent with that fact.

Article II

Legislative

SECTION 1

Legislative power. The legislative power of the State shall be vested in the General Assembly, which shall consist of a Senate and a House of Representatives.

Following Article I, the Declaration of Rights, and its statement of fundamental principles, Article II begins a series of articles concerned with the structure of state government. True to the principle of separation of powers prescribed in Article I, Section 6, Articles II through IV assign the legislative, executive, and judicial powers to distinct branches of government. The legislative power is vested in the General Assembly, so called because all the people are present there in the persons of their representatives. The General Assembly has had a continuous existence since 1776; it has always consisted of two chambers, although the lower house from 1776 until 1868 was named (in accordance with English custom) the house of commons. The upper chamber, a republican version of the English House of Lords, was named the senate in imitation of the ancient Roman Senate, familiar to revolutionary leaders from their classical education.

Although originally the sole source of legislation, the General Assembly in modern times began to share its rule-making power with administrative agencies, executive branch bodies that combine otherwise separated powers. The judicial article expressly permits the delegation to administrative agencies of "such judicial powers as may be reasonably necessary as an incident to the accomplishment of the purposes for which the agencies were created" (Article IV, Section 3). In the absence of a comparable provision in the legislative article, the state supreme court has rationalized the delegation of legislative power by distinguishing between "supreme legislative power," vested exclusively by the present section in the General Assembly, and limited legislative power, sometimes called quasi-legislative power, which may be delegated so long as adequate guiding standards are provided (North Carolina Turnpike Authority v. Pine Island, Inc., 1965).

Not all questions of legislative power implicate the principle of separation of powers. Even in areas in which its power is supreme, the legislature cannot restrict the power of a succeeding legislature; what one session of the General Assembly may do may be undone by another (Plemmer v. Matthewson, 1971). Nor can a majority of the General Assembly delegate its power to make laws to a select group of legislators (Advisory Opinion in re Separation of Powers, 1982). The ultimate explanation of these rules lies in the concept of "legislative power" itself.

SECTION 2

Number of Senators. The Senate shall be composed of 50 Senators, biennially chosen by ballot.

The number of senators was set at fifty by amendment in 1835 and has not varied since then. The original plan in the state's first constitution allotted one senator to each county, so the number increased as western counties were organized and eastern counties divided. At first, senators were elected annually, but the 1835 amendment lengthened the term to two years, another change that has endured. Although not specified here, the ballot by which senators are chosen has elsewhere been held to mean a secret ballot (see Article VI, Section 5).

SECTION 3

Senate districts; apportionment of Senators. The Senators shall be elected from districts. The General Assembly, at the first regular session convening after the return of every decennial census of population taken by order of Congress, shall revise the senate districts and the apportionment of Senators among those districts, subject to the following requirements:

1. Each Senator shall represent, as nearly as may be, an equal number of inhabitants, the number of inhabitants that each Senator represents being determined for this purpose by dividing the population of the district that he represents by the number of Senators apportioned to that district;

2. Each senate district shall at all times consist of contiguous territory;

3. No county shall be divided in the formation of a senate district;

4. When established, the senate districts and the apportionment of Senators shall remain unaltered until the return of another decennial census of population taken by order of Congress.

The 1776 Constitution provided one senator for each county. Although that arrangement was dropped in 1835, the amenders were under instructions from the General Assembly not to divide a county between two or more senatorial districts, an early precursor of Clause 3 above. From 1835 senatorial districts were based on wealth, as measured by the amount of taxes paid. The 1868 Constitution changed the basis of representation to population—at first, as determined by a state-conducted census, and since an 1873 amendment, as determined by the federal census conducted every ten years on the anniversary of the first enumeration in 1790.

SECTION 4

Number of Representatives. The House of Representatives shall be composed of 120 Representatives, biennially chosen by ballot.

Just as the size of the senate has not varied since 1835, so, too, the size of the lower house (originally called the house of commons) has been constant since then. The 1776 Constitution had provided for two representatives from each county and one each from a few designated "borough towns." In the original plan, the representatives were elected annually; biennial elections, first provided in 1835, have been the rule ever since. Choice "by ballot" has been interpreted to mean "by secret ballot" (see Article VI, Section 5).

SECTION 5

Representative districts; apportionment of Representatives. The Representatives shall be elected from districts. The General Assembly, at the first regular session convening after the return of every decennial census of population taken by order of Congress, shall revise the representative districts and the apportionment of Representatives among those districts, subject to the following requirements:

1. Each Representative shall represent, as nearly as may be, an equal number of inhabitants, the number of inhabitants that each Representative represents being determined for this purpose by dividing the population of the district that he represents by the number of Representatives apportioned to that district;

2. Each representative district shall at all times consist of contiguous territory;

3. No county shall be divided in the formation of a representative district;

4. When established, the representative districts and the apportionment of Representatives shall remain unaltered until the return of another decennial census of population taken by order of Congress.

From 1776 representation in the lower house was based on counties (and borough towns); since 1835 it has been based on population. When the switch was made, the General Assembly instructed the amenders to guarantee each county at least one representative. That guarantee was dropped in 1968 by an amendment that conformed the apportionment of the house of representatives to the federal requirement of one person–one vote, although an echo of it can still be heard in Clause 3, forbidding the division of counties between representative districts.

SECTION 6

> **Qualifications for Senator.** Each Senator, at the time of his election, shall be not less than 25 years of age, shall be a qualified voter of the State, and shall have resided in the State as a citizen for two years and in the district for which he is chosen for one year immediately preceding his election.

See the commentary following Section 7.

SECTION 7

> **Qualifications for Representative.** Each Representative, at the time of his election, shall be a qualified voter of the State, and shall have resided in the district for which he is chosen for one year immediately preceding his election.

Under the state's first constitution there were significant property qualifications for elective office, higher for senators than for representatives, but these were abolished by the second constitution in 1868. In one of the few additions made at that time to the declaration of rights, property qualifications, either for voting or for office holding, were forbidden, "as political rights and privileges are not dependent upon or modified by property" (Article I, Section 11). The senate has always been a smaller body, and during the period from 1835 to 1868 senatorial districts were based on wealth, as measured by the amount of taxes paid. Once population alone became the basis of representation in both houses, the distinctiveness of senators was reduced; it lingers in the somewhat higher age qualification and the two-year residency requirement. Other minimal qualifications are imposed by the requirement that each senator and representative be a "qualified voter of the State." (For voter qualifications, see Article VI, Section 2.) Although the voting age is now eighteen, the minimum age for elective office remains twenty-one (Article VI, Section 6), except as otherwise specified—as for senators. The governor and lieutenant governor must be at least thirty (Article III, Section 2, Subsection 2). Disqualifications for office are set out in Article VI, Section 8.

SECTION 8

Elections. The election for members of the General Assembly shall be held for the respective districts in 1972 and every two years thereafter, at the places and on the day prescribed by law.

Sections 2 and 4 of this article provide that senators and representatives, respectively, shall be "biennially chosen." This section provides for those elections to be held in even-numbered years.

SECTION 9

Term of office. The term of office of Senators and Representatives shall commence on the first day of January next after their election.

From 1868 until a constitutional amendment in 1982 the term of office of senators and representatives commenced "at the time of their election." By the present wording, all terms begin alike on New Year's Day of odd-numbered years.

SECTION 10

Vacancies. Every vacancy occurring in the membership of the General Assembly by reason of death, resignation, or other cause shall be filled in the manner prescribed by law.

Rather than order a new election in case of a legislative vacancy, the General Assembly has prescribed a process guaranteed to leave the political balance unchanged: The governor is required to appoint the person recommended by the political party executive committee for the district (North Carolina General Statutes § 163-11).

SECTION 11

Sessions.

1. Regular Sessions. The General Assembly shall meet in regular session in 1973 and every two years thereafter on the day prescribed by law. Neither house shall proceed upon public business unless a majority of all of its members are actually present.

2. Extra sessions on legislative call. The President of the Senate and the Speaker of the House of Representatives shall convene the General Assembly in extra session by their joint proclamation upon receipt by the President of the Senate of written requests therefor signed by three-fifths of all the members of the Senate and upon receipt by the Speaker of the House of

Representatives of written requests therefor signed by three-fifths of all the members of the House of Representatives.

While their term of office begins on January 1 of odd-numbered years, senators and representatives do not begin to function in their legislative capacity until their respective houses are convened. The day prescribed by law is the "first Wednesday after the second Monday in January" (North Carolina General Statutes § 120-11.1). The requirement that a majority of its members be "actually present" before a house commences to take up public business is designed to prevent a lesser number from usurping the powers of the whole. In theory, a majority of one house, by refusing to attend the opening session, could prevent that house from operating and thereby prevent the General Assembly from enacting legislation. Regular sessions may (and now usually do) extend over two years, so a bill may take that long to pass into law.

Extra sessions must be convened at the request of three-fifths of the members of both houses, a provision added by amendment at the same time the 1971 Constitution was approved. The president of the senate and the speaker of the house are without discretion in the matter: They "shall convene" the General Assembly on receipt of the proper number of requests. Extra sessions may also be convened by a majority of the Council of State in case the mental capacity of the governor is in question (Article III, Section 3) or by the governor "on extraordinary occasions" (Article III, Section 5, Subsection 7).

SECTION 12

Oath of members. Each member of the General Assembly, before taking his seat, shall take an oath or affirmation that he will support the Constitution and laws of the United States and the Constitution of the State of North Carolina, and will faithfully discharge his duty as a member of the Senate or House of Representatives.

The words of the oath are set out in Article VI, Section 7 and make express what would be the case in any event under the supremacy clause of the U.S. Constitution (art. VI, cls. 2–3): that the U.S. Constitution and laws come first, then the state constitution and laws "not inconsistent therewith." In addition, Article I, Section 5 proclaims the "paramount allegiance" of every North Carolinian, not just legislators, to the Constitution and government of the United States and declares invalid any state law "in contravention or subversion thereof." The option of affirmation (as opposed to oath) was originally offered in North Carolina and elsewhere as an accommodation to Quakers and other Christian sects that took literally Jesus' command in the Sermon on the Mount, "Swear not at all" (Matt. 5:34), and refused to take oaths. An affirmation is a solemn declaration of equal legal effect.

SECTION 13

President of the Senate. The Lieutenant Governor shall be President of
the Senate and shall preside over the Senate, but shall have no vote unless
the Senate is equally divided.

The office of lieutenant governor was first created by the 1868 Constitution.
Under the 1776 Constitution the governor was elected by the General Assembly
for a term of one year; by amendment in 1835 the office was made directly
elected, and the term was lengthened to two years. The duties of the governor
remained modest, and it was not until the office received enhanced power and
a four-year term in 1868 that a second in command was called for. Although
an officer in the executive branch, the lieutenant governor has an anomalous
legislative role as the senate's presiding officer. Out of respect for the principle
of separation of powers, the lieutenant governor has no vote in the senate, except
in case of a tie. (The house of representatives, which also has an even number
of members, has no constitutional tie breaker.) Because of this dual role, the
lieutenant governor's office as president of the senate is repeated among the
duties of the lieutenant governor in Article III, Section 6.

SECTION 14

Other officers of the Senate.

1. President Pro Tempore—succession to presidency. The Senate shall
elect from its membership a President Pro Tempore, who shall become
President of the Senate upon the failure of the Lieutenant Governor-elect to
qualify, or upon succession by the Lieutenant Governor to the office of
Governor, or upon the death, resignation, or removal from office of the
President of the Senate, and who shall serve until the expiration of his term
of office as Senator.

2. President Pro Tempore—temporary succession. During the physical or
mental incapacity of the President of the Senate to perform the duties of his
office, or during the absence of the President of the Senate, the President
Pro Tempore shall preside over the Senate.

3. Other Officers. The Senate shall elect its other officers.

Before 1868 the senate's presiding officer had been its speaker, elected from its
membership; since 1868 the lieutenant governor, in the capacity of president of
the senate, has presided. The president pro tempore ("for the time being"),
successor to the antebellum speaker of the senate, performs that function during
the lieutenant governor's incapacity or absence. Like all legislative officers, the
president pro tempore must be chosen by voice vote, *viva voce* (Article VI,
Section 5). In case the office of lieutenant governor is vacant, the president pro

tempore becomes president of the senate, presumably without losing the right
to vote in the capacity of senator.

SECTION 15

Officers of the House of Representatives. The House of Representatives
shall elect its Speaker and other officers.

Unlike the Senate, the lower house has always chosen its own presiding officer.
Although not expressly required, the speaker is in fact elected from its membership. Unlike the president of the senate, the speaker of the house is not
deprived by the constitution of the right to vote. All elections by the General
Assembly must be by voice vote, *viva voce* (Article VI, Section 5).

SECTION 16

Compensation and allowances. The members and officers of the General
Assembly shall receive for their services the compensation and allowances
prescribed by law. An increase in the compensation or allowances of
members shall become effective at the beginning of the next regular session
of the General Assembly following the session at which it was enacted.

By its silence the 1868 Constitution as originally drafted and adopted authorized
the members of the General Assembly to set their own compensation. By amendment in 1876 the constitution set the amount, originally four dollars a day for
a sixty-day session. Over the years the rate was gradually raised by amendment
until in 1967 the members were once again entrusted with the power of determining the value of their own services. To prevent abuse of this power, no
increase becomes effective until the members have renewed their mandate from
the people, a provision similar to that in the long-gestating Twenty-Seventh
Amendment (1992) to the U.S. Constitution.

SECTION 17

Journals. Each house shall keep a journal of its proceedings, which shall
be printed and made public immediately after the adjournment of the General
Assembly.

See the commentary following Section 19.

SECTION 18

Protests. Any member of either house may dissent from and protest
against any act or resolve which he may think injurious to the public or to
any individual, and have the reasons of his dissent entered on the journal.

See the commentary following Section 19.

SECTION 19

> **Record votes.** Upon motion made in either house and seconded by one fifth of the members present, the yeas and nays upon any question shall be taken and entered upon the journal.

From the state's first constitution in 1776, printed journals of the proceedings of both houses have been required. The purpose is not only to create a public record, but also to permit the voters to hold their representatives accountable; to the latter end, protests including a statement of reasons must be entered at the request of any member, and roll call votes "upon any question" must be recorded if one-fifth of the members vote to require it. Votes on the second and third readings of revenue bills in each house must be entered on the journal (Article II, Section 23).

SECTION 20

> **Powers of the General Assembly.** Each house shall be judge of the qualifications and elections of its own members, shall sit upon its own adjournment from day to day, and shall prepare bills to be enacted into laws. The two houses may jointly adjourn to any future day or other place. Either house may, of its own motion, adjourn for a period not in excess of three days.

Each house is empowered to judge the qualifications and elections of its own members; the judicial branch has determined that this power is exclusive, so the courts lack jurisdiction over such questions (State ex rel. Alexander v. Pharr, 1920). Both houses by joint ballot are empowered to determine contested elections to executive offices (Article VI, Section 5); no provision is made by the constitution for contested judicial elections. Once in session, the two houses are in control of their own meetings; together they may adjourn "to any future day or other place." Each house separately possesses the power to order temporary adjournments of no more than three days. Even if one house exceeded its authority by adjourning for longer, it is unlikely to invalidate legislation passed during that session (Abbott v. Town of Highlands, 1981).

The supreme power of the General Assembly is, of course, the power to make laws. Conferred by Section 1 of this article, the legislative power must be exercised according to a prescribed form. Acts begin as bills prepared by the General Assembly. The remainder of Article II particularizes the process by which bills become laws.

SECTION 21

> **Style of the acts.** The style of the acts shall be: "The General Assembly
> of North Carolina enacts:".

Although this section refers to the "style" of the acts, its meaning is the "enacting clause," the form of words signaling the beginning of the effective portion of a statute. Whatever precedes the enacting clause—the title or caption, the preamble or "whereases"—is not law, although it may be subsequently used by courts as an aid in interpretation. Without an enacting clause no law has been made (In re Advisory Opinion, 1947). Unlike the constitutions of some states, the North Carolina Constitution includes no requirement that the title of a bill accurately summarize its contents.

SECTION 22

> **Action on bills.** All bills and resolutions of a legislative nature shall be
> read three times in each house before they become laws, and shall be signed
> by the presiding officers of both houses.

The requirement of three readings comes from English parliamentary procedure, anciently designed to prevent spur-of-the-moment legislation. The entire bill is not usually read aloud, but referred to by number or title. The bill must not only be "read" (in that sense), but also be passed three times in each house. Proof positive that these requirements were met is provided by the signatures of the two presiding officers, the president of the senate (Article II, Section 13) and the speaker of the house of representatives (Article II, Section 15). Their signatures form what is commonly called the ratification certificate; just as the enacting clause signals the beginning of an act, the ratification certificate marks its end. Although all action on a bill should be entered in the journals of the two houses, a court will not look beyond the ratification certificate with respect to ordinary legislation (State ex rel. Dyer v. City of Leaksville, 1969)—revenue bills, the subject of the next section, are an exception.

Bills become laws on the execution of the ratification certificate; there is no requirement that the governor sign or otherwise approve acts of the General Assembly. In the absence of such a requirement, the governor has no power to veto legislation. Although no law may be made without a ratification certificate (State ex rel. Scarborough v. Robinson, 1879), the requirement that the presiding officers sign all enacted legislation is not intended to give them a veto power (State ex rel. Cook v. Meares, 1895).

SECTION 23

> **Revenue bills.** No laws shall be enacted to raise money on the credit of
> the State, or to pledge the faith of the State directly or indirectly for the

payment of any debt, or to impose any tax upon the people of the State, or to allow the counties, cities, or towns to do so, unless the bill for the purpose shall have been read three several times in each house of the General Assembly and passed three several readings, which readings shall have been on three different days, and shall have been agreed to by each house respectively, and unless the yeas and nays on the second and third readings of the bill shall have been entered on the journal.

As Chief Justice John Marshall long ago reminded Americans, "the power to tax involves the power to destroy" (McCulloch v. Maryland, 1819). Even in the hands of the people's representatives, this awesome power must be carefully hedged so this section prescribes special procedures for the enactment of revenue bills. (Finance is also the subject of a separate constitutional article, Article V.) Not only must revenue bills be given three readings, but also the readings must be on three different days and the votes on the second and third readings entered in the journal. With respect to revenue measures, unlike all others, courts will not accept the ratification certificates as conclusive proof that the requirements have been met, but will require the journals themselves as sources of proof (Frazier v. Board of Commissioners of Guilford County, 1927). Not only must the number of those voting be entered in the record, but also their names must appear (Commissioners of New Hanover County v. DeRosset, 1901).

Revenue bills are defined by the present section to be bills that have any one of four effects: (1) "to raise money on the credit of the State," (2) "to pledge the faith of the State directly or indirectly for the payment of any debt," (3) "to impose any tax upon the people of the State," or (4) "to allow the counties, cities, or towns to do so [i.e., to impose a tax]." Although some of these terms are defined in the finance article (Article V, Section 3, Subsection 3 and Article V, Section 4, Subsection 5), the definitions therein are expressly limited to the sections in which they appear. Whether the same or similar definitions apply to the present section is unclear. In general, state revenue comes from borrowing or taxes. Raising money on the credit of the state or pledging its faith implicates borrowing—that is, securing money in the present by promising future repayment, usually with interest. A tax is a forced contribution to government; it differs from a fee in that it has no necessary immediate relationship to a benefit conferred. Although the only units of local government expressly mentioned in the present section are counties, cities, and towns, it has been held applicable to townships (Wittkowsky v. Board of Commissioners of Jackson County, 1908) and seems likely to apply equally to any other municipal subdivision.

Failure to comply with the required formalities renders an act void as a revenue measure, although it may be valid in other respects (Rodman-Heath Cotton Mills v. Town of Waxhaw, 1902). Revenue bills that have been subject to material amendment must be treated as new bills and therefore read three times on three different days, but the courts will presume an amendment to be not material unless proven otherwise (Frazier v. Board of Commissioners of Guilford County, 1927).

SECTION 24

Limitations on local, private, and special legislation.

1. Prohibited subjects. The General Assembly shall not enact any local, private, or special act or resolution:

   a. Relating to health, sanitation, and the abatement of nuisances;

   b. Changing the names of cities, towns, and townships;

   c. Authorizing the laying out, opening, altering, maintaining, or discontinuing of highways, streets, or alleys;

   d. Relating to ferries or bridges;

   e. Relating to non-navigable streams;

   f. Relating to cemeteries;

   g. Relating to pay of jurors;

   h. Erecting new townships, or changing township lines, or establishing or changing the lines of school districts;

   i. Remitting fines, penalties, and forfeitures, or refunding moneys legally paid into the public treasury;

   j. Regulating labor, trade, mining, or manufacturing;

   k. Extending the time for the levy or collection of taxes or otherwise relieving any collector of taxes from the due performance of his official duties or his sureties from liability;

   l. Giving effect to informal wills and deeds;

   m. Granting a divorce or securing alimony in any individual case;

   n. Altering the name of any person, or legitimating any person not born in lawful wedlock, or restoring to the rights of citizenship any person convicted of a felony.

2. Repeals. Nor shall the General Assembly enact any such local, private, or special act by partial repeal of a general law; but the General Assembly may at any time repeal local, private, or special laws enacted by it.

3. Prohibited acts void. Any local, private, or special act or resolution enacted in violation of the provisions of this Section shall be void.

4. General laws. The General Assembly may enact general laws regulating the matters set out in this Section.

English parliamentary practice at the time of the American Revolution drew a distinction between general or public acts, on the one hand, and special or private acts, on the other. Sir William Blackstone put it this way in 1765: ''A general or public act is an universal rule, that regards the whole community. . . . Special or private acts are rather exceptions than rules, being those which only operate upon particular persons, and private concerns.''[12] North Carolina's first constitution placed no limits on the types of private or special acts that could be passed, but the constitutional convention in 1835, concerned about the amount of time the General Assembly had spent on such legislation and the opportunities it provided for abuse, proposed a number of detailed prohibitions that the voters approved. The 1868 constitutional convention, itself distracted by a plethora of petitions for divorce, carried forward the provisions, similar to Subsection 1(m) and (n) above, prohibiting private "bills of divorcement" and private acts changing personal names, legitimating bastards, or relieving person from the effects of a conviction for felony. In 1916 concern that the legislature was still spending too much time on local, private, or special acts led the voters to adopt a constitutional amendment confining the General Assembly to general legislation on a further dozen subjects, many of them concerning local government. A definition of "general laws," permitting legislation based on classes, is in Article XIV, Section 3.

Over the years the North Carolina Supreme Court has struggled to devise a test for determining whether a given law is general or local. An early test counted the number of counties affected and held "general" a law that applied to a majority (In re Harris, 1922). Later the court replaced this simplistic test with one focusing on the reasonableness of any legislation that applied to a class within the state; this included both the reasonableness of legislating for a class in the first place and the reasonableness of the particular class described (Adams v. North Carolina Department of Natural and Economic Resources, 1978). In 1987 the court abandoned this test, too, in favor of one that focused on whether the subject matter, however confined, affects the "general public interests and concerns"; the new test proved sufficiently generous to uphold as general a law that closed part of a named street in one town (Town of Emerald Isle ex rel. Smith v. State, 1987). The key to this generosity may perhaps be found in the judicial recognition that legislative drafters had grown adept at defining classes general in form, but local in fact; the court announced that "tortured classifications" would no longer be necessary.

Article III

Executive

SECTION 1

Executive power. The executive power of the State shall be vested in the Governor.

Although the governorship as a state office is as old as the General Assembly, dating from the 1776 Constitution, it assumed its present dimensions only in the 1868 Constitution. Just as legislative power connotes the power to legislate or make laws, so executive power connotes the power to execute or enforce the laws: The governor is duty-bound to "take care that the laws be faithfully executed" (Article III, Section 5, Subsection 4).

SECTION 2

Governor and Lieutenant Governor: election, term, and qualifications.

1. Election and term. The Governor and Lieutenant Governor shall be elected by the qualified voters of the State in 1972 and every four years thereafter, at the same time and places as members of the General Assembly are elected. Their term of office shall be four years and shall commence on the first day of January next after their election and continue until their successors are elected and qualified.

2. Qualifications. No person shall be eligible for election to the office of Governor or Lieutenant Governor unless, at the time of his election, he shall have attained the age of 30 years and shall have been a citizen of the United States for five years and a resident of this State for two years immediately

preceding his election. No person elected to the Office of Governor or Lieutenant Governor shall be eligible for election to more than two consecutive terms of the same office.

Under the 1776 Constitution the governor was indirectly elected: The voters elected the members of the General Assembly, who in turn elected the governor. At first the term of office was one year, and the same person could not serve more than three years out of six. In 1835 the governorship was made directly elected, and the term was lengthened to two years; the same person could not serve more than four years out of six. In 1868 the term of office was lengthened again, attaining its present four-year period. Also in 1868 the office of lieutenant governor was first created, with a four-year elective term coinciding with that of the governor. Elections for governor and lieutenant governor are held in even-numbered years beginning with 1972 so they coincide with elections for the General Assembly every second election. Until 1977 governors and lieutenant governors were ineligible to serve successive terms; by amendment in that year they are now permitted two consecutive terms.

From 1776 governors were required to meet a substantial property qualification. Indeed, at the constitutional convention in 1835 Judge Gaston wryly observed of the state's chief executive that "all that is required from him is, that he should be a gentleman in character and manners, and exercise a liberal hospitality."[13] The property qualification was abolished in 1868 (see Article I, Section 11). More maturity has always been required of governors: Ever since 1776 the age qualification has been thirty, higher than for any other state officer. Senators must be at least twenty-five (Article II, Section 6); all other elected officers must be at least twenty-one (Article VI, Section 6). Under the 1776 Constitution the governor had to have been a resident of the state for five years; this is now reduced to two, although he or she must have been a citizen of the United States for at least five years. Unlike the president of the United States, the governor need not be a native-born citizen.

SECTION 3

Succession to office of Governor.

1. Succession as Governor. The Lieutenant Governor-elect shall become Governor upon the failure of the Governor-elect to qualify. The Lieutenant Governor shall become Governor upon the death, resignation, or removal from office of the Governor. The further order of succession to the office of Governor shall be prescribed by law. A successor shall serve for the remainder of the term of the Governor whom he succeeds and until a new Governor is elected and qualified.

2. Succession as Acting Governor. During the absence of the Governor from the State, or during the physical or mental incapacity of the Governor to perform the duties of his office, the Lieutenant Governor shall be Acting

Governor. The further order of succession as Acting Governor shall be prescribed by law.

3. Physical incapacity. The Governor may, by a written statement filed with the Attorney General, declare that he is physically incapable of performing the duties of his office, and may thereafter in the same manner declare that he is physically capable of performing the duties of his office.

4. Mental incapacity. The mental incapacity of the Governor to perform the duties of his office shall be determined only by joint resolution adopted by a vote of two-thirds of all of the members of each house of the General Assembly. Thereafter, the mental capacity of the Governor to perform the duties of his office shall be determined only by joint resolution adopted by a vote of a majority of all the members of each house of the General Assembly. In all cases, the General Assembly shall give the Governor such notice as it may deem proper and shall allow him an opportunity to be heard before a joint session of the General Assembly before it takes final action. When the General Assembly is not in session, the Council of State, a majority of its members concurring, may convene it in extra session for the purpose of proceeding under this paragraph.

5. Impeachment. Removal of the Governor from office for any other cause shall be by impeachment.

When the gubernatorial term was short and the duties of office minimal, the problem of succession on death, disability, or absence was minor. Under the 1776 Constitution the office devolved on the speaker of the senate; in case the speakership of the senate was vacant, it passed to the speaker of the house. The longer term and greater duties prescribed by the 1868 Constitution made necessary more elaborate provisions for succession. The prime executive duty of the lieutenant governor is to succeed to the governorship if it is vacant and to serve as acting governor in case of the temporary absence or incapacity of the governor. The further order of succession is prescribed by statute: president of the senate (since the lieutenant governor is unavailable, this would be the president pro tempore; Article II, Section 14, Subsection 1), speaker of the house, secretary of state, auditor, treasurer, superintendent of public instruction, attorney general, commissioner of agriculture, commissioner of labor, and commissioner of insurance (North Carolina General Statutes § 147-11.1). The successor is to serve the remainder of the term, not just until the next regularly scheduled election, thus maintaining the quadrennial schedule set out in the preceding section.

Physical incapacity is to be determined by the governor alone; mental incapacity, by joint resolution of two-thirds of the members of each house of the General Assembly. If the General Assembly is not in session, it may be convened in extra session by a majority of the Council of State, an executive body composed of elected officers (Article III, Section 8). Other than physical or mental incapacity, the only ground for removing the governor from office is the commission

of an impeachable offense. The procedures for impeachment are spelled out in
Article IV, Section 4.

SECTION 4

Oath of office for Governor. The Governor, before entering upon the
duties of his office, shall, before any Justice of the Supreme Court, take an
oath or affirmation that he will support the Constitution and laws of the
United States and of the State of North Carolina, and that he will faithfully
perform the duties pertaining to the office of governor.

The words of the oath are set out in Article VI, Section 7 and make express
what would be the case in any event under the supremacy clause of the U.S.
Constitution (art. VI, cls. 2–3): that the U.S. Constitution and laws come first,
then the state constitution and laws "not inconsistent therewith." In addition,
Article I, Section 5 proclaims the "paramount allegiance" of every North Carolinian, not just elected officials, to the Constitution and government of the
United States and declares invalid any state law "in contravention or subversion
thereof." The option of affirmation (as opposed to oath) was originally offered
in North Carolina and elsewhere as an accommodation to Quakers and other
Christian sects that took literally Jesus' command in the Sermon on the Mount,
"Swear not at all" (Matt. 5:34), and refused to take oaths. An affirmation is a
solemn declaration of equal legal effect. The duties of the governor are listed
in the next section.

SECTION 5

Duties of Governor.

1. Residence. The Governor shall reside at the seat of government of
this State.

2. Information to General Assembly. The Governor shall from time to
time give the General Assembly information of the affairs of the State and
recommend to their consideration such measures as he shall deem expedient.

3. Budget. The Governor shall prepare and recommend to the General
Assembly a comprehensive budget of the anticipated revenue and proposed
expenditures of the State for the ensuing fiscal period. The budget as enacted
by the General Assembly shall be administered by the Governor.

The total expenditures of the State for the fiscal period covered by the
budget shall not exceed the total of receipts during that fiscal period and the
surplus remaining in the State Treasury at the beginning of the period. To
insure that the State does not incur a deficit for any fiscal period, the Governor
shall continually survey the collection of the revenue and shall effect the
necessary economies in State expenditures, after first making adequate
provision for the prompt payment of the principal of and interest on bonds

and notes of the State according to their terms, whenever he determines that receipts during the fiscal period, when added to any surplus remaining in the State Treasury at the beginning of the period, will not be sufficient to meet budgeted expenditures. This section shall not be construed to impair the power of the State to issue its bonds and notes within the limitations imposed in Article V of this Constitution, nor to impair the obligation of bonds and notes of the State now outstanding or issued hereafter.

4. Execution of laws. The Governor shall take care that the laws be faithfully executed.

5. Commander in Chief. The Governor shall be Commander in Chief of the military forces of the State except when they shall be called into the service of the United States.

6. Clemency. The Governor may grant reprieves, commutations, and pardons, after conviction, for all offenses (except in cases of impeachment), upon such conditions as he may think proper, subject to regulations prescribed by law relative to the manner of applying for pardons. The terms reprieves, commutations, and pardons shall not include paroles.

7. Extra sessions. The Governor may, on extraordinary occasions, by and with the advice of the Council of State, convene the General Assembly in extra session by his proclamation, stating therein the purpose or purposes for which they are thus convened.

8. Appointments. The Governor shall nominate and by and with the advice and consent of a majority of the Senators appoint all officers whose appointments are not otherwise provided for.

9. Information. The Governor may at any time require information in writing from the head of any administrative department or agency upon any subject relating to the duties of his office.

10. Administrative reorganization. The General Assembly shall prescribe the functions, powers, and duties of the administrative departments and agencies of the State and may alter them from time to time, but the Governor may make such changes in the allocation of offices and agencies and in the allocation of those functions, powers, and duties as he considers necessary for efficient administration. If those changes affect existing law, they shall be set forth in executive orders, which shall be submitted to the General Assembly not later than the sixtieth calendar day of its session, and shall become effective and shall have the force of law upon adjournment sine die of the session, unless specifically disapproved by resolution of either house of the General Assembly or specifically modified by joint resolution of both houses of the General Assembly.

The history of the duties of the governor of North Carolina is of an ever-lengthening list. The 1776 Constitution gave the governor command of the state militia, the power to draw and spend money appropriated by the General Assembly, and the power to grant reprieves and pardons. The 1868 Constitution spelled out the governor's role vis-à-vis the General Assembly, requiring him or her to report periodically on the affairs of state, to recommend measures, and to convene extra sessions on extraordinary occasions. The second constitution also confirmed the governor's role as head of the administration, empowering him or her to appoint executive officers, but post-Reconstruction amendments curtailed the power of appointment. The 1971 Constitution restated these duties, and constitutional amendments have enhanced the governor's power over the budget and administrative reorganization. The veto power, perhaps the greatest of all, has continued to elude the state's chief executive.

1. "Residence." The governor must reside at "the seat of government," elsewhere defined as Raleigh (Article XIV, Section 1). This requirement is apparently imposed to ensure the continuity of state government. The General Assembly is not in permanent session, but the governor is always "on duty."

2. "Information to General Assembly." The governor must periodically report to the General Assembly on the "state of the State"; he or she may also recommend legislative action.

3. "Budget." Whatever else the governor recommends to the General Assembly, he or she must recommend a "comprehensive budget," although the legislature has no duty to adopt it as recommended. Whatever budget is adopted the governor must administer, a specific application of the general duty to execute the laws. In the opinion of the state supreme court justices, a statute authorizing a joint legislative commission to make budgetary decisions would interfere with this gubernatorial duty (Advisory Opinion in re Separation of Powers, 1982); it seems on analysis to be instead an improper delegation of legislative power. The second paragraph of this subsection, requiring a balanced budget, was added by amendment in 1977. It empowers the governor to make "necessary economies in State expenditures," without consulting the General Assembly, whenever he determines them to be necessary to avoid a deficit within the budgetary period.

4. "Execution of laws." The governor must enforce the laws. Lacking a veto, the state's chief executive has no role in the legislative process, nor may he or she refuse to enforce any law. Suspending laws or their execution is expressly prohibited by Article I, Section 7. In the capacity of commander in chief of the state's military forces, the governor is expressly authorized to call out the troops when necessary "to execute the law" (Article XII, Section 1).

5. "Commander in Chief." In keeping with American traditions of civilian control of the armed forces, "the military shall be kept under strict subordination to, and governed by, the civil power" (Article I, Section 30). The present subsection implements that requirement by making the governor commander in chief of the state's military forces, "except when they shall be called into the service of the United States." The exception is necessary because of the provision in the U.S. Constitution appointing the president of the United States commander in chief of "the Militia of the several States, when called into the actual Service of the United States" (art. II, § 2, cl. 1). The governor's command of the state militia is repeated in Article XII, Section 1, where the permissible uses of troops

are listed as follows: "to execute the law, suppress riots and insurrections, and repel invasion."

Conferring an office, rather than imposing a duty strictly speaking, this subsection marks a shift within the present section: The remaining subsections (except for Subsection 8 on appointments) empower the governor to act, rather than requiring him or her to do so. On the linguistic level the shift is from what the governor "shall" do to what the governor "may" do.

6. "Clemency." The governor may grant convicted criminals reprieves, commutations, and pardons. A reprieve is a temporary suspension of sentence; a commutation, a reduction of sentence; and a pardon, a complete revocation of sentence. Clemency may be exercised only "after conviction," defined by the state supreme court as verdict and judgment in the trial court, not the final rejection of all appeals (State v. Mathis, 1891). Clemency may be upon condition, either precedent (e.g., that the convicted person must first pay the costs of trial) or subsequent (e.g., that the convicted person must remain sober and industrious) (In re Williams, 1908). The power of the governor to exercise clemency in individual cases does not preclude a power in the legislature to pass a general amnesty act (State v. Bowman, 1907), and the clemency clause itself contemplates "regulations prescribed by law relative to the manner of applying for pardons." (The current provisions are in North Carolina General Statutes § 147-21.) The governor's exercise of the power of clemency, granting it in one case and denying it in another, is not ordinarily subject to judicial review (State v. Jarrette, 1974).

The power to parole—that is, to grant an early release from prison subject to certain conditions—had been exercised by the governor, but was transferred by a 1954 amendment to a statutory Board of Paroles (now the Parole Commission). It is noteworthy that the governor's power of clemency does not extend to cases of impeachment. Curiously, Article VI, Section 8 contemplates the removal of an incident of impeachment and conviction—disqualification for office—"in the manner prescribed by law."

7. "Extra sessions." The governor may convene extra sessions of the General Assembly "on extraordinary occasions." He or she must first seek the advice (but apparently not the consent) of the Council of State, an executive body created by Article III, Section 8.

8. "Appointments." The appointments subsection is mandatory, not permissive: The governor "shall" nominate officers whose appointments are not otherwise provided for. In such cases appointment is dependent on the advice *and consent* of a majority of senators. By contrast, when any of the eight executive offices created by Article III, Section 7 becomes vacant, the governor appoints a temporary officer; likewise, the unexpired terms of vacant judicial offices (unless otherwise provided for) are to be filled by the governor's appointees (Article IV, Section 19). In neither case is senatorial consent required. With respect to the State Board of Education, the governor appoints eleven

members, subject to confirmation not by the senate, but by "the General Assembly in joint session"; in case of subsequent vacancies the governor's appointees fill the unexpired terms "and shall not be subject to confirmation" (Article IX, Section 4).

The 1868 Constitution had originally included a specific prohibition of legislative appointments: "and no such officer shall be appointed or elected by the General Assembly." This phrase was dropped by amendment in 1876, when the General Assembly reclaimed some of the powers it had lost in the Reconstruction Constitution. The prohibition did not reappear in the 1971 Constitution, and the state supreme court has held that its absence implies that the General Assembly may provide for someone other than the governor to make appointments to offices not specifically reserved for him or her. In terms of separation of powers, this means that the power to appoint someone to execute the laws is not itself the exercise of executive power. Thus, the General Assembly can empower the chief justice to appoint the head of the Office of Administrative Hearings (State ex rel. Martin v. Melott, 1987).

9. "Information." The governor may require the head of any administrative department or agency to furnish information in writing on any subject relating to executive duties.

10. "Administrative reorganization." Coincident with adopting the 1971 Constitution, the voters approved an amendment adding this subsection; the same amendment added Section 11 of this article, also concerning administrative reorganization. The governor may reorganize the administration by executive orders submitted to the General Assembly and not disapproved by either house. This clause confers a legislative power on the governor: Unless disapproved, executive orders have "the force of law." The arrangement may be described as conferring a "legislative veto"; since disapproval by either house would prevent effectiveness, it could be called more particularly a "one-house veto." Although found unconstitutional on the federal level as a violation of separation of powers (Chadha v. Immigration and Naturalization Service, 1983), it is presumptively valid in state government in this case because of its express constitutional authorization.

In addition to the above, the governor has the further duty of keeping the Great Seal of the State of North Carolina (Article III, Section 10). He or she is empowered by the finance article to authorize state or local government borrowing without prior voter approval in case of emergencies threatening public health or safety (Article V, Section 3, Subsection 1(e) and Article V, Section 4, Subsection 2(e)).

SECTION 6

Duties of the Lieutenant Governor. The Lieutenant Governor shall be President of the Senate, but shall have no vote unless the Senate is equally divided. He shall perform such additional duties as the General Assembly or the Governor may assign to him. He shall receive the compensation and allowances prescribed by law.

The office of lieutenant governor was created in 1868. Unique among executive officers, the lieutenant governor has regular legislative as well as executive duties. Although the General Assembly or governor may assign him or her additional duties, the only one specifically assigned by this article is to succeed to the governorship if it is vacant and to serve as acting governor in case of the temporary absence or incapacity of the governor (Article III, Section 3). The education article makes the lieutenant governor an ex officio member of the State Board of Education (Article IX, Section 4, Subsection 1). Because the lieutenant governor has a legislative duty—to serve as president of the senate—and a vote in case the senate is equally divided, the office is mentioned in the legislative article (Article II, Section 13) in words almost identical to the first sentence of the present section. The lieutenant governor is entitled to compensation, which a later section prohibits from being reduced during the term of office (Article III, Section 9).

SECTION 7

Other elective officers.

1. Officers. A Secretary of State, an Auditor, a Treasurer, a Superintendent of Public Instruction, an Attorney General, a Commissioner of Agriculture, a Commissioner of Labor, and a Commissioner of Insurance shall be elected by the qualified voters of the State in 1972 and every four years thereafter at the same time and places as members of the General Assembly are elected. Their term of office shall be four years and shall commence on the first day of January next after their election and continue until their successors are elected and qualified.

2. Duties. Their respective duties shall be prescribed by law.

3. Vacancies. If the office of any of these officers is vacated by death, resignation, or otherwise, it shall be the duty of the Governor to appoint another to serve until his successor is elected and qualified. Every such vacancy shall be filled by election at the first election for members of the General Assembly that occurs more than 60 days after the vacancy has taken place, and the person chosen shall hold the office for the remainder of the unexpired term fixed in this Section. When a vacancy occurs in the office of any of the officers named in this Section and the term expires on the first day of January succeeding the next election for members of the General Assembly, the Governor shall appoint to fill the vacancy for the unexpired term of the office.

4. Interim officers. Upon the occurrence of a vacancy in the office of any one of these officers for any of the causes stated in the preceding paragraph, the Governor may appoint an interim officer to perform the duties of that

office until a person is appointed or elected pursuant to this Section to fill the vacancy and is qualified.

5. Acting officers. During the physical or mental incapacity of any one of these officers to perform the duties of his office, as determined pursuant to this Section, the duties of his office shall be performed by an acting officer who shall be appointed by the Governor.

6. Determination of incapacity. The General Assembly shall by law prescribe with respect to those officers, other than the Governor, whose offices are created by this Article, procedures for determining the physical or mental incapacity of any officer to perform the duties of his office, and for determining whether an officer who has been temporarily incapacitated has sufficiently recovered his physical or mental capacity to perform the duties of his office. Removal of those officers from office for any other cause shall be by impeachment.

7. Special qualifications for Attorney General. Only persons duly authorized to practice law in the courts of this State shall be eligible for appointment or election as Attorney General.

Although the offices of secretary of state, treasurer, and attorney general date from the 1776 Constitution, they became directly elected only in 1868. The offices of auditor and superintendent of public instruction, directly elected from the first, were created at the same time—as was the short-lived office of superintendent of public works, abolished by amendment in 1873. The increasing role of the executive led to the steady increase of executive offices: The office of commissioner of agriculture, created by statute in 1877, became directly elected in 1899; the office of commissioner of labor, created by statute in 1887, was first directly elected in 1900; and the office of commissioner of insurance, created by statute in 1899, became directly elected in 1908. The latter three became constitutional offices in 1944.

Although in general their duties are prescribed by law, a few of these officers do have specific constitutional assignments. The superintendent of public instruction is the secretary and chief administrative officer of the State Board of Education, of which the treasurer (as well as the lieutenant governor) is an ex officio member (Article IX, Section 4).

In case of vacancies in these offices, the governor has a duty to appoint a successor. Unlike the offices referred to in Section 5, Subsection 8 of this article, appointment is not conditioned on the consent of a majority of senators. The present section provides for succession in case of vacancy or incapacity; Section 3 of this article is equally detailed concerning such eventualities with respect to the office of governor. Nowhere is comparable provision made for the office of lieutenant governor, so the state supreme court has held that that office remains vacant in case of the incumbent's death (Thomas v. State Board of Elections, 1962). Of course, the lieutenant governor's role as president of the senate is filled by the president pro tempore (Article II, Section 14).

In 1984 the voters approved a constitutional amendment that added Subsection 7, requiring the attorney general, the state's chief law officer, to be licensed to practice law in the state; the amendment imposed the same requirement for district attorneys (Article IV, Section 18, Subsection 1). The effect was to make a formal qualification of what had been generally required as a practical matter. In 1980 the voters had imposed the same requirement on the state's judges, although with a "grandfather clause" for lay persons who had previously held office (Article IV, Section 22), a provision apparently unnecessary in the present case.

SECTION 8

Council of State. The Council of State shall consist of the officers whose offices are established by this Article.

Although the Council of State figured in the 1776 Constitution, it underwent a radical redesign in 1868. The original Council of State was composed of seven persons elected by the General Assembly for one-year terms "who shall advise the Governor in the execution of his office." Under the 1868 Constitution the Council of State became a body of directly elected officers, with executive duties of their own. Today it includes the ten officers whose offices are established by Article III: the governor and lieutenant governor (Section 2), and the secretary of state, auditor, treasurer, superintendent of public instruction, attorney general, commissioner of agriculture, commissioner of labor, and commissioner of insurance (Section 7). Its constitutional powers are vestigial: Under Article III, Section 3, Subsection 4, it may itself convene an extra session of the General Assembly for the purpose of considering the governor's mental incapacity; under Article III, Section 5, Subsection 7 it must be consulted before the governor may convene extra sessions. Today its most significant powers are statutory, such as approving the governor's acquisition of property on behalf of the state.

SECTION 9

Compensation and allowances. The officers whose offices are established by this Article shall at stated periods receive the compensation and allowances prescribed by law, which shall not be diminished during the time for which they have been chosen.

Ten offices are established by Article III: the governor and lieutenant governor (Section 2) and the secretary of state, auditor, treasurer, superintendent of public instruction, attorney general, commissioner of agriculture, commissioner of labor, and commissioner of insurance (Section 7). The reason their compensation may not be diminished during their terms is to preserve their independence from the legislature, a practical application of the principle of separation of powers. The same security is accorded judges in Article IV, Section 21.

SECTION 10

> **Seal of State.** There shall be a seal of the State, which shall be kept by the Governor and used by him as occasion may require, and shall be called "The Great Seal of the State of North Carolina". All grants and commissions shall be issued in the name and by the authority of the State of North Carolina, sealed with "The Great Seal of the State of North Carolina", and signed by the Governor.

Although a state seal has been required by all three constitutions, its design has been determined by statute; in all, five distinct seals have been used. The present design, adopted in 1971, shows two female figures, representing liberty and plenty. Liberty holds in her right hand a scroll on which is the word "Constitution." Above the figures appears "May 20, 1775," the date of the supposed Mecklenburg Declaration of Independence; below them is the state motto, "*Esse Quam Videri*" ("to be rather than to seem"), a quotation from the Roman orator Cicero.

SECTION 11

> **Administrative departments.** Not later than July 1, 1975, all administrative departments, agencies, and offices of the State and their respective functions, powers, and duties shall be allocated by law among and within not more than 25 principal administrative departments so as to group them as far as practicable according to major purposes. Regulatory, quasi-judicial, and temporary agencies may, but need not, be allocated within a principal department.

Coincident with adopting the 1971 Constitution, the voters also adopted an amendment adding this section and Section 5, Subsection 10 of this article (empowering the governor to implement administrative reorganization). Effective July 1, 1971, the present section gave the General Assembly four years within which to reorganize the administration into no more than twenty-five departments, this number being thought the maximum that can be effectively supervised.

Article IV

Judicial

SECTION 1

Judicial power. The judicial power of the State shall, except as provided in Section 3 of this Article, be vested in a Court for the Trial of Impeachments and in a General Court of Justice. The General Assembly shall have no power to deprive the judicial department of any power or jurisdiction that rightfully pertains to it as a coordinate department of the government, nor shall it establish or authorize any courts other than as permitted by this Article.

Just as the legislative power is vested in the General Assembly and the executive power in the office of the governor, the judicial power is vested in courts: the Court for the Trial of Impeachments and the General Court of Justice. Impeachment is an allegation of wrongdoing by a public officer, and its punishment is limited by Section 4 of this article to removal from office and disqualification from future office holding. While an undoubted exercise of judicial power, impeachment and removal from office are far less common than criminal prosecution and civil adjudication, the province of the General Court of Justice. It was to make of the latter a "unified judicial system" (see the next section) that the judicial article of the 1868 Constitution was largely rewritten by amendment in 1962; the amended article was carried over without substantial change in the 1971 Constitution. The only exception to this unified system is the judicial power conferred by law on administrative agencies (see Section 3 of this article).

Although the general principle of separation of powers enshrined in Article I, Section 6 would seem to provide adequate protection for the judicial department from encroachments by the General Assembly, the principle is given particular application in the second sentence of the present section, perhaps because the judiciary is recognized to be, as Alexander Hamilton put it in *The Federalist* (No. 78), ''beyond comparison the weakest of the three departments of power.''[14] Judicial power is exclusively the courts': The legislature may not revise by statute a final judicial decision (Gardner v. Gardner, 1980). Although the present section expressly forbids only the deprivation of judicial power, the underlying principle equally forbids its enlargement (Smith v. State, 1976): Jurisdiction conferred by the constitution cannot be increased by the legislature, a principle as old as Marbury v. Madison (1803).

SECTION 2

General Court of Justice. The General Court of Justice shall constitute a unified judicial system for purposes of jurisdiction, operation, and administration, and shall consist of an Appellate Division, a Superior Court Division, and a District Court Division.

The desirability of a ''unified judicial system'' might seem self-evident—it recommended itself to the drafters of the 1868 Constitution—but it was lacking in North Carolina for almost a century, after amendments adopted in 1876 restored to the General Assembly the power to determine the jurisdiction of all courts below the supreme court and to establish inferior courts as it saw fit. The resulting hodgepodge was not eliminated until 1962 when the basis of the present article was adopted. The various divisions of the General Court of Justice are the subject of later sections of this article: Section 5 (Appellate Division), Section 9 (Superior Court Division), and Section 10 (District Court Division).

SECTION 3

Judicial powers of administrative agencies. The General Assembly may vest in administrative agencies established pursuant to law such judicial powers as may be reasonably necessary as an incident to the accomplishment of the purposes for which the agencies were created. Appeals from administrative agencies shall be to the General Court of Justice.

Administrative agencies are bodies within the executive branch of state government; as such, they could not ordinarily be given judicial power without violating the fundamental principle of separation of powers. This section expressly authorizes the General Assembly to confer such power on administrative agencies when it is ''reasonably necessary'' to their effective functioning. The state supreme court has the final word on the reasonableness of any claimed necessity (In re Appeal from Civil Penalties, 1989). Appeals from administrative agencies are ''to the General Court of Justice,'' defined in the previous section as a ''unified judicial system'' of trial and appellate courts; as such, appeals from agencies must begin in the lower courts. The legislature may not in general authorize appeals from agencies directly to the supreme court (State ex rel. Utilities Commission v. Old Fort Finishing Plant, 1965); only in case of appeals from the North Carolina Utilities Commission may such authority be granted and then only by virtue of a specific constitutional exception (Article IV, Section 12, Subsection 1).

It is noticeable that there is no counterpart to the present section in Article II on the legislative power; nonetheless, it has often been held that the General Assembly may delegate limited legislative power to administrative agencies. The delegated power, sometimes described as quasi-legislative, must be accompanied by standards adequate to guide administrative discretion (see Article II, Section 1).

SECTION 4

Court for the Trial of Impeachments. The House of Representatives solely shall have the power of impeaching. The Court for the Trial of Impeachments shall be the Senate. When the Governor or Lieutenant Governor is impeached, the Chief Justice shall preside over the Court. A majority of the members shall be necessary to a quorum, and no person shall be convicted without the concurrence of two-thirds of the Senators present. Judgment upon conviction shall not extend beyond removal from and disqualification to hold office in this State, but the party shall be liable to indictment and punishment according to law.

Impeachment is a criminal charge (Article I, Section 22); its trial, the exercise of judicial power. Without special provision, the trial of impeachments by a legislative body would violate the principle of separation of powers (Article I, Section 6). This section confers the exclusive power of impeaching on the house of representatives, constituting it a sort of grand jury in cases of official misconduct. The senate is the judge and jury, but unlike an ordinary jury, its verdict need not be unanimous, and unlike an ordinary panel of judges, a simple majority is not sufficient: Two-thirds of the senators present must concur in a conviction. The punishment of the crime is political: removal from office and disqualification for further office holding. Criminal punishments are possible, but must be meted out after a separate proceeding in the General Court of Justice. By virtue of the express language of this section, the two rounds could not possibly constitute double jeopardy (see Article I, Section 19).

Because impeachment is a criminal proceeding, it is unsuitable for use in removing officers for physical or mental incapacity. Alternatives to impeachment are provided by the constitution for the governor (Article III, Section 3, Subsections 3 and 4), justices and judges (Article IV, Section 17, Subsections 1 and 2), and superior court clerks (Article IV, Section 17, Subsection 4). The General Assembly is directed to prescribe alternatives by statute for elective executive officers other than the governor (Article III, Section 7, Subsection 6), for magistrates (Article IV, Section 17, Subsection 3), and for sheriffs (Article VII, Section 2).

SECTION 5

Appellate division. The Appellate Division of the General Court of Justice shall consist of the Supreme Court and the Court of Appeals.

The Appellate Division forms the apex of the judicial pyramid. At the very top is the supreme court, first created by statute in 1818; before then, the state's highest court had been the court of conference, composed of superior court judges. As a court created directly by the constitution, the supreme court dates to the state's second constitution, that of 1868. The court of appeals, first authorized by constitutional amendment in 1962, was created by statute, effective January 1, 1967 (North Carolina General Statutes § 7A-16).

SECTION 6

Supreme Court.

1. Membership. The Supreme Court shall consist of a Chief Justice and six Associate Justices, but the General Assembly may increase the number of Associate Justices to not more than eight. In the event the Chief Justice is unable, on account of absence or temporary incapacity, to perform any of the duties placed upon him, the senior Associate Justice available may discharge these duties.

2. Sessions of the Supreme Court. The sessions of the Supreme Court shall be held in the City of Raleigh unless otherwise provided by the General Assembly.

For its first half-century, from 1818 until 1868, the supreme court consisted of three judges: the chief justice and two side judges. The 1868 Constitution, the first to give the court constitutional status, increased the total to five, but the post-Reconstruction amendments of 1876 reduced it again to three. Since then, the size of the court has grown steadily: to five in 1888 by constitutional amendment; to seven in 1937 by statute authorized by constitutional amendment in 1935. The court remains today at a total membership of seven, the chief justice and six associate justices, although the General Assembly is empowered by the present section to increase the total size to nine if it sees fit.

The chief justice has many administrative duties, some inherent in the office of presiding judge, some imposed directly by the constitution, and others imposed by statute. The constitutional duties are to preside over the Court for the Trial of Impeachments if the governor or lieutenant governor is impeached (Article IV, Section 4), to designate one of the district judges as the chief district judge when more than one district judge is provided for a single district (Article IV, Section 10), to supervise the assignment of district judges made by the chief district judges (Article IV, Section 11), and to assign superior court judges (Article IV, Section 11). In addition, the chief justice may transfer district judges from one district to another for temporary or specialized duty (Article IV, Section 11). In case the chief justice is unable to perform any of these duties, the senior available associate justice—that is, the one with the longest tenure on the court—shall act in the chief justice's place.

The supreme court sits in Raleigh, the "permanent seat of government" (Article XIV, Section 1), unless the General Assembly directs otherwise.

SECTION 7

> **Court of Appeals.** The structure, organization, and composition of the Court of Appeals shall be determined by the General Assembly. The Court shall have not less than five members, and may be authorized to sit in divisions, or other than en banc. Sessions of the Court shall be held at such times and places as the General Assembly may prescribe.

Unlike the supreme court, established directly by the constitution, the court of appeals is a statutory court. First authorized by constitutional amendment in 1965, it was created by statute, effective January 1, 1967 (North Carolina General Statutes § 7A-16). As presently constituted, the court of appeals has twelve members: a chief judge and eleven judges. The court regularly sits in divisions consisting of three members each, rather than all together (*en banc*)—as the Supreme Court does. Like its structure, organization, and composition, its jurisdiction is defined by statute (Article IV, Section 12, Subsection 2).

SECTION 8

> **Retirement of Justices and Judges.** The General Assembly shall provide by general law for the retirement of Justices and Judges of the General Court of Justice, and may provide for the temporary recall of any retired Justice or Judge to serve on the court or courts of the division from which he was retired. The General Assembly shall also prescribe maximum age limits for service as a Justice or Judge.

The first sentence of this section, new with the 1971 Constitution, directs the General Assembly to provide for judicial retirement and empowers it to provide for the temporary recall of retired justices or judges. The second sentence, added by amendment in 1972, directs the General Assembly to set maximum age limits for judicial service—that is, to require retirement at a certain age. Discharging its duty under the second sentence, the General Assembly has prescribed retirement at age seventy-two (North Carolina General Statutes § 7A-4.20). The effect of this statute (and the second sentence of the present section that mandated it) is to terminate the service of any justice or judge who reaches the maximum age (Martin v. State, 1991); otherwise, justices and judges serve terms of eight years (Article IV, Section 16).

SECTION 9

Superior Courts.

1. Superior Court districts. The General Assembly shall, from time to time, divide the State into a convenient number of Superior Court judicial districts and shall provide for the election of one or more Superior Court Judges for each district. Each regular Superior Court Judge shall reside in the district for which he is elected. The General Assembly may provide by general law for the selection or appointment of special or emergency Superior Court Judges not selected for a particular judicial district.

2. Open at all times; sessions for trial of cases. The Superior Court shall be open at all times for the transaction of all business except the trial of issues of fact requiring a jury. Regular trial sessions of the Superior Court shall be held at times fixed pursuant to a calendar of courts promulgated by the Supreme Court. At least two sessions for the trial of jury cases shall be held annually in each county.

3. Clerks. A Clerk of the Superior Court for each county shall be elected for a term of four years by the qualified voters thereof, at the same time and places as members of the General Assembly are elected. If the office of Clerk of the Superior Court becomes vacant otherwise than by the expiration of the term, or if the people fail to elect, the senior regular resident Judge of the Superior Court serving the county shall appoint to fill the vacancy until an election can be regularly held.

Like the court of appeals, the Superior Court Division of the General Court of Justice owes its existence to statute (North Carolina General Statutes § 7A-40). Superior court districts are based on counties (or parts of counties), as befits the successor to the antebellum county-based system. Subsection 2, requiring the court to be "open at all times," is reminiscent of the open-courts requirement of Article I, Section 18. It does not require the court to be in round-the-clock session, but it does empower superior court judges to exercise judicial power, as needed, at any time of the day or night, the practical application of the principle that justice shall not be denied or delayed. The superior court is open for "all business," as befits a court of "original general jurisdiction" (Article IV, Section 12, Subsection 3).

The clerks of the superior courts are judicial officers in their own right, with such "jurisdiction and powers" as are prescribed by law (Article IV, Section 12, Subsection 3). In case of a vacancy in the office of clerk, the senior regular resident superior court judge appoints a successor to serve "until an election can be regularly held," meaning until the next election for members of the General Assembly, not the next election for the regular term of clerk (Rodwell v. Rowland, 1905). As provided by the next section, the clerk nominates magistrates, who are appointed by the senior regular resident superior court judge.

SECTION 10

District Courts. The General Assembly shall, from time to time, divide the State into a convenient number of local court districts and shall prescribe where the District Courts shall sit, but a District Court must sit in at least one place in each county. District Judges shall be elected for each district for a term of four years, in a manner prescribed by law. When more than one District Judge is authorized and elected for a district, the Chief Justice of the Supreme Court shall designate one of the judges as Chief District Judge. Every District Judge shall reside in the district for which he is elected. For each county, the senior regular resident Judge of the Superior Court serving the county shall appoint for a term of two years, from nominations submitted by the Clerk of the Superior Court of the county, one or more Magistrates who shall be officers of the District Court. The number of District Judges and Magistrates shall, from time to time, be determined by the General Assembly. Vacancies in the office of District Judge shall be filled for the unexpired term in a manner prescribed by law. Vacancies in the office of Magistrate shall be filled for the unexpired term in the manner provided for original appointment to the office.

The District Court Division of the General Court of Justice is created by statute (North Carolina General Statutes § 7A-130) and consists of various district courts organized in territorial districts based on counties. The District Court Division replaced the haphazard collection of recorder's courts. By statute the local district court is required to sit in the county seat and in a few designated additional seats of court. In case of a vacancy the governor is empowered by statute to fill the unexpired term, but only from nominations submitted by the district bar; nominees must be of the same political party as the elected district judge (North Carolina General Statutes § 7A-142, held constitutional in Baker v. Martin, 1991), an arrangement similar to that for filling a vacancy in the General Assembly (Article II, Section 10).

Magistrates, successors to the time-hallowed justices of the peace, are appointed by the regular resident superior court judge on the nomination of the clerk of the superior court; vacancies are filled in the same manner.

SECTION 11

Assignment of Judges. The Chief Justice of the Supreme Court, acting in accordance with rules of the Supreme Court, shall make assignments of

Judges of the Superior Court and may transfer District Judges from one district to another for temporary or specialized duty. The principle of rotating Superior Court Judges among the various districts of a division is a salutary one and shall be observed. For this purpose the General Assembly may divide the State into a number of judicial divisions. Subject to the general supervision of the Chief Justice of the Supreme Court, assignment of District Judges within each local court district shall be made by the Chief District Judge.

Two of the constitutional duties of the chief justice are to assign superior court judges and, if necessary, to transfer district judges. District judges are assigned by the chief district judge, designated by the chief justice pursuant to Section 10 of this article. As required by Sections 9 and 10, the General Assembly has divided the state into superior court districts and local court districts. In addition, as authorized by the present section, the General Assembly has created larger units known as "judicial divisions," the thirty superior court districts being arranged in four judicial divisions (North Carolina General Statutes § 7A-41). Within a division superior court judges are rotated, keeping the judges in touch with a larger geographical area and promoting uniformity of justice.

SECTION 12

Jurisdiction of the General Court of Justice.

1. Supreme Court. The Supreme Court shall have jurisdiction to review upon appeal any decision of the courts below, upon any matter of law or legal inference. The jurisdiction of the Supreme Court over "issues of fact" and "questions of fact" shall be the same exercised by it prior to the adoption of this Article, and the Court may issue any remedial writs necessary to give it general supervision and control over the proceedings of the other courts. The Supreme Court also has jurisdiction to review, when authorized by law, direct appeals from a final order or decision of the North Carolina Utilities Commission.

2. Court of Appeals. The Court of Appeals shall have such appellate jurisdiction as the General Assembly may prescribe.

3. Superior Court. Except as otherwise provided by the General Assembly, the Superior Court shall have original general jurisdiction throughout the State. The Clerks of the Superior Court shall have such jurisdiction and powers as the General Assembly shall prescribe by general law uniformly applicable in every county of the State.

4. District Courts; Magistrates. The General Assembly shall, by general law uniformly applicable in every local court district of the State, prescribe the jurisdiction and powers of the District Courts and Magistrates.

5. Waiver. The General Assembly may by general law provide that the jurisdictional limits may be waived in civil cases.

6. Appeals. The General Assembly shall by general law provide a proper system of appeals. Appeals from Magistrates shall be heard de novo, with the right of trial by jury as defined in this Constitution and the laws of this State.

In 1868 the North Carolina Supreme Court became for the first time a constitutional court, in the sense that it owed its existence as an institution directly to the constitution and not to any statute; in 1868 it also received its first direct grant by the constitution of appellate jurisdiction. Like American appellate courts generally, the state supreme court is largely limited to review of matters of law, as opposed to those of fact. Prior to the merger of legal and equitable jurisdictions in 1868 (Article IV, Section 13), the court had reviewed findings of fact in equitable proceedings; in equity all the evidence was in writing, and the appellate court had available to it all the information on which the lower court had based its findings. After 1868 for a few years uncertainty prevailed concerning the authority of the court to continue to review matters of fact in equitable appeals. By amendment adopted in 1876 it was made clear that the court had the same jurisdiction over equitable "questions of fact" as it had had before 1868; that rule continues in effect today. The clause obviously gives the supreme court no jurisdiction to review "issues of fact" in actions at law, the historical preserve of the jury; trial by jury is guaranteed by Article I, Sections 24 and 25.

The principal object of the revision of the judicial article in 1962 was to provide a "unified judicial system" (Article IV, Section 2). To this end, the General Assembly lost its power to multiply courts and authorize special appeals. Review of administrative agencies in their exercise of delegated judicial power must begin in the trial courts (State ex rel. Utilities Commission v. Old Fort Finishing Plant, 1965). By virtue of a constitutional amendment adopted in 1982, the North Carolina Utilities Commission was granted an exemption from this rule: The General Assembly in the case of final orders in general rate cases has authorized direct appeals as of right to the supreme court (North Carolina General Statutes § 7A-29(b)).

Unlike the supreme court, the court of appeals owes its existence to legislation (Article IV, Section 7); its appellate jurisdiction, too, is defined by statute, as authorized in Subsection 2 of the present section. At the next level below the court of appeals is the superior court, a court of statewide "original general jurisdiction" (except as otherwise provided by law). Clerks of the superior courts, district courts, and magistrates have such jurisdiction as provided by "general law," a concept described in Article XIV, Section 3. Magistrates may hear and decide cases, but appeals from their decisions must be heard de novo (anew); the appeal becomes, in other words, a new trial, complete with defendant's right to trial by jury (Article I, Section 24).

SECTION 13

Forms of action; rules of procedure.

1. Forms of Action. There shall be in this State but one form of action for the enforcement or protection of private rights or the redress of private wrongs, which shall be denominated a civil action, and in which there shall be a right to have issues of fact tried before a jury. Every action prosecuted by the people of the State as a party against a person charged with a public offense, for the punishment thereof, shall be termed a criminal action.

2. Rules of procedure. The Supreme Court shall have exclusive authority to make rules of procedure and practice for the Appellate Division. The General Assembly may make rules of procedure and practice for the Superior Court and District Court Divisions, and the General Assembly may delegate this authority to the Supreme Court. No rule of procedure or practice shall abridge substantive rights or abrogate or limit the right of trial by jury. If the General Assembly should delegate to the Supreme Court the rule-making power, the General Assembly may, nevertheless, alter, amend, or repeal any rule of procedure or practice adopted by the Supreme Court for the Superior Court or District Court Divisions.

The English legal system, inherited by the state of North Carolina, had recognized actions at law and suits in equity, the distinction being largely historical and technical. In 1868 North Carolina joined the trend of progressive states and merged the two into a single form of civil action. Implementing the guarantee of trial by jury in civil cases in Article I, Section 25, the present section guarantees the right in such actions ''to have issues of fact tried before a jury.'' Criminal prosecutions, defined here as actions ''prosecuted by the people of the State as a party against a person charged with a public offense, for the punishment thereof,'' are termed criminal, as opposed to civil, actions. Although not expressly reserved in the present section, the right to a jury trial in criminal cases is guaranteed in Article I, Section 24. Criminal punishments are listed in Article XI, Section 1.

Proper procedure is as important as proper rules in the administration of justice. Relying on the principle of separation of powers, the state supreme court a century ago asserted its power to prescribe its own rules of procedure (Herndon v. Imperial Fire Insurance Co., 1892). Subsection 2 of the present section expressly confirms that power: The supreme court alone may make rules of procedure for the Appellate Division of the General Court of Justice, defined in Section 5 of this article as the supreme court itself and the court of appeals. The General Assembly may legislate rules of procedure for the trial courts (the superior and district courts) or may delegate the task to the supreme court; in fact, it has done the latter (North Carolina General Statutes § 7A-34). Because of the potential for rules of procedure to affect substantive rights, the present section expressly saves all such rights, especially the ''sacred right'' to trial by jury.

SECTION 14

Waiver of jury trial. In all issues of fact joined in any court, the parties in any civil case may waive the right to have the issues determined by a jury, in which case the finding of the judge upon the facts shall have the force and effect of a verdict by a jury.

Trial by jury in civil cases respecting property is proclaimed to be "one of the best securities of the rights of the people" (Article I, Section 25). What is technically tried before the jury are "issues of fact," that is, matters of fact put in issue by the pleadings. Trial by jury is a right, not a duty, so it may be waived. In addition to express waiver, failure by a party to appear waives the right. If trial by jury is waived, the judge's findings of fact have the same effect as a jury verdict; that is, they are conclusive if there is any evidence to support them (Cauble v. Bell, 1959). Trial by jury in criminal cases is guaranteed by Article I, Section 24; it may be waived by pleading guilty.

SECTION 15

Administration. The General Assembly shall provide for an administrative office of the courts to carry out the provisions of this Article.

Discharging its constitutional duty, the General Assembly established the Administrative Office of the Courts (North Carolina General Statutes § 7A-340). Its director, appointed by the chief justice and serving "at his pleasure," is considered to be an officer of the General Court of Justice; as such, he or she is protected by judicial immunity (Fowler v. Alexander, 1973).

SECTION 16

Terms of office and election of Justices of the Supreme Court, Judges of the Court of Appeals, and Judges of the Superior Court. Justices of the Supreme Court, Judges of the Court of Appeals, and regular Judges of the Superior Court shall be elected by the qualified voters and shall hold office for terms of eight years and until their successors are elected and qualified. Justices of the Supreme Court and Judges of the Court of Appeals shall be elected by the qualified voters of the State. Regular Judges of the Superior Court may be elected by the qualified voters of the State or by the voters of their respective districts, as the General Assembly may prescribe.

Under the 1776 Constitution judges were elected by the General Assembly and served for life; the 1868 Constitution first provided for direct election and eight-year terms. Judges may be removed for cause before the end of their terms, as provided in the next section. They must retire when they reach the maximum age set by statute pursuant to Section 8 of this article.

Justices of the supreme court and judges of the court of appeals must be elected in statewide elections, and the General Assembly has opted for statewide elections for superior court judges (North Carolina General Statutes § 163-1). Until 1987 superior court judges were elected under a system that provided for staggered terms in some multi-seat districts. A statute adopted in that year postponed certain judicial elections in order to secure uniformity in the beginning of terms; the effect was to lengthen the service of some incumbents beyond eight years. Using reasoning that even the supreme court justices admitted might "appear artificial at first," the court upheld the statute:

Once the incumbent judges' terms of office expire, their service ends when their successors are elected and qualified. . . . Where, as here, the incumbents' terms end without successors having been elected and qualified, and new terms of office have not begun, the Constitution's "hold over" provision operates and allows the incumbents to continue serving in the interim. . . . The constitutional provision, not the legislative act, allows the judges to remain in office. (State ex rel. Martin v. Preston, 1989.)

Since no vacancies technically occurred, the governor was given no opportunity to make interim appointments.

SECTION 17

Removal of Judges, Magistrates and Clerks.

1. Removal of Judges by the General Assembly. Any Justice or Judge of the General Court of Justice may be removed from office for mental or physical incapacity by joint resolution of two-thirds of all the members of each house of the General Assembly. Any Justice or Judge against whom the General Assembly may be about to proceed shall receive notice thereof, accompanied by a copy of the causes alleged for his removal, at least 20 days before the day on which either house of the General Assembly shall act thereon. Removal from office by the General Assembly for any other cause shall be by impeachment.

2. Additional method of removal of Judges. The General Assembly shall prescribe a procedure, in addition to impeachment and address set forth in this Section, for the removal of a Justice or Judge of the General Court of Justice for mental or physical incapacity interfering with the performance of his duties which is, or is likely to become, permanent, and for the censure and removal of a Justice or Judge of the General Court of Justice for wilful misconduct in office, wilful and persistent failure to perform his duties, habitual intemperance, conviction of a crime involving moral turpitude, or conduct prejudicial to the administration of justice that brings the judicial office into disrepute.

3. Removal of Magistrates. The General Assembly shall provide by

general law for the removal of Magistrates for misconduct or mental or physical incapacity.

4. Removal of Clerks. Any Clerk of the Superior Court may be removed from office for misconduct or mental or physical incapacity by the senior regular resident Superior Court Judge serving the county. Any Clerk against whom proceedings are instituted shall receive written notice of the charges against him at least 10 days before the hearing upon the charges. Any Clerk so removed from office shall be entitled to an appeal as provided by law.

Without this section, the only way to remove a judicial officer would be by impeachment (Article IV, Section 4), and removal would carry with it disqualification for further office holding (Article VI, Section 8). Because impeachment is a slow and cumbersome procedure, involving the senate and the house of representatives and necessarily taking time from legislative business, repeated efforts have been made to find simpler alternatives that nonetheless protect the judiciary from vexatious or politically motivated charges. Physical or mental incapacity was the most difficult to deal with by a system designed for the punishment of crime: Impeachment initiates a criminal prosecution (Article I, Section 22). The amendments of 1876 added the procedure in Subsection 1, removal by address—that is, "joint resolution of two-thirds of all the members of each house of the General Assembly." Special procedures for the removal of the governor in such cases are provided in Article III, Section 3, Subsections 3 and 4; other elective executive officers are covered by Article III, Section 7, Subsection 6 and sheriffs by Article VII, Section 2.

In 1972 an amendment added Subsection 2, mandating legislation to create yet another means for removal of justices or judges for mental or physical incapacity. In discharge of its duty the General Assembly established the Judicial Standards Commission (North Carolina General Statutes § 7A-375). Of more significance, this new system is also directed to deal with "wilful misconduct in office, wilful and persistent failure to perform [official] duties, habitual intemperance, conviction of a crime involving moral turpitude, or conduct prejudicial to the administration of justice that brings the judicial office into disrepute"—all offenses traditionally handled only by impeachment. Indeed, since removal from office for such causes is a criminal punishment (see Article XI, Section 1), without the express language in the present clause authorizing it "in addition to impeachment and address," it would appear to conflict with the constitutional sections on impeachment. As it is, it appears that removal from office by the procedures legislated under Subsection 2 would not disqualify the person from further elective office since Article VI, Section 8 applies only to removal "by impeachment."

The removal of magistrates is governed by statute (North Carolina General Statutes § 7A-173): They may be removed by any regular superior court judge holding court in the county. Grounds for removal are the same as those for justices or judges.

SECTION 18

District Attorney and Prosecutorial Districts.

1. District Attorneys. The General Assembly shall, from time to time, divide the State into a convenient number of prosecutorial districts, for each of which a District Attorney shall be chosen for a term of four years by the qualified voters thereof, at the same time and places as members of the General Assembly are elected. Only persons duly authorized to practice law in the courts of this State shall be eligible for election or appointment as a District Attorney. The District Attorney shall advise the officers of justice in his district, be responsible for the prosecution on behalf of the State of all criminal actions in the Superior Courts of his district, perform such duties related to appeals therefrom as the Attorney General may require, and perform such other duties as the General Assembly may prescribe.

2. Prosecution in District Court Division. Criminal actions in the District Court Division shall be prosecuted in such manner as the General Assembly may prescribe by general law uniformly applicable in every local court district of the State.

Section 13 of this article defines a criminal action as one "prosecuted by the people of the State as a party against a person charged with a public offense, for the punishment thereof." The people's lawyer in such cases is a district attorney, called a solicitor until the name was changed by amendment in 1974. Although legal training was always a practical necessity, it became a legal requirement only in 1983 when the second sentence of Subsection 1 was added by constitutional amendment—the amendment that added the same requirement for the attorney general (Article III, Section 7, Subsection 7). A law license had been made a qualification for judicial office by amendment in 1980 (Article IV, Section 22).

SECTION 19

Vacancies. Unless otherwise provided in this Article, all vacancies occurring in the offices provided for by this Article shall be filled by appointment of the Governor, and the appointees shall hold their places until the next election for members of the General Assembly that is held more than 60 days after the vacancy occurs, when elections shall be held to fill the offices. When the unexpired term of any of the offices named in this Article of the Constitution in which a vacancy has occurred, and in which it is herein provided that the Governor shall fill the vacancy, expires on the first day of January succeeding the next election for members of the General Assembly, the Governor shall appoint to fill that vacancy for the unexpired term of the office. If any person elected or appointed to any of these offices shall fail to qualify, the office shall be appointed to, held and filled as provided in case of vacancies occurring therein. All incumbents of these offices shall hold until their successors are qualified.

The governor fills vacancies in the judicial branch, "unless otherwise provided in this Article"; senatorial consent is not mentioned, so none is required. The governor's power of appointment does not extend to vacancies in the office of clerk of the superior court, which are filled by the senior regular resident judge of the superior court for the county (Article IV, Section 9, Subsection 3); in the office of district judge, which are filled as prescribed by statute (Article IV, Section 10); or in the office of magistrate, which are filled in the manner provided for original appointment to the office—that is, by the senior regular resident judge of the superior court for the county from nominations by the clerk of the superior court (Article IV, Section 10).

Gubernatorial appointees hold their offices "until the next election for members of the General Assembly that is held more than 60 days after the vacancy occurs." The sixty-day period is presumably designed to prevent too rapid turnover; it was lengthened to sixty from thirty days by constitutional amendment in 1987. Elections for members of the General Assembly are held in even-numbered years (Article II, Section 8), so appointees may serve as long as two years plus sixty days. Once an election is held, those elected "fill the offices," which the state supreme court has determined to mean "finish the unexpired terms," rather than "begin new eight-year terms" (Brannon v. North Carolina State Board of Elections, 1992).

SECTION 20

Revenues and expenses of the judicial department. The General Assembly shall provide for the establishment of a schedule of court fees and costs which shall be uniform throughout the State within each division of the General Court of Justice. The operating expenses of the judicial department, other than compensation to process servers and other locally paid non-judicial officers, shall be paid from State funds.

Justice is the responsibility of government, so the operating expenses of the judicial branch are borne by the state, although court fees and costs may be charged to individual litigants.

SECTION 21

Fees, salaries and emoluments. The General Assembly shall prescribe and regulate the fees, salaries, and emoluments of all officers provided for in this Article, but the salaries of Judges shall not be diminished during their continuance in office. In no case shall the compensation of any Judge or Magistrate be dependent upon his decision or upon the collection of costs.

The General Assembly sets the compensation of all officers in the judicial branch. To preserve judicial independence, the salaries of judges (including justices) may not be reduced during their service. The distinction between "all officers," on the one hand, and "Judges," on the other, is significant: Officers who are not judges may suffer salary cuts. Judicial compensation may not be made dependent on the outcome of cases; neither judge nor magistrate, for instance, may be paid a percentage of fines. Once used as a means of keeping the costs of government low, "payment by results" is now viewed as a breach of due process guaranteed by the U.S. Constitution (Tumey v. Ohio, 1927); it has long been viewed as a violation of natural law because rewarding judges for conviction gives them an interest in the outcome, making each in a sense a "judge in his own case" (Dr. Bonham's Case, 1610).

SECTION 22

Qualification of Justices and Judges. Only persons duly authorized to practice law in the courts of this State shall be eligible for election or appointment as a Justice of the Supreme Court, Judge of the Court of Appeals, Judge of the Superior Court, or Judge of District Court. This section shall not apply to persons elected to or serving in such capacities on or before January 1, 1981.

As a practical matter, the vast majority of North Carolina judges have been licensed to practice law in this state, but until this section was added by amendment in 1980, it was not a formal qualification for office. In 1983 another amendment added the same qualification for service as attorney general (Article III, Section 7, Subsection 7) and district attorney (Article IV, Section 18, Subsection 1). The second sentence of the present section is a "grandfather clause," exempting non-lawyers serving as judges prior to the effective date. The attorney general has issued a formal opinion that one who had been a judge at the relevant time, even though he or she resigned or did not seek immediate reelection, may still qualify for judicial office; that is, the exemption conferred by the second sentence can last a lifetime (Opinion of Attorney General to Hon. Arnold O. Jones, 1981).

Article V

Finance

Incident to the thorough constitutional reform of 1971, Article V was completely rewritten. Ratified apart from the rest of the constitution, it became effective only on July 1, 1973, the delay being necessary to permit implementation without disruption of state finances. Because the principal sources of state revenue are taxes and borrowing, those topics occupy the bulk of the article: Sections 1, 2, and 5 on taxes; Sections 3, 4, and 6 on debt and repayment. Section 7, prohibiting withdrawals from the treasury except ''in consequence of appropriations made by law,'' is the article's logical conclusion. Sections 8 to 13, granting authority to borrow for half a dozen favored projects, were added by a series of later amendments and constitute a sort of appendix.

SECTION 1

> **No capitation tax to be levied.** No poll or capitation tax shall be levied by the General Assembly or by any county, city or town, or other taxing unit.

A poll or capitation tax is a ''head tax,'' a flat rate charged on each individual. Unrelated to income or the ownership of land or other assets, it bears hardest on the poor. Because of the correlation in the United States between race and poverty—black Americans as a class have always been poorer than whites—the poll tax was the only tax that blacks were sure to owe. In Jim Crow days, non-payment of the poll tax was used, along with failure of the literacy test (Article VI, Section 4), to disfranchise blacks. By constitutional amendment in 1919 North Carolina eliminated payment of the poll tax as a qualification for voting; federal law followed suit with the Twenty-Fourth Amendment in 1964. Although the tie with voting was broken, the poll tax as a means to raise revenue remained constitutional until the effective date of this article.

A further type of tax barred by the constitution appears in Article I, Section 16. Incident to its ban on ex post facto laws, the declaration of rights has included since 1868 this sentence: "No law taxing retrospectively sales, purchases, or other acts previously done shall be enacted."

SECTION 2

State and local taxation.

1. Power of taxation. The power of taxation shall be exercised in a just and equitable manner, for public purposes only, and shall never be surrendered, suspended, or contracted away.

2. Classification. Only the General Assembly shall have the power to classify property for taxation, which power shall be exercised only on a State-wide basis and shall not be delegated. No class of property shall be taxed except by uniform rule, and every classification shall be made by general law uniformly applicable in every county, city and town, and other unit of local government.

3. Exemptions. Property belonging to the State, counties, and municipal corporations shall be exempt from taxation. The General Assembly may exempt cemeteries and property held for educational, scientific, literary, cultural, charitable, or religious purposes, and, to a value not exceeding $300, any personal property. The General Assembly may exempt from taxation not exceeding $1,000 in value of property held and used as the place of residence of the owner. Every exemption shall be on a State-wide basis and shall be made by general law uniformly applicable in every county, city and town, and other unit of local government. No taxing authority other than the General Assembly may grant exemptions, and the General Assembly shall not delegate the powers accorded to it by this subsection.

4. Special tax areas. Subject to the limitations imposed by Section 4, the General Assembly may enact general laws authorizing the governing body of any county, city, or town to define territorial areas and to levy taxes within those areas, in addition to those levied throughout the county, city, or town, in order to finance, provide, or maintain services, facilities, and functions in addition to or to a greater extent than those financed, provided, or maintained for the entire county, city, or town.

5. Purposes of property tax. The General Assembly shall not authorize any county, city or town, special district, or other unit of local government to levy taxes on property, except for purposes authorized by general law uniformly applicable throughout the State, unless the tax is approved by a majority of the qualified voters of the unit who vote thereon.

6. Income tax. The rate of tax on incomes shall not in any case exceed ten percent, and there shall be allowed personal exemptions and deductions so that only net incomes are taxed.

7. Contracts. The General Assembly may enact laws whereby the State, any county, city or town, and any other public corporation may contract with and appropriate money to any person, association, or corporation for the accomplishment of public purposes only.

Taxes may be levied for "public purposes only"; the North Carolina Supreme Court has read this restriction broadly as a limitation on all forms of government expenditure (In re Housing Bonds, 1982). In a leading case the court held that this means the "ultimate net gain or advantage must be the public's as contra-distinguished from that of an individual or private entity" (Mitchell v. North Carolina Industrial Development Financing Authority, 1968). The line proved difficult to draw; for instance, a municipality has been permitted to operate its own cable television system (Madison Cablevision, Inc. v. City of Morganton, 1989). At a minimum, taxes paid by A must not be handed over to B simply to enrich the latter. All taxes and government expenditures have a redistributive effect, however, and that is constitutional so long as the primary purpose is "public." The provision that the power to tax shall never be "surrendered, suspended, or contracted away" is addressed to an abuse in the nineteenth century when business corporations often secured tax exemptions as part of their state charters.

Subsection 2 permits classification of property for tax purposes, but only by "general law uniformly applicable in every county, city and town, and other unit of local government." This phrase, which is repeated in Subsection 3, is explained in Article XIV, Section 3 to exclude special or local acts; the same section repeats the obvious, that such laws must themselves be "without clas-sification or exemption."

State property is exempted from taxation by Subsection 3, regardless of the use to which it is put; thus, for example, municipalities may not tax property of the University of North Carolina even if it is not being used for public purposes (In re University of North Carolina, 1980). Certain other property may be ex-empted by legislation. Since property held for "religious purposes" is expressly listed among those that may be exempted, no credible argument can be made under the state constitution that such an exemption would violate the guarantee of religious liberty in Article I, Section 13. The General Assembly may exempt from taxation up to $300 worth of personal property and up to $1,000 worth of residential property as a concession to poverty. Elsewhere, the constitution itself confers an exemption from the claims of private creditors: no less than $500 worth of personalty and no less than $1,000 worth of realty (Article X, Sections 1 and 2). The list of permitted exemptions is exclusive: The General Assembly may not grant exemptions for property held for other purposes (Sir Walter Lodge, No. 411, I.O.O.F. v. Swain, 1940).

The authorization of special tax areas by "general laws" is permitted by Subsection 4. The permission is made expressly "subject to the limitations imposed by Section 4"; since the latter concerns local government borrowing rather than taxing, the limitation is of no consequence. Special tax areas were expected to be of particular utility to consolidated city-counties (see Article VII, Section 3), permitting them to define "urban service districts" with more services and higher taxes. Since no consolidated city-counties have been formed so far, the present subsection remains dormant.

Property taxes, the mainstay of local government, are limited by Subsection 5 to purposes authorized by "general law uniformly applicable throughout the State," a phrase explained in Article XIV, Section 3. The money may be applied to other purposes only if approved by popular vote, an instance in which "no taxation without representation" yields to direct democracy.

The income tax, not available to the federal government until the Sixteenth Amendment in 1913, was always constitutional in North Carolina. Subsection 6—a limitation, not a grant, of power—sets the maximum rate of income taxation at 10 percent of net income.

Subsection 7 permits all levels of state government to enter into contracts with private parties so long as the object of the contract is a "public purpose."

SECTION 3

Limitations upon the increase of State debt.

1. Authorized purposes; two-thirds limitation. The General Assembly shall have no power to contract debts secured by a pledge of the faith and credit of the State, unless approved by a majority of the qualified voters of the State who vote thereon, except for the following purposes:

   a. to fund or refund a valid existing debt;

   b. to supply an unforeseen deficiency in the revenue;

   c. to borrow in anticipation of the collection of taxes due and payable within the current fiscal year to an amount not exceeding 50 per cent of such taxes;

   d. to suppress riots or insurrections, or to repel invasions;

   e. to meet emergencies immediately threatening the public health or safety, as conclusively determined in writing by the Governor;

   f. for any other lawful purpose, to the extent of two-thirds of the amount by which the State's outstanding indebtedness shall have been reduced during the next preceding biennium.

2. Gift or loan of credit regulated. The General Assembly shall have no power to give or lend the credit of the State in aid of any person, association, or corporation, except a corporation in which the State has a controlling interest, unless the subject is submitted to a direct vote of the people of the State, and is approved by a majority of the qualified voters who vote thereon.

3. Definitions. A debt is incurred within the meaning of this Section when the State borrows money. A pledge of the faith and credit within the meaning of this Section is a pledge of the taxing power. A loan of credit within the

meaning of this Section occurs when the State exchanges its obligations with
or in any way guarantees the debts of an individual, association, or private
corporation.

4. Certain debts barred. The General Assembly shall never assume or pay
any debt or obligation, express or implied, incurred in aid of insurrection
or rebellion against the United States. Neither shall the General Assembly
assume or pay any debt or bond incurred or issued by authority of the
Convention of 1868, the special session of the General Assembly of 1868,
or the General Assemblies of 1868–69 and 1869–70, unless the subject is
submitted to the people of the State and is approved by a majority of all of
the qualified voters at a referendum held for that sole purpose.

5. Outstanding debt. Except as provided in subsection (4), nothing in this
Section shall be construed to invalidate or impair the obligation of any bond,
note, or other evidence of indebtedness outstanding or authorized for issue
as of July 1, 1973.

Apart from taxes—the subject of Sections 1 and 2 of this article—the only other
major source of state finance is borrowing. The present section on state debt is
closely paralleled by the following section on local government debt; between
them, they impose a strict discipline on public borrowing. Unless within six
specified exceptions, all debts must be approved by the voters, specifically by
"a majority of the qualified voters of the State who vote thereon"—another
example of direct as opposed to representative democracy. Debts properly approved are secured by "a pledge of the faith and credit of the State," defined
in Subsection 3 as "a pledge of the taxing power." Bonds issued on such security
are commonly called "general obligation bonds"; the interest paid on them is
usually exempt from state and federal income taxation. Not requiring voter
approval are debts "to fund or refund" an existing debt—that is, to convert one
debt into another with different terms (funding) or to contract a new debt in
order to pay off an old one (refunding); the theory of this exception seems to
be that no additional obligation is incurred, although that is not spelled out. (A
judicial decision concerning local government debt seems to bear out this conclusion. See the commentary on Article V, Section 4.)

Another type of debt not requiring voter approval is "anticipation borrowing"—that is, borrowing on the security of revenue not yet received. Anticipation
borrowing can free ordinary spending from the fluctuations of income—at the
cost, of course, of paying the current rate of interest. Without voter approval,
anticipation borrowing is limited to a conservative 50 percent of anticipated
revenue. In addition, the state may borrow without a vote of the people up to
two-thirds of the amount by which it reduced outstanding debt within the last
preceding biennial budget, putting the state on the path of ever-decreasing debt.
Finally, various emergencies threatening the public health or safety may be met
by borrowing without the time-consuming process of voter approval. The governor's determination of what constitutes such a threat is made "conclusive,"
the object being to reassure bond counsel, lawyers specializing in finance who

issue opinions concerning the validity of bonds, that voter approval is not required; otherwise, a supreme court decision might be demanded.

Subsection 2 prohibits the gift or loan to private parties of the state's credit without approval by the voters. A "loan of credit" is defined in Subsection 3 to mean the exchange of state obligations for private ones or any form of loan guarantee; a gift of credit presumably means the conferral of such benefits without consideration. Like the surrender of the taxing power, prohibited by Section 2 of this article, the present prohibition addresses an abuse of the nineteenth century when private corporations backed up their debts with public credit. Hoping to encourage economic development and lulled by assurances that no money would be required, the public often ended up owing large sums. An exception to the prohibition is made in favor of corporations "in which the State has a controlling interest," such as the North Carolina Railroad.

Subsection 4, like the declaration of rights' prohibitions of secession and slavery (Article I, Sections 4 and 17), is an obvious relic of the Civil War. The prohibition on payment of debts "incurred in aid of insurrection or rebellion" repeats the words of the Fourteenth Amendment to the U.S. Constitution (amend. XIV, § 4) and is the state's solemn repudiation of its share of the Confederate war debt. In the section that follows, units of local government are likewise prohibited from assuming such debts. The second sentence of the present subsection, incorporating a post-Reconstruction amendment ratified in 1880, repudiates debts incurred by the constitutional convention of 1868 that drafted the state's second constitution and those incurred by the General Assembly during Reconstruction. Repayment of such debts must be approved by the voters, specifically by "a majority of all the qualified voters at a referendum," arguably a higher standard than for borrowing, which requires "a majority of those actually voting." While repudiation would seem to violate the contracts clause of the U.S. Constitution (art. I, § 10, cl. 1), the state's creditors generally found federal courts closed to them by the Eleventh Amendment to the U.S. Constitution.

The borrowing covered by this section (and the following) is secured by a pledge of the state's taxing power; money borrowed on other security is not covered. If a public authority, such as the North Carolina Turnpike Authority, borrows money on the security of its revenue, no voter approval is required (North Carolina Turnpike Authority v. Pine Island, Inc., 1965). This fact has led to the proliferation of entities, including some non-profit private corporations, authorized to borrow on the security of their revenues for a variety of favored projects, such as health care and higher education. (See Sections 8 to 13 of this article.)

SECTION 4

Limitations upon the increase of local government debt.

1. Regulation of borrowing and debt. The General Assembly shall enact

general laws relating to the borrowing of money secured by a pledge of the faith and credit and the contracting of other debts by counties, cities and towns, special districts, and other units, authorities, and agencies of local government.

2. Authorized purposes; two-thirds limitation. The General Assembly shall have no power to authorize any county, city or town, special district, or other unit of local government to contract debts secured by a pledge of its faith and credit unless approved by a majority of the qualified voters of the unit who vote thereon, except for the following purposes:

a. to fund or refund a valid existing debt;

b. to supply an unforeseen deficiency in the revenue;

c. to borrow in anticipation of the collection of taxes due and payable within the current fiscal year to an amount not exceeding 50 per cent of such taxes;

d. to suppress riots or insurrections;

e. to meet emergencies immediately threatening the public health or safety, as conclusively determined in writing by the Governor;

f. for purposes authorized by general laws uniformly applicable throughout the State, to the extent of two-thirds of the amount by which the unit's outstanding indebtedness shall have been reduced during the next preceding fiscal year.

3. Gift or loan of credit regulated. No county, city or town, special district, or other unit of local government shall give or lend its credit in aid of any person, association, or corporation, except for public purposes as authorized by general law, and unless approved by a majority of the qualified voters of the unit who vote thereon.

4. Certain debts barred. No county, city or town, or other unit of local government shall assume or pay any debt or the interest thereon contracted directly or indirectly in aid or support of rebellion or insurrection against the United States.

5. Definitions. A debt is incurred within the meaning of this Section when a county, city or town, special district, or other unit, authority, or agency of local government borrows money. A pledge of faith and credit within the meaning of this Section is a pledge of the taxing power. A loan of credit within the meaning of this Section occurs when a county, city or town, special district, or other unit, authority, or agency of local government exchanges its obligations with or in any way guarantees the debts of an individual, association, or private corporation.

6. Outstanding debt. Except as provided in subsection (4), nothing in this Section shall be construed to invalidate or impair the obligation of any bond, note, or other evidence of indebtedness outstanding or authorized for issue as of July 1, 1973.

The present section begins with a clear announcement of principle: There shall be no local legislation on local government debt. All laws on the subject must be "general laws," defined in Article XIV, Section 3 to exclude special acts, but to permit classified general laws—that is, general laws limited to "classes defined by population or other criteria."

Most of what is said concerning the previous section on state debt is equally applicable to the present section on local government debt. In a few cases local government practices testing the limits of constitutional power have been upheld by the state supreme court, creating precedents relevant to state finance as well. In City of Concord v. All Owners of Taxable Property (1991), a municipal bond offer made without voter approval was upheld to refund an existing debt even though the bonds were in an amount greater than the bonds to be refunded; falling interest rates made the overall cost to the municipality less than the original bonds. In Wayne County Citizens Association v. Wayne County Board of Commissioners (1991), an installment contract for the purchase of a jail was upheld despite the lack of voter approval. The transaction did not involve a pledge of the local government's "faith and credit" because the contract explicitly stated that the taxing power was not implicated. Although annual payments stretching over many years, and thus resembling debt repayments, would be required, the crucial difference was that the sellers, unlike creditors, had no more security than the contract itself provided.

SECTION 5

Acts levying taxes to state objects. Every act of the General Assembly levying a tax shall state the special object to which it is to be applied, and it shall be applied to no other purpose.

Revenue bills require special solemnities for adoption (Article II, Section 23); in addition, the present section requires the legislation to state the "special object" for which the revenue is to be raised. The final clause—"and it shall be applied to no other purpose"—requires that substance follows form.

SECTION 6

Inviolability of sinking funds and retirement funds.

1. Sinking funds. The General Assembly shall not use or authorize to be used any part of the amount of any sinking fund for any purpose other than the retirement of the bonds for which the sinking fund has been created, except that these funds may be invested as authorized by law.

2. Retirement funds. Neither the General Assembly nor any public officer, employee, or agency shall use or authorize to be used any part of the funds of the Teachers' and State Employees' Retirement System or the Local Governmental Employees' Retirement System for any purpose other than retirement system benefits and purposes, administrative expenses, and

refunds; except that retirement system funds may be invested as authorized by law, subject to the investment limitation that the funds of the Teachers' and State Employees' Retirement System and the Local Governmental Employees' Retirement System shall not be applied, diverted, loaned to, or used by the State, any State agency, State officer, public officer, or public employee.

Borrowing money is easy; it is repayment that is difficult. The sinking fund, an invention of eighteenth-century economists, is an attempt to reduce the difficulty by making repayment automatic. The classic scheme began with a sum used to purchase bonds; rather than retiring the individual bonds purchased, these were held, and the interest they earned was used to purchase still more bonds. If left unaltered, the system would over time result in the purchase of all outstanding bonds. Modern sinking funds speed up the process with regular appropriations. To remain creditworthy, the legislature must obviously resist the temptation to "raid" the sinking fund. The first subsection of the present section is a constitutional prohibition of using the fund (or any part of it) for any other than its intended purpose.

Once retirement plans for state employees were created, a comparable problem arose: how to guarantee that the funds would not be "raided." By constitutional amendment, approved in 1950 and carried forward into the 1971 Constitution, teachers and state employees secured constitutional protection for their retirement funds; in 1971 local government employees were given the same protection. Money in the funds may not even be loaned to the state.

SECTION 7

Drawing public money.

1. State treasury. No money shall be drawn from the State Treasury but in consequence of appropriations made by law, and an accurate account of the receipts and expenditures of State funds shall be published annually.

2. Local treasury. No money shall be drawn from the treasury of any county, city or town, or other unit of local government except by authority of law.

The power of the purse is the exclusive prerogative of the General Assembly, and Subsection 1 dates from the 1776 Constitution. As the functions of local governments have increased, so have local government revenues, necessitating local treasuries. By amendment in 1962 expenditures of these funds, too, were expressly made subject to the "authority of law."

SECTION 8

Health care facilities. Notwithstanding any other provisions of this Constitution, the General Assembly may enact general laws to authorize the

State, counties, cities or towns, and other State and local governmental entities to issue revenue bonds to finance or refinance for any such governmental entity or any nonprofit private corporation, regardless of any church or religious relationship, the cost of acquiring, constructing, and financing health care facility projects to be operated to serve and benefit the public; provided, no cost incurred earlier than two years prior to the effective date of this section shall be refinanced. Such bonds shall be payable from the revenues, gross or net, of any such projects and any other health care facilities of any such governmental entity or nonprofit private corporation pledged therefor; shall not be secured by a pledge of the full faith and credit, or deemed to create an indebtedness requiring voter approval of any governmental entity; and may be secured by an agreement which may provide for the conveyance of title of, with or without consideration, any such project or facilities to the governmental entity or nonprofit private corporation. The power of eminent domain shall not be used pursuant hereto for nonprofit private corporations.

Sections 3 and 4 of this article deal with borrowing by the state and local governments, respectively. The present section, added by amendment in 1975, is an exception to both. It empowers the General Assembly to authorize state and local governments to borrow for health care facilities without voter approval. The dispensation is justified because the bonds to be issued do not pledge the "faith and credit" of the state; that is, they do not pledge the taxing power. Instead, these are "revenue bonds," secured by the revenue generated by the facilities in question (and, if necessary, by a mortgage on the property). Although the bonds may be used to refinance existing debt, they may not be used to cover costs incurred more than two years prior to the section's effective date; this is to prevent the "grandfathering" of old debt, incurred before the governmental role was permitted. Since historically many churches have provided hospitals and other health care facilities, many eligible projects would have a religious affiliation. To preclude any argument that such involvement violates the state's commitment to religious liberty (Article I, Section 13), the present section expressly approves such ties.

SECTION 9

Capital projects for industry. Notwithstanding any other provision of this Constitution, the General Assembly may enact general laws to authorize counties to create authorities to issue revenue bonds to finance, but not refinance, the cost of capital projects consisting of industrial, manufacturing and pollution control facilities for industry and pollution control facilities for public utilities, and to refund such bonds.

In no event shall such revenue bonds be secured by or payable from any public moneys whatsoever, but such revenue bonds shall be secured by and payable only from revenues or property derived from private parties. All

such capital projects and all transactions therefor shall be subject to taxation
to the extent such projects and transactions would be subject to taxation if
no public body were involved therewith; provided, however, that the General
Assembly may provide that the interest on such revenue bonds shall be
exempt from income taxes within the State.

The power of eminent domain shall not be exercised to provide any
property for any such capital project.

Unlike the preceding section that authorizes state and local debt, the present
section, added in 1976, authorizes only county debt; it is, in other words, an
exception to part of Section 4 of this article. Like Section 8, it permits revenue
bonds without voter approval, in this case limited to financing capital projects
for industry. Unlike Section 8 bonds, these bonds may not be used to refinance
any costs incurred earlier, although the bonds, once issued, may later be refunded.
Capital projects remain taxable, although the interest paid on the bonds may be
exempted from income taxation; by making the bonds "tax-free" a lower rate
of interest is usually secured. The effect, obviously, is to transfer some wealth
from the state to the borrowing counties since state revenues from income taxes
are reduced, while the counties save money on interest charges.

SECTION 10

Joint ownership of generation and transmission facilities. In addition
to other powers conferred upon them by law, municipalities owning or
operating facilities for the generation, transmission or distribution of electric
power and energy and joint agencies formed by such municipalities for the
purpose of owning or operating facilities for the generation and transmission
of electric power and energy (each, respectively, "a unit of municipal
government") may jointly or severally own, operate and maintain works,
plants and facilities, within or without the State, for the generation and
transmission of electric power and energy, or both, with any person, firm,
association or corporation, public or private, engaged in the generation,
transmission or distribution of electric power and energy for resale (each,
respectively, "a co-owner") within this State or any state contiguous to this
State, and may enter into and carry out agreements with respect to such
jointly owned facilities. For the purpose of financing its share of the cost
of any such jointly owned electric generation or transmission facilities, a
unit of municipal government may issue its revenue bonds in the manner
prescribed by the General Assembly, payable as to both principal and interest
solely from and secured by a lien and charge on all or any part of the revenue
derived, or to be derived, by such unit of municipal government from the
ownership and operation of its electric facilities; provided, however, that
no unit of municipal government shall be liable, either jointly or severally,
for any acts, omissions or obligations of any co-owner, nor shall any money
or property of any unit of municipal government be credited or otherwise

applied to the account of any co-owner or be charged with any debt, lien
or mortgage as a result of any debt or obligation of any co-owner.

Unlike Section 9 which applies only to counties, the present section, added in
1977, applies only to municipalities, a further exception to Section 4 of this
article on local government debt. Again no voter approval is required for certain
bond issues because the bonds are revenue bonds, not implicating the state's
taxing power. Municipalities owning electric utilities are permitted, together or
separately ("jointly or severally"), to associate with other utilities, public or
private, in North Carolina or any contiguous state (Virginia, Tennessee, Georgia,
and South Carolina).

SECTION 11

Capital projects for agriculture. Notwithstanding any other provision
of the Constitution the General Assembly may enact general laws to authorize
the creation of an agency to issue revenue bonds to finance the cost of capital
projects consisting of agricultural facilities, and to refund such bonds.

In no event shall such revenue bonds be secured by or payable from any
public moneys whatsoever, but such revenue bonds shall be secured by and
payable only from revenues or property derived from private parties. All
such capital projects and all transactions therefor shall be subject to taxation
to the extent such projects and transactions would be subject to taxation if
no public body were involved therewith; provided, however, that the General
Assembly may provide that the interest on such revenue bonds shall be
exempt from income taxes within the State.

The power of eminent domain shall not be exercised to provide any
property for any such capital project.

Once capital projects for industry became eligible for support by revenue bonds
(Section 9), it was perhaps only a matter of time until comparable provisions
were made for agriculture, the state's other (and older) economic mainstay.
Added in 1984, the present section parallels Section 9 with only one exception:
Rather than empowering the General Assembly to authorize counties to borrow
for such capital projects, it empowers the General Assembly to create new
agencies for such purposes.

SECTION 12

Higher Education Facilities. Notwithstanding any other provisions of
this Constitution, the General Assembly may enact general laws to authorize
the State or any State entity to issue revenue bonds to finance and refinance
the cost of acquiring, constructing, and financing higher education facilities
to be operated to serve and benefit the public for any nonprofit private

corporation, regardless of any church or religious relationship provided no cost incurred earlier than five years prior to the effective date of this section shall be refinanced. Such bonds shall be payable from any revenues or assets of any such nonprofit private corporation pledged therefor, shall not be secured by a pledge of the full faith and credit of the State or such State entity or deemed to create an indebtedness requiring voter approval of the State or such entity, and, where the title to such facilities is vested in the State or any State entity, may be secured by an agreement which may provide for the conveyance of title to, with or without consideration, such facilities to the nonprofit private corporation. The power of eminent domain shall not be used pursuant hereto.

In 1986 higher education caught up with health care: The present section, modeled on Section 8, empowers the General Assembly to authorize revenue bonds for such purposes without voter approval. In this case old debt may be refinanced if the costs were incurred within the preceding five years. (In Section 8 the limit is two years.) Education, like health care, was often provided by religious organizations, so an express declaration that any support from revenue bonds would not violate religious liberty (Article I, Section 13) is included.

SECTION 13

Seaport and airport facilities.

1. Notwithstanding any other provision of this Constitution, the General Assembly may enact general laws to grant to the State, counties, municipalities, and other State and local governmental entities all powers useful in connection with the development of new and existing seaports and airports, and to authorize such public bodies.

a. To acquire, construct, own, own jointly with public and private parties, lease as lessee, mortgage, sell, lease as lessor or otherwise dispose of lands and facilities and improvements, including undivided interests therein;

b. To finance and refinance for public and private parties seaport and airport facilities and improvements which relate to, develop or further waterborne or airborne commerce and cargo and passenger traffic, including commercial, industrial, manufacturing, processing, mining, transportation, distribution, storage, marine, aviation and environmental facilities and improvements; and

c. To secure any such financing or refinancing by all or any portion of their revenues, income or assets or other available monies associated with any of their seaport or airport facilities and with the facilities and improvements to be financed or refinanced, and by foreclosable liens on all or any part of their properties associated with any of their seaport or airport facilities and with the facilities and improvements to be financed or refinanced, but in no event to create a debt secured by a pledge of the faith and credit of the State or any other public body in the State.

Like Section 8 concerning the financing of health care facilities, the present section, added in 1986, constitutes an exception to both Sections 3 and 4 of this article on state and local government debt. Again, the justification—aside from the benefits of improved transportation facilities—is that revenue bonds alone are involved; the faith and credit of the state are not implicated.

Note: As proposed to the voters and ratified by them, this section contained a Subsection 1, but no other subsections.

Article VI

Suffrage and Eligibility to Office

SECTION 1

Who may vote. Every person born in the United States and every person who has been naturalized, 18 years of age, and possessing the qualifications set out in this Article, shall be entitled to vote at any election by the people of the State, except as herein otherwise provided.

The sections of this article divide neatly in half: Sections 1 to 5 concern suffrage, the right to vote, while Sections 6 to 10 concern eligibility to be voted into office. United States citizenship is the first requirement for North Carolina voters and is governed by federal law. Every person born in the United States is automatically a citizen (United States v. Wong Kim Ark, 1897); persons not born in this country may become citizens by naturalization, a process prescribed by statute (see U.S. Const. art. I, § 8, cl. 4). The minimum age for voting was set at twenty-one in the 1776 Constitution and remained there until 1971 when the ratification of the Twenty-Sixth Amendment to the U.S. Constitution lowered the age to eighteen; the state constitution incorporated the change by an amendment approved in 1972.

SECTION 2

Qualifications of voter.

1. Residence period for State elections. Any person who has resided in the State of North Carolina for one year and in the precinct, ward, or other election district for 30 days next preceding an election, and possesses the other qualifications set out in this Article, shall be entitled to vote at any

election held in this State. Removal from one precinct, ward, or other election district to another in this State shall not operate to deprive any person of the right to vote in the precinct, ward, or other election district from which that person has removed until 30 days after the removal.

2. Residence period for presidential elections. The General Assembly may reduce the time of residence for persons voting in presidential elections. A person made eligible by reason of a reduction in time of residence shall possess the other qualifications set out in this Article, shall only be entitled to vote for President and Vice President of the United States or for electors for President and Vice President, and shall not thereby become eligible to hold office in this State.

3. Disqualification of felon. No person adjudged guilty of a felony against this State or the United States, or adjudged guilty of a felony in another state that also would be a felony if it had been committed in this State, shall be permitted to vote unless that person shall be first restored to the rights of citizenship in the manner prescribed by law.

"Residence," for purposes of voting, is synonymous with domicile—that is, a permanent dwelling place to which one, when absent, intends to return (Hall v. Wake County Board of Elections, 1972). The constitutional plan is to require one year of residence to vote in state elections—less may be required by statute for voting in presidential elections—and thirty days' residence in the election district. The last requirement is artfully worded to prevent the loss of the right to vote because of a change of residence within the state shortly before an election: One who moves may continue to vote in the former district until eligible to vote in the new district.

The subsection on presidential elections concludes with the proviso that any legislative dispensation from ordinary residence requirements does not make one "eligible to hold office in this State," a proviso necessitated by the blanket qualification for office in Article VI, Section 6 of everyone twenty-one years of age or older (not otherwise disqualified) who is a "qualified voter in North Carolina." The constitutional scheme was severely compromised by a federal ruling that the one-year residence requirement for voting in state elections is invalid under the equal protection clause of the Fourteenth Amendment to the U.S. Constitution (Andrews v. Cody, 1972). Because of its express requirement by the present section, it could not possibly have been found in violation of the state's similarly worded equal protection clause (Article I, Section 19).

Convicted felons are disqualified, presumably because they voluntarily breached a major duty of citizenship. Their exclusion is not, however, a punishment for crime—all permissible punishments are catalogued in Article XI, Section 1—but rather a consequence of conviction (State v. Jones, 1880). "Felony" is left undefined by the present section, just as "misdemeanor" is given no constitutional definition in Article I, Section 24 which permits trial without jury for misdemeanors. Because a judgment of guilt is required, it is believed that a plea of *nolo contendere* or "no contest" to a felony charge does not result in disqualification to vote (Opinion of Attorney General to Ms. Bessie J. Cherry, 1980). A felon's rights of citizenship can be restored only by general law (Article II, Section 24, Subsection 1(n)).

SECTION 3

Registration. Every person offering to vote shall be at the time legally registered as a voter as herein prescribed and in the manner provided by law. The General Assembly shall enact general laws governing the registration of voters.

See the commentary following Section 4.

SECTION 4

Qualification for registration. Every person presenting himself for registration shall be able to read and write any section of the Constitution in the English language.

Registration is not itself one of the qualifications for voting; those are set out in Sections 1 and 2. Instead, it is a process for determining who is qualified to vote before the actual polling day. Registered voters have established their qualifications beforehand.

The literacy test, first imposed by amendment in 1900, was part of the scheme to disfranchise black voters, who were less likely because of unequal educational opportunities to be able to read; a "grandfather clause" originally saved the voting privileges of illiterate whites. Abuses in the administration of the test further widened the gap in results between the races. Literacy tests are now prohibited by federal law, so Section 4 is a dead letter (Gaston County v. United States, 1969).

Reflecting the realities of federal law with respect to both residency and literacy, the oath now required by statute as a prerequisite to registration obliges applicants to swear (or affirm) only that they will support both the federal and the state constitutions, will have resided in the state for thirty days preceding the election, and have not registered elsewhere (North Carolina General Statutes § 163-72).

SECTION 5

Elections by people and General Assembly. All elections by the people shall be by ballot, and all elections by the General Assembly shall be viva voce. A contested election for any office established by Article III of this

Constitution shall be determined by joint ballot of both houses of the General
Assembly in the manner prescribed by law.

At first, voters at the polls declared their choices openly. This section, requiring
popular elections to be "by ballot," has been held to imply a requirement of
secret ballots only (Withers v. Board of County Commissioners, 1929). Secrecy
is meant to free voters from intimidation and to reduce corruption by denying
those who would buy votes a ready means of knowing whether they got what
they paid for. By contrast, elections of officers by the General Assembly (Article
II, Sections 14 and 15) must be by voice vote (*viva voce*) in order to ensure
public accountability.

The second sentence of this section, stemming from a constitutional amendment in 1926, makes the two houses of the General Assembly the judge of
contested elections for executive offices. Article II, Section 20 empowers each
house separately to determine contested legislative elections. There is no provision in the constitution concerning contested judicial elections.

SECTION 6

Eligibility to elective office. Every qualified voter in North Carolina who
is 21 years of age, except as in this Constitution disqualified, shall be eligible
for election by the people to office.

Although the Twenty-Sixth Amendment to the U.S. Constitution in 1971 lowered
the voting age to eighteen, the state's minimum age for office holding remains
twenty-one. Higher age qualifications are set for three offices: twenty-five for
senator (Article II, Section 6) and thirty for governor and lieutenant governor
(Article III, Section 2, Subsection 2). Although in logic the statement that
"[e]very qualified voter . . . shall be eligible for election" does not necessarily
mean that no one else is eligible, the present section seems to have been intended
to be exclusive—that is, to mean that no one but a qualified voter shall be eligible
for election.

SECTION 7

Oath. Before entering upon the duties of an office, a person elected or
appointed to the office shall take and subscribe the following oath:
"I, ..., do solemnly swear (or affirm) that I will support and maintain
the Constitution and laws of the United States, and the Constitution and
laws of North Carolina not inconsistent therewith, and that I will faithfully discharge the duties of my office as . . . ., so help me God."

An oath of office is explicitly required of members of the General Assembly
(Article II, Section 12) and of the governor (Article III, Section 4). This section

spells out the oath required of them, and of all other state officers. The oath must be both taken (i.e., sworn to) and subscribed (i.e., signed). Persons with religious scruples about swearing are permitted to affirm the oath—that is, to make a solemn undertaking with the same legal effect. The oath makes express what would otherwise be the case under the supremacy clause of the U.S. Constitution (art. VI, cls. 2–3): that the U.S. Constitution and laws made under it take precedence over the state constitution and laws. Without taking the oath, every North Carolina citizen still owes "paramount allegiance" to the national government (Article I, Section 5).

SECTION 8

Disqualifications for office. The following persons shall be disqualified for office:

First, any person who shall deny the being of Almighty God.

Second, with respect to any office that is filled by election by the people, any person who is not qualified to vote in an election for that office.

Third, any person who has been adjudged guilty of treason or any other felony against this State or the United States, or any person who had been adjudged guilty of a felony in another state that also would be a felony if it had been committed in this State, or any person who has been removed by impeachment from any office, and who has not been restored to the rights of citizenship in the manner prescribed by law.

Ever since its 1776 Constitution the state has imposed some kind of religious test for office. At first the list of those excluded was long: atheists, Roman Catholics, Jews, and Christian pacifists. In 1835 the constitutional ban on Catholic officeholders was lifted; in 1861–62 Jews were permitted to serve. The 1868 Constitution pared the list to atheists only. The proximity of this section to that spelling out the oath of office explains the remaining disqualification: Delegates to the constitutional convention in 1868 were convinced that "no oath would bind a man who denied the existence of a higher power."[15] Despite its carryover in the 1971 Constitution, the religious test for office was already a dead letter because it was held to violate the religious liberty guaranteed by the First and Fourteenth Amendments to the U.S. Constitution (Torcaso v. Watkins, 1961; Opinion of Attorney General to Mr. Clyde Smith, 1972). Obviously, it is not violative of the state's similarly worded guarantee of religious liberty (Article I, Section 13).

Elective offices are limited to those qualified to vote in elections for that office. In general, that excludes non-citizens (Article VI, Section 1). Traitors, against either the state or the federal government, are also excluded. (On treason against the state, see Article I, Section 29.) The disqualification for office of convicted felons repeats their disqualification for voting (Article VI, Section 2, Subsection

3). It is not a punishment for crime—all permissible punishments are listed in Article XI, Section 1—but rather a consequence of conviction (State v. Jones, 1880). Because a judgment of guilt is required, it is believed that a plea of *nolo contendere* or "no contest" to a felony charge does not result in disqualification for office (Opinion of Attorney General to Ms. Bessie J. Cherry, 1980). The disqualification of those who had earlier been removed from office by impeachment makes plain what is elsewhere ambiguous: that removal from office automatically entails disqualification from future office holding. See Article IV, Section 4 and Article XI, Section 1. A felon's rights of citizenship can be restored only by general law (Article II, Section 24, Subsection 1(n)). Restoring the rights of persons removed from office "in the manner prescribed by law" expressly contemplates the removal of a judicially imposed punishment by legislative means.

The list of disqualifications for office in the present section is exclusive: The General Assembly may not add to it by statute (Moore v. Knightdale Board of Elections, 1992).

SECTION 9

Dual office holding.

1. Prohibitions. It is salutary that the responsibilities of self-government be widely shared among the citizens of the State and that the potential abuse of authority inherent in the holding of multiple offices by an individual be avoided. Therefore, no person who holds any office or place of trust or profit under the United States or any department thereof, or under any other state or government, shall be eligible to hold any office in this State that is filled by election by the people. No person shall hold concurrently any two offices in this State that are filled by election of the people. No person shall hold concurrently any two or more appointive offices or places of trust or profit, or any combination of elective and appointive offices or places of trust or profit, except as the General Assembly shall provide by general law.

2. Exceptions. The provisions of this Section shall not prohibit any officer of the military forces of the State or of the United States not on active duty for an extensive period of time, any notary public, or any delegate to a Convention of the People from holding concurrently another office or place of trust or profit under this State or the United States or any department thereof.

The ban on dual office holding is justified in terms of increasing participation in government and preventing abuse of authority. The effect is to disqualify for elective office in North Carolina anyone holding an office in the federal government or in another state government. The ban on holding two elective state offices at the same time reinforces the principle of separation of powers since elective offices are found in each of the three branches. Absent a general law permitting it, two appointive offices or one appointive office and one elective office may not be held by the same person at the same time. Violation of this section by accepting a second state office or a federal office automatically vacates the first (Barnhill v. Thompson, 1898).

Subsection 2 makes three exceptions in favor of a few offices that would be unlikely to risk "abuse of authority": (1) military officers not on active duty, (2) notaries public, and (3) delegates to a Convention of the People, an extraordinary assembly to propose amendments to the constitution described in Article XIII, Sections 1 and 3.

SECTION 10

> **Continuation in office.** In the absence of any contrary provision, all officers in this State, whether appointed or elected, shall hold their positions until other appointments are made or, if the offices are elective, until their successors are chosen and qualified.

Despite the existence of fixed terms, officers retain their positions until successors are chosen and qualified. The reason, of course, is to prevent an abeyance of office. With respect to the governor and lieutenant governor, this section repeats the provision of Article III, Section 2, Subsection 1; with respect to the other elected executive officers, it repeats Article III, Section 7, Subsection 1; with respect to justices of the supreme court, judges of the court of appeals, and regular judges of the superior court, it repeats Article IV, Section 16. Although no comparable provision is found in Article II on the legislative branch, it is assumed that the present section makes the same rule applicable to senators and representatives.

This provision has been put to extraordinary use in a case challenging a statute ending staggered terms for superior court judges. Because the General Assembly could not shorten constitutional terms of office, it delayed certain elections. By virtue of this "holdover" provision, the judges in districts without elections continued to serve until their successors were "chosen and qualified." The effect was to lengthen the time of service, if not the term of office (State ex rel. Martin v. Preston, 1989).

Article VII

Local Government

SECTION 1

General Assembly to provide for local government. The General Assembly shall provide for the organization and government and the fixing of boundaries of counties, cities and towns, and other governmental subdivisions, and except as otherwise prohibited by this Constitution, may give such powers and duties to counties, cities and towns, and other governmental subdivisions as it may deem advisable.

The General Assembly shall not incorporate as a city or town, nor shall it authorize to be incorporated as a city or town, any territory lying within one mile of the corporate limits of any other city or town having a population of 5,000 or more according to the most recent decennial census of population taken by order of Congress, or lying within three miles of the corporate limits of any other city or town having a population of 10,000 or more according to the most recent decennial census of population taken by order of Congress, or lying within four miles of the corporate limits of any other city or town having a population of 25,000 or more according to the most recent decennial census of population taken by order of Congress, or lying within five miles of the corporate limits of any other city or town having a population of 50,000 or more according to the most recent decennial census of population taken by order of Congress. Notwithstanding the foregoing limitations, the General Assembly may incorporate a city or town by an act adopted by vote of three-fifths of all the members of each house.

Created by the state, units of local government draw their powers from charters; in this they resemble modern business corporations which also derive their legal existence from state charters. This similarity explains the proximity of Article

VII on local government and Article VIII on corporations. In the 1868 Constitution they were entitled, respectively, Municipal Corporations and Corporations Other than Municipal. The original provisions in the Reconstruction Constitution devolved considerable power to local governments based on townships, units then new to the state, but by post-Reconstruction amendments in 1876 the General Assembly resumed much of its former control—in order to prevent black voters from controlling townships (mainly in the east) in which they formed the majority. As instrumentalities of the state, units of local government have only such powers as the General Assembly gives them.

Added by amendment in 1972, the second sentence of the present section limits the power of the legislature to charter ("incorporate") new cities or towns in close proximity to existing units, presumably to prevent "new arrivals" from foreclosing the possibilities of growth by the older units. A super majority of three-fifths is required to override this restriction.

SECTION 2

> **Sheriffs.** In each county a Sheriff shall be elected by the qualified voters thereof at the same time and places as members of the General Assembly are elected and shall hold his office for a period of four years, subject to removal for cause as provided by law.

As a state office, the county sheriff dates to the 1776 Constitution. Directly elected, the sheriff has the inherent power to appoint deputy sheriffs (Gowens v. Alamance County, 1939). An unfit sheriff may be removed by the resident superior court judge for the county (North Carolina General Statutes § 128–16).

SECTION 3

> **Merged or consolidated counties.** Any unit of local government formed by the merger or consolidation of a county or counties and the cities and towns therein shall be deemed both a county and a city for the purposes of this Constitution, and may exercise any authority conferred by law on counties, or on cities and towns, or both, as the General Assembly may provide.

New in the 1971 Constitution, this section makes clear that a consolidated city-county would for constitutional purposes be both a city and a county. Although occasionally discussed with respect to the state's most populous cities such as Charlotte, no such consolidation has yet occurred, so the section remains dormant.

Article VIII

Corporations

SECTION 1

Corporate charters. No corporation shall be created, nor shall its charter be extended, altered, or amended by special act, except corporations for charitable, educational, penal, or reformatory purposes that are to be and remain under the patronage and control of the State; but the General Assembly shall provide by general laws for the chartering, organization, and powers of all corporations, and for the amending, extending, and forfeiture of all charters, except those above permitted by special act. All such general acts may be altered from time to time or repealed. The General Assembly may at any time by special act repeal the charter of any corporation.

The earliest corporations known to the common law were "bodies politic," groups of persons empowered by charter to act as a single person for purposes of suing and being sued (see the next section). Originally the corporate form was used most commonly for purposes of local government; indeed, Article VII on local government was entitled Municipal Corporations in the 1868 Constitution. By contrast, the present article was entitled Corporations Other than Municipal. Today the association in the public mind of corporations and business makes the old terms confusing.

Originally business corporations were chartered one by one, an arrangement which, with the increasing frequency of incorporation and the possibilities for gain incident to greater economic activity, led to time-consuming legislative proceedings, rife with opportunities for corruption. An amendment ratified in 1917 prohibited the chartering of business corporations by special act, a prohibition carried forward in 1971. General incorporation acts permit incorporation "on demand." The express reservation of the power to alter or repeal such acts responds to a particular historical development. In the celebrated case of Trustees of Dartmouth College v. Woodward (1819), the U.S. Supreme Court in an opinion by Chief Justice John Marshall held that charters of incorporation were contracts and, as such, could not be impaired without violating the contracts clause of the U.S. Constitution (art. I, § 10, cl. 1). In an important concurring opinion Mr. Justice Story observed that no impairment would occur if the state had originally reserved the power to alter the charter. The purpose of the present section is precisely that: to enable the state to alter or repeal corporate powers without violating federal law (Elizabeth City Water & Power Co. v. City of Elizabeth City, 1924).

This section has been construed to apply only to private business associations, not to state agencies even if organized as public corporations (Webb v. Port Commission of Morehead City, 1934).

SECTION 2

> **Corporations defined.** The term "corporation" as used in this Section shall be construed to include all associations and joint-stock companies having any of the powers and privileges of corporations not possessed by individuals or partnerships. All corporations shall have the right to sue and shall be subject to be sued in all courts, in like cases as natural persons.

As a definition of "corporation," this section, dating from the 1868 Constitution, is almost useless, tautological in fact: Corporations are associations having the powers of corporations. The purpose, however, was not originally to provide a dictionary definition, but rather to confine the General Assembly's power of incorporation to general laws only. The legislature could not evade this rule by labelling its creation something other than "corporation": If it has the powers of a corporation, it is one. All associations with powers and privileges in excess of those possessed by individuals or partnerships are to be construed to be corporations. At a minimum, corporations are groups that may sue and be sued as one person; in old-fashioned terms they are for purposes of suit "artificial persons," as contrasted with ordinary mortals, "natural persons."

The real problem with this section is not its failure to define the word, but rather its express limitation of what it has to say about "corporation" to the term "as used in this Section." Literally that means the so-called definition is applicable only to the second sentence of the present section. Unless it is construed to apply to the word as used in Section 1, it is truly useless. In fact, from 1868 until 1971 the definition of "corporation" applied to the term "as used in this Article."

Article IX

Education

SECTION 1

Education encouraged. Religion, morality, and knowledge being necessary to good government and the happiness of mankind, schools, libraries, and the means of education shall forever be encouraged.

The declaration of rights, in a section new in 1868, proclaimed the people's "right to the privilege of education" (Article I, Section 15). Article IX implements that right, leading off with a general statement on the utility of knowledge (as well as religion and morality) copied from the venerable Northwest Ordinance of 1787.[16]

SECTION 2

Uniform system of schools.

1. General and uniform system; term. The General Assembly shall provide by taxation and otherwise for a general and uniform system of free public schools, which shall be maintained at least nine months in every year, and wherein equal opportunities shall be provided for all students.

2. Local responsibility. The General Assembly may assign to units of local government such responsibility for the financial support of the free public schools as it may deem appropriate. The governing boards of units of local government with financial responsibility for public education may use local revenues to add to or supplement any public school or post-secondary school program.

Although the 1776 Constitution had called for publicly supported schools "for the convenient Instruction of Youth," a statewide system of public or, as they were then called, common schools was not established until legislation in 1839. In 1868 free public schools with at least a four-month term were enshrined in the constitution, although in practice the goal was not achieved for decades. The minimum term was lengthened to six months by amendment in 1918, by which time ideal and reality were at last congruent. The 1971 Constitution raised the minimum to nine months, where it had in fact been fixed by statute for years since 1943.

The Reconstruction Constitution had eschewed any mention of race, but a post-Reconstruction amendment in 1876 required segregated schooling ("separate but equal"). Outlawed in 1954 by the U.S. Supreme Court's ruling in Brown v. Board of Education, racially segregated education was forbidden by the 1971 Constitution. If the non-discrimination clause added to Article I, Section 19 were not enough, the present section firmly requires the public schools to provide equal opportunities to "all students."

Recently attention has shifted from the question of racial discrimination as such to the question of economic discrimination. (Given the unequal distribution of wealth between the races, the two generally go together.) Specifically the question is whether a system of financing public schools that leaves poorer districts with less money to spend per pupil passes constitutional muster. The North Carolina Court of Appeals has held that it does: What is guaranteed is equal access, not equal expenditure (Britt v. North Carolina State Board of Education, 1987).

The requirement that public education be "free" has not been interpreted to exclude absolutely all charges. Modest and reasonable fees for supplementary instructional materials, such as laboratory equipment or art supplies, may be required of all students able to pay (Sneed v. Greensboro City Board of Education, 1980).

Not only must the public schools be free and equal, but also they must form a "general and uniform system." The challenge in interpreting this requirement is to reconcile it with the permission expressly given in Subsection 2 to local government (if authorized by the General Assembly) to use local revenues "to add to or supplement any public school or post-secondary school program." The problem of unequal funding is exacerbated by the express grant to each county by Article IX, Section 7 of fines, penalties, and forfeitures for use by the local schools.

SECTION 3

School attendance. The General Assembly shall provide that every child of appropriate age and of sufficient mental and physical ability shall attend the public schools, unless educated by other means.

The General Assembly must enact a compulsory school attendance law, but the school a child attends need not be part of the state's public school system. The requisite education may be acquired at a private school, or even at a properly supervised "home school" (Delconte v. State, 1985).

SECTION 4

State Board of Education.

1. Board. The State Board of Education shall consist of the Lieutenant Governor, the Treasurer, and eleven members appointed by the Governor, subject to confirmation by the General Assembly in joint session. The General Assembly shall divide the State into eight educational districts. Of the appointive members of the Board, one shall be appointed from each of the eight educational districts and three shall be appointed from the State at large. Appointments shall be for overlapping terms of eight years. Appointments to fill vacancies shall be made by the Governor for the unexpired terms and shall not be subject to confirmation.

2. Superintendent of Public Instruction. The Superintendent of Public Instruction shall be the secretary and chief administrative officer of the State Board of Education.

See the commentary following Section 5.

SECTION 5

Powers and duties of Board. The State Board of Education shall supervise and administer the free public school system and the educational funds provided for its support, except the funds mentioned in Section 7 of this Article, and shall make all needed rules and regulations in relation thereto, subject to laws enacted by the General Assembly.

The State Board of Education is in charge of the public school system. Because the duty to attend school may be satisfied at schools other than the public schools (Article IX, Section 3), the state has the authority to make reasonable regulations for those schools; it may delegate its authority in this regard to the State Board of Education (State v. Williams, 1960).

SECTION 6

State school fund. The proceeds of all lands that have been or hereafter may be granted by the United States to this State, and not otherwise appropriated by this State or the United States; all moneys, stocks, bonds, and other property belonging to the State for purposes of public education;

the net proceeds of all sales of the swamp lands belonging to the State; and all other grants, gifts, and devises that have been or hereafter may be made to the State; and not otherwise appropriated by the State or by the terms of the grant, gift, or devise, shall be paid into the State Treasury and, together with so much of the revenue of the State as may be set apart for that purpose, shall be faithfully appropriated and used exclusively for establishing and maintaining a uniform system of free public schools.

See the commentary following Section 7.

SECTION 7

County school fund. All moneys, stocks, bonds, and other property belonging to a county school fund, and the clear proceeds of all penalties and forfeitures and of all fines collected in the several counties for any breach of the penal laws of the State, shall belong to and remain in the several counties, and shall be faithfully appropriated and used exclusively for maintaining free public schools.

The public schools are "free" because they are paid for by the public. Two funds exist: one at the level of state government, funded from a variety of sources, but principally from appropriations; the other at the level of local (specifically county) government, funded largely from the "profits" of justice—that is, fines, penalties, and forfeitures. While the state school fund is dedicated to "maintaining a uniform system of free public schools," the county school fund is set apart simply for "maintaining free public schools." The wording itself suggests that "uniform" (at least in this regard) does not mean uniformly funded.

As education has grown increasingly expensive, attention has focused on the revenue generated by the successful prosecution of crime. "Clear proceeds" has been held to mean the total amount of the fine, penalty, or forfeiture less the cost of collection; it does not include the overall cost of enforcing the law in question (Cauble v. City of Asheville, 1985), nor does it include money set aside for future law enforcement (Shore v. Edmisten, 1976). In 1985 the General Assembly stepped in with a legislative definition, limiting the allowable cost of collection to no more than 10 percent of the total (North Carolina General Statutes § 115C-437).

It is violation of state "penal laws" that produces fines, penalties, and forfeitures for the benefit of the county school fund; the state supreme court has interpreted this phrase expansively to mean "laws that impose a monetary payment for their violation . . . regardless of whether the . . . proceeding is civil or criminal" (Mussallam v. Mussallam, 1988). No benefit accrues from violation of federal laws. This is unexceptionable; more troublesome is the provision of federal forfeiture law, permitting the sharing of proceeds with local law enforcement officers (United States v. Alston, 1989). Given the extent of overlap between state and federal penal laws, this means a local police department ends up with considerably more revenue in case it invites federal involvement; the county school fund is the only loser.

SECTION 8

> **Higher education.** The General Assembly shall maintain a public system of higher education, comprising The University of North Carolina and such other institutions of higher education as the General Assembly may deem wise. The General Assembly shall provide for the selection of trustees of The University of North Carolina and of the other institutions of higher education, in whom shall be vested all the privileges, rights, franchises, and endowments heretofore granted to or conferred upon the trustees of these institutions. The General Assembly may enact laws necessary and expedient for the maintenance and management of The University of North Carolina and the other public institutions of higher education.

The idea of a public university was first mentioned in the 1776 Constitution, and the University of North Carolina was duly chartered in 1789. In 1805 the charter was amended, replacing the original co-optative board of trustees with one appointed by the General Assembly and chaired by the governor (at that time elected by the legislature). As part of the enhancement of executive power in the 1868 Constitution, the State Board of Education was authorized to appoint the University's trustees, but with the resurgence of legislative power after Reconstruction, the General Assembly reclaimed control by amendment in 1873. The provision, permitting the General Assembly to provide for the selection of trustees (now members of the Board of Governors) allows it to keep the power of appointment for itself (North Carolina General Statutes § 116-6).

SECTION 9

> **Benefits of public institutions of higher education.** The General Assembly shall provide that the benefits of The University of North Carolina and other public institutions of higher education, as far as practicable, be extended to the people of the State free of expense.

See the commentary following Section 10.

SECTION 10

> **Escheats.**
>
> 1. Escheats prior to July 1, 1971. All property that prior to July 1, 1971, accrued to the State from escheats, unclaimed dividends, or distributive

shares of the estates of deceased persons shall be appropriated to the use of The University of North Carolina.

2. Escheats after June 30, 1971. All property that, after June 30, 1971, shall accrue to the State from escheats, unclaimed dividends, or distributive shares of the estates of deceased persons shall be used to aid worthy and needy students who are residents of this State and are enrolled in public institutions of higher education in this State. The method, amount, and type of distribution shall be prescribed by law.

The idea that higher education could be provided "free of expense," capping the free public school system, was first mentioned as a goal in 1868. Although never realized in practice—it was always promised only to the extent "practicable"—the state has strived to keep charges for state residents low. Public funding of the university began in 1789 with the assignment of the state's right to escheats—that is, the real property of those who die without a will or known heirs. Like escheats is the state's right to unclaimed personal property ("unclaimed dividends, or [unclaimed] distributive shares of the estates of deceased persons"). Until June 30, 1971, all such property belonged to the university outright, although since 1946 it had been held as an endowment fund for scholarships; thereafter it benefits higher education indirectly, by aiding "worthy and needy" state residents enrolled in any public institution of higher education in the state.

Article X

Homesteads and Exemptions

SECTION 1

Personal property exemptions. The personal property of any resident of this State, to a value fixed by the General Assembly but not less than $500, to be selected by the resident, is exempted from sale under execution or other final process of any court, issued for the collection of any debt.

Economics has its casualties, no less than war. Article X on homesteads and exemptions aims to protect economic losers from utter destitution. The state's first constitution prohibited the imprisonment of a debtor once he had surrendered "all his estate, real and personal, for the use of his creditors," and statutes passed before the Civil War exempted small amounts of property even then, so the debtor would not be deprived of necessities. Defeat in the Civil War and the consequent economic dislocation greatly increased the number of defaults and bankruptcies, and legislation granted debtors further relief. The 1868 Constitution retained the ban on imprisonment for debt (except in cases of fraud), moving it to the declaration of rights, where it may still be found in Article I, Section 28; also added was an article concerning homesteads and exemptions, on which the present article is modeled. A once lively debate centered on whether the constitutional protections covered debts contracted before April 24, 1868, the effective date of the Reconstruction Constitution. State supreme court decisions upholding such protections were overruled by the U.S. Supreme Court in Edwards v. Kearzey (1878), which held that they violated the contracts clause of the U.S. Constitution (art. I, § 10, cl. 1). The protections accorded by Article X are therefore prospective only.

Because American law recognizes two types of property, real and personal, two exemptions are granted. The first, in the present section, concerns personal property; the second, in the following section, concerns real property. The latter, including land and buildings, is properly the "homestead exemption," principally designed to secure a dwelling from the claims of creditors. The personal property exemption is designed to secure a minimum of those things other than shelter necessary for existence. Although personal property is generally money or goods, its actual legal definition is whatever property would not at common law have descended at death to a person's heirs. Real property went to the heirs; all else went to the deceased's personal representative for disposal in the due course of administering the estate.

The personal property exemption is granted directly by the constitution (Board of Commissioners of Montgomery County v. Riley, 1876). Although the General Assembly is empowered to raise the amount, it may not lower it, and no implementing legislation is required for its effectiveness. Rather than raising the personal property exemption as such, the General Assembly has passed a somewhat more generous Exemptions Act, better geared to the modern world, making detailed provisions for (among other things) motor vehicles, professional implements, and necessary health aids (North Carolina General Statutes § 1C-1601). The debtor may choose to rely on the Exemptions Act in lieu of the constitutional provisions. Although the personal property exemption is not available against the tax collector, the General Assembly is elsewhere empowered to exempt up to $300 worth of personal property from taxation (Article V, Section 2, Subsection 3).

The constitutional exemption guarantees the debtor $500 worth of personal property at all times; as the property is diminished by use, the debtor is entitled to add to it, if possible, up to the exempted amount (Campbell v. White, 1886). In other words, the personal property exemption is not granted once and for all, but may be asserted again and again (New Amsterdam Casualty Co. v. Waller, 1962). The term "any debt" has been held to include more than contract debts, so the exemption may be asserted against claims based on tort (Dellinger v. Tweed, 1872). By contrast, the guarantee against imprisonment for "debt" in Article I, Section 28 has been limited to causes of action based on contract.

By its nature, the personal property exemption may not be waived by an agreement not to claim it (Branch v. Tomlinson, 1877). The exemption (like the homestead exemption) is, however, expressly subordinated by Section 3 of this article to mechanics' and laborers' liens. Unlike the homestead exemption, it ceases at the death of the debtor (Johnson v. Cross, 1872). Available only to a "resident of this State," the exemption also terminates on a permanent change of residence to another state.

SECTION 2

Homestead exemptions.

1. Exemption from sale; exceptions. Every homestead and the dwellings

and buildings used therewith, to a value fixed by the General Assembly but not less than $1,000, to be selected by the owner thereof, or in lieu thereof, at the option of the owner, any lot in a city or town with the dwellings and buildings used thereon, and to the same value, owned and occupied by a resident of the State, shall be exempt from sale under execution or other final process obtained on any debt. But no property shall be exempt from sale for taxes, or for payment of obligations contracted for its purchase.

2. Exemption for benefit of children. The homestead, after the death of the owner thereof, shall be exempt from the payment of any debt during the minority of the owner's children, or any of them.

3. Exemption for benefit of surviving spouse. If the owner of a homestead dies, leaving a surviving spouse but no minor children, the homestead shall be exempt from the debts of the owner, and the rents and profits thereof shall inure to the benefit of the surviving spouse until he or she remarries, unless the surviving spouse is the owner of a separate homestead.

4. Conveyance of homestead. Nothing contained in this Article shall operate to prevent the owner of a homestead from disposing of it by deed, but no deed made by a married owner of a homestead shall be valid without the signature and acknowledgement of his or her spouse.

The homestead exemption guarantees an impecunious debtor a minimum quantum of real estate. Like the personal property exemption, it is granted directly by the constitution and vests independently of legislation (Adrian v. Shaw, 1880). Although the General Assembly has not seen fit to increase the value of the homestead exemption as such, it has offered the debtor the choice of electing the somewhat more generous protections of the Exemptions Act (North Carolina General Statutes § 1C-1601). Because the homestead exemption attaches only to real property that is "occupied" by the debtor, it does not protect any future interests, such as remainders (Stern v. Lee, 1894). Once allotted, the homestead is not a new estate in land, but only a determinable exemption. Should the homestead subsequently rise in value, the creditor may demand a reallotment (Citizens National Bank v. Green, 1878).

The particular property subject to the exemption is to be "selected by the owner." Although probably intended to preserve a dwelling for the debtor, the state supreme court has not required that an existing dwelling be selected; the homestead exemption has been recognized in vacant lots (Equitable Life Assurance Society v. Russos, 1936). Because a dwelling may exceed the value of the exemption, the possibility exists that the debtor will be limited to selecting only a portion of the building (Campbell v. White, 1886). In one case the debtor selected the hallway adjacent to the front door (Seeman Printery, Inc. v. Schinhan, 1977). While secure from general creditors, the homestead is liable to sale for unpaid taxes, although elsewhere in the constitution the General Assembly is empowered to exempt up to $1,000 worth of real property used as the owner's residence (Article V, Section 2, Subsection 3). The homestead is also liable to sale for payment of delinquent "obligations contracted for its purchase," normally a mortgage, deed of trust, or installment land contract. Section 3 of this article expressly subordinates the exemption to mechanics' and laborers' liens.

Unlike the personal property exemption, the homestead exemption inures to the benefit of the debtor's family. On the debtor's death, any minor children succeed to the homestead; if there is none, a surviving spouse succeeds. In the 1868 Constitution the exemption was limited to widows; the 1971 Constitution carried the limitation forward, but in 1977 an amendment extended the benefit to a surviving spouse of either sex. Minor children hold the exemption in a survivorship tenancy; in other words, when one minor child dies or attains majority, the whole homestead accrues to siblings still under age. No inquiry is made into the financial condition of the children; they succeed to the homestead regardless of whether they possess other assets (Allen v. Shields, 1875). When the youngest child arrives at full age, the exemption terminates; it does not then pass to a surviving spouse (Barnes v. Cherry, 1925).

As originally drafted in 1868 (and carried forward in 1971), the widow succeeded to the homestead exemption only if the deceased debtor left "no children." The case of Simmons v. Respass (1909) demonstrated a probably unintended consequence of such phrasing. A debtor was survived by two adult children by his first wife and also by his widow by a second marriage. Neither the children nor the widow was entitled to the homestead exemption: not the children because they were adults, not the widow because there were surviving children.

This anomalous result was belatedly altered by amendment in 1977, inserting the adjective "minor" to modify children: Today the widow would have been entitled to the homestead because the children were not minors. In case there are no minor children and a surviving spouse succeeds, the survivor is expressly granted the "rents and profits" from the estate; in this regard the surviving spouse is better off than the deceased debtor (Citizens National Bank v. Green, 1878). Unlike the case with children, the financial condition of a surviving spouse is relevant; the exemption is lost if the survivor is the owner of a separate homestead. If available, the homestead exemption of a surviving spouse continues until remarriage or death. Because the exemption is granted only to a "resident of the State," a debtor can terminate it by permanent removal to another state; even if minor children or a spouse is left behind in North Carolina, they are not entitled to the debtor's homestead (Finley v. Saunders, 1887). Homesteads are transferable; in case the debtor is married, however, the spouse must join in the conveyance since there is a constitutionally guaranteed right of survivorship in homestead property.

SECTION 3

Mechanics' and laborers' liens. The General Assembly shall provide by proper legislation for giving to mechanics and laborers an adequate lien on the subject-matter of their labor. The provisions of Sections 1 and 2 of this

Article shall not be so construed as to prevent a laborer's lien for work done
and performed for the person claiming the exemption or a mechanic's lien
for work done on the premises.

While the prior sections of this article confer exemptions and empower the
General Assembly to increase them as it sees fit, this section is mandatory,
directing the legislature to provide for mechanics' and laborers' liens (American
Bridge Division, United States Steel Corp. v. Brinkley, 1961). (The present
provisions are in North Carolina General Statutes § 44A-7 *et seq.*) Liens, securing
payment for work done, are the opposite of exemptions, and the original mandate
in the 1868 Constitution appeared in Article XIV on miscellaneous topics; its
placement in the present article in the 1971 Constitution is explained by the
second sentence, making the liens superior even to the homestead and personal
property exemptions.

A laborer's lien secures payment for work done (presumably anywhere), while
a mechanic's lien is limited to work done "on the premises"—that is, on the
real property subject to the lien. Although part of a national movement in the
nineteenth century to protect workers and thereby encourage economic development, laborers' and mechanics' liens in North Carolina originated in the special
conditions after the Civil War. In 1879, holding that a plantation overseer was
ineligible for a laborer's lien, the state supreme court explained that the constitutional provision was intended to protect those who had recently been "released
from thraldom" (i.e., ex-slaves), now "totally dependant upon their manual toil
for subsistence" (Whitaker v. Smith, 1879).

SECTION 4

Property of married women secured to them. The real and personal
property of any female in this State acquired before marriage, and all
property, real and personal, to which she may, after marriage, become in
any manner entitled, shall be and remain the sole and separate estate and
property of such female, and shall not be liable for any debts, obligations,
or engagements of her husband, and may be devised and bequeathed and
conveyed by her, subject to such regulations and limitations as the General
Assembly may prescribe. Every married woman may exercise powers of
attorney conferred upon her by her husband, including the power to execute
and acknowledge deeds to property owned by herself and her husband or
by her husband.

This section applies to only one class of persons in the state: married women.
Its most important provisions go back to the 1868 Constitution and are intended
to equalize the positions of husbands and wives with respect to property ownership. According to the common law rules in effect before 1868, on marriage
a woman lost control of her property to her husband. He could dispose of her

personal property as he saw fit; in her real property he acquired what amounted to a life estate, and any rents or profits were his, without a duty to account to his wife. Under such circumstances creditors of the husband were free to attach the property.

The only means at that time to prevent the application of common law rules lay in the creation of a trust to hold the property for the woman's "sole and separate use," an arrangement available as a practical matter only to the well-to-do. The effect of the present section is to make what had once been the case for a privileged few the rule for all: Every married woman now retains the sole and separate estate in her own property. What is hers is not liable for her husband's debts; to that extent, recognition of a married woman's property creates an exemption from the claims of creditors. The second sentence of the present section, permitting a married woman to exercise powers of attorney conferred on her by her husband, negates the old rule that a married woman lacked legal personality and was in effect her husband's ward.

This section has not been interpreted to prevent a husband and wife from holding real property together as tenants by the entirety (Bank of Greenville v. Gornto, 1913). In such case, the property is subject to the claims of creditors of both spouses and upon the death of either spouse remains the property of the survivor. Nor does it prevent a surviving spouse from claiming a share in separately owned property pursuant to statutes making the survivor a "forced heir" or permitting the election of an interest in the nature of common law dower or curtesy.

SECTION 5

> **Insurance.** A person may insure his or her own life for the sole use and benefit of his or her spouse or children or both, and upon his or her death the proceeds from the insurance shall be paid to or for the benefit of the spouse or children or both, or to a guardian, free from all claims of the representatives or creditors of the insured or his or her estate. Any insurance policy which insures the life of a person for the sole use and benefit of that person's spouse or children or both shall not be subject to the claims of creditors of the insured during his or her lifetime, whether or not the policy reserves to the insured during his or her lifetime any or all rights provided for by the policy and whether or not the policy proceeds are payable to the estate of the insured in the event the beneficiary or beneficiaries predecease the insured.

Life insurance was still a relatively new business when the drafters of the 1868 Constitution inserted the original of this section, but its potential as a means to provide for surviving family members was already obvious. Obvious, too, was the attraction of the proceeds to creditors of the insured. In the male-dominated world of 1868, the drafters provided an exemption for a husband who insured his life for the benefit of his wife and children; the 1971 Constitution carried the provision forward, but a 1977 amendment rewrote the section, making it applicable to insurance on the life of either spouse. Given the niggardly amount of the personal property and homestead exemptions, as well as the subordination of the latter to tax and purchase money liens and of both to mechanics' and laborers' liens, the insurance exemption probably offers the greatest relief to survivors of an impecunious debtor, assuming he was able to pay the premiums. The second sentence, added in the 1971 Constitution, secures the cash value of the policy from claims by creditors during the lifetime of the insured.

Article XI

Punishments, Corrections, and Charities

SECTION 1

Punishments. The following punishments only shall be known to the laws of this State: death, imprisonment, fines, removal from office, and disqualification to hold and enjoy any office of honor, trust, or profit under this State.

Criminal prosecutions generally begin with indictment or impeachment (see Article I, Section 22); criminal convictions can result only in the punishments listed in the present section: death, imprisonment, fines, and removal from and disqualification for state office. Because expressly listed here, none can possibly be considered "cruel or unusual" within the prohibition of Article I, Section 27. Although the common law provided certain extraordinary punishments for treason—corruption of blood and forfeiture of estate—these are expressly prohibited by Article I, Section 29 and impliedly prohibited by the present section. Indictable offenses are punishable by death, imprisonment, or fines. (Fine and imprisonment are often combined in the punishment for the same offense.) Imprisonment for debt is prohibited by Article I, Section 28. Impeachable offenses, limited to official misconduct, may be punished only by removal from office and disqualification for future office holding (Article IV, Section 4). While appearing to be two punishments, removal and disqualification are in fact only one because any officer removed by impeachment is automatically disqualified for office (Article VI, Section 8). A consequence of (but not a punishment for) conviction of a felony is also disqualification for voting and office holding (Article VI, Section 2, Subsection 3 and Article VI, Section 8).

Since none of the permissible punishments may be inflicted posthumously, there is no possible punishment for suicide, although attempted suicide may be punished (State v. Willis, 1961). Permitted punishments may be suspended if the convicted criminal agrees to satisfy certain conditions, and these are not unconstitutional punishments so long as the conditions themselves are constitutional, related to the purposes of punishment, and otherwise reasonable (Shore v. Edmisten, 1976).

SECTION 2

> **Death punishment.** The object of punishments being not only to satisfy justice, but also to reform the offender and thus prevent crime, murder, arson, burglary, and rape, and these only, may be punishable with death, if the General Assembly shall so enact.

This section opens with a statement of the dual purpose of punishment: (1) "to satisfy justice" and (2) "to reform the offender," the latter being justified as a means of preventing the offender from committing further crime. Deterrence as such does not figure in the list. The conclusion drawn from this twofold rationale is that capital punishment must be limited to the most heinous offenses: murder, arson, burglary, and rape. When death is the punishment, there is no possibility of reforming the offender. Curiously, treason is not included on the list of possible capital offenses, although it was the crime for which the gruesome sentence "hanged, drawn, and quartered" was invented. Perhaps it was thought that any treason worth punishing with death would include one of the other offenses as well. At present the only capital offense in North Carolina is murder in the first degree (North Carolina General Statutes § 14-17).

SECTION 3

> **Charitable and correctional institutions and agencies.** Such charitable, benevolent, penal, and correctional institutions and agencies as the needs of humanity and the public good may require shall be established and operated by the State under such organization and in such manner as the General Assembly may prescribe.

Despite the mandatory form—certain institutions and agencies "shall be established"—this section does not in fact require any particular action by the General Assembly because the legislature is itself the final judge of what the "needs of humanity" and the "public good" require. Nor is it properly considered a grant of power since the legislature would be competent to establish these institutions and agencies even in its absence. In fact, this section, although new in 1971, represents the last residue of the 1868 Constitution's ambitious program of social welfare. The Reconstruction Constitution had recommended to the General Assembly the care of vagrants, orphans, idiots, and inebriates and had required the General Assembly to provide for the care of deaf mutes, the blind, and the insane; when even the latter proved to be beyond the state's will and resources, an amendment in 1880, rather than deleting the section entirely, changed the requirement to a permission.

SECTION 4

Welfare policy; board of public welfare. Beneficent provision for the poor, the unfortunate, and the orphan is one of the first duties of a civilized and a Christian state. Therefore the General Assembly shall provide for and define the duties of a board of public welfare.

Although an embarrassment to those who prefer to have no public recognition of religion, the declaration in this section that North Carolina is (or ought to be) a civilized and Christian state is of no legal consequence. In context it merely explains why the section goes on to impose on the General Assembly the obligation to create a board of public welfare, now actually the Social Services Commission (North Carolina General Statutes § 143B-153). Of far more substance, the state supreme court has located in this section a duty of the state to pay the cost of medical care incurred by indigents (Board of Managers v. City of Wilmington, 1953).

Article XII

Military Forces

SECTION 1.

Governor is Commander in Chief. The Governor shall be Commander in Chief of the military forces of the State and may call out those forces to execute the law, suppress riots and insurrections, and repel invasion.

The declaration of rights requires that ''the military shall be kept under strict subordination to, and governed by, the civil power'' (Article I, Section 30). The present section (and Article III, Section 5, Subsection 5 on the duties of the governor) implements that requirement by naming the governor commander in chief of the state's military forces. The governor loses command to the president of the United States—as the executive article makes plain—in case the state militia is ''called into the actual service of the United States'' (U.S. Const. art. II, § 2, cl. 1).

Conventions; Constitutional Amendment and Revision

SECTION 1

Convention of the People. No Convention of the People of this State shall ever be called unless by the concurrence of two-thirds of all the members of each house of the General Assembly, and unless the proposition "Convention or No Convention" is first submitted to the qualified voters of the State at the time and in the manner prescribed by the General Assembly. If a majority of the votes cast upon the proposition are in favor of a Convention, it shall assemble on the day prescribed by the General Assembly. The General Assembly shall, in the act of submitting the convention proposition, propose limitations upon the authority of the Convention; and if a majority of the votes cast upon the proposition are in favor of a Convention, those limitations shall become binding upon the Convention. Delegates to the Convention shall be elected by the qualified voters at the time and in the manner prescribed in the act of submission. The Convention shall consist of a number of delegates equal to the membership of the House of Representatives of the General Assembly that submits the convention proposition and the delegates shall be apportioned as is the House of Representatives. A Convention shall adopt no ordinance not necessary to the purpose for which the Convention has been called.

The state's first constitution, drafted and adopted by a provincial congress and never thereafter referred to the voters, included no provision for amendment. When Fayetteville was made a borough town entitled to its own representative in the house of commons in 1789, the change was made by the constitutional convention called to ratify the U.S. Constitution; again, the voters were not consulted directly. By contrast, the more momentous amendments in 1835 were the product of a process very much like that described in this section: a call by the General Assembly, confirmed by the voters, who elected delegates on the same basis as members of the lower house, the proposed amendments being subsequently submitted to the voters.

The main procedural concern in 1835 was whether the General Assembly could limit the powers of the convention; the only expedient then available was to impose an oath on the delegates to abide by the restrictions. After some cavilling, the delegates took the oath and never thereafter attempted to exercise plenary power. A similar problem emerged in 1875, at the state's last constitutional convention, and was similarly resolved (or unresolved) by the delegates' taking the oath after a protest and never thereafter seeking to violate its terms. The present section addresses the problem directly: "The General Assembly shall . . . propose limitations upon the authority of the Convention; and if a majority of the votes cast upon the proposition are in favor of a Convention, those limitations shall become binding upon the Convention."

A related problem is that of a constitutional convention exercising legislative power; acts of a constitutional convention are technically labeled "ordinances," rather than "statutes." While the convention of 1835 refrained, those of 1860–61 and 1868 passed numerous ordinances, ranging from the momentous, such as chartering railroads and authorizing bond issues, to the mundane, such as granting individual divorces. The present section forbids the practice by tying ordinances to the business of amendment: "A Convention shall adopt no ordinance not necessary to the purpose for which the Convention has been called." The double negative of the provision may have been deliberately chosen since a positive formulation—a convention shall adopt only ordinances necessary to the purpose for which the convention has been called—might suggest that *some* ordinances are required.

Voter qualifications are the same as those for other elections: U.S. citizenship and North Carolina residency (Article VI, Sections 1 and 2). The delegates, equal in number to the membership of the house of representatives (now set at 120 by Article II, Section 4), are to be apportioned as are the members of the house of representatives, for which see Article II, Section 5. Although the constitution generally forbids the concurrent holding of two elective offices, an exception is expressly made when one of the two is a place in a Convention of the People (Article VI, Section 9, Subsection 2).

Note: The third sentence of the present section, referring to the limitations on the convention proposed by the General Assembly "in the act of submitting the convention proposition," is set out as proposed to the voters and ratified by them. The act in question would seem to be the act or statute passed by the legislature. In the draft constitution proposed by the State Constitution Study Commission, the phrase more sensibly read "in the act submitting the convention proposition."

SECTION 2

Power to revise or amend Constitution reserved to people. The people of this State reserve the power to amend this Constitution and to adopt a new or revised Constitution. This power may be exercised by either of the methods set out hereinafter in this Article, but in no other way.

The first sentence of this section repeats the substance of Section 3 in Article I, the Declaration of Rights: "The people of this State have the inherent, sole, and exclusive right . . . of altering or abolishing their Constitution and form of government whenever it may be necessary to their safety and happiness. . . . " That same section goes on to recognize the necessary consequence of membership in a federal union: "but every such right shall be exercised in pursuance of law and consistently with the Constitution of the United States." The same limitation, although unexpressed, applies to the present section.

The second sentence channels the awesome power of constitution making (or re-making) into two alternatives: the convention described in the preceding section (and again in the following section) and legislative initiation, described in Section 4 of this article.

SECTION 3

Revision or amendment by Convention of the People. A Convention of the People of this State may be called pursuant to Section 1 of this Article to propose a new or revised Constitution or to propose amendments to this Constitution. Every new or revised Constitution and every constitutional amendment adopted by a Convention shall be submitted to the qualified voters of the State at the time and in the manner prescribed by the Convention. If a majority of the votes cast thereon are in favor of ratification of the new or revised Constitution or the constitutional amendment or amendments, it or they shall become effective January first next after ratification by the qualified voters unless a different effective date is prescribed by the Convention.

See the commentary following Section 4.

SECTION 4

Revision or amendment by legislative initiation. A proposal of a new or revised Constitution or an amendment or amendments to this Constitution may be initiated by the General Assembly, but only if three-fifths of all the members of each house shall adopt an act submitting the proposal to the qualified voters of the State for their ratification or rejection. The proposal shall be submitted at the time and in the manner prescribed by the General Assembly. If a majority of the votes cast thereon are in favor of the proposed new or revised Constitution or constitutional amendment or amendments, it or they shall become effective January first next after ratification by the voters unless a different effective date is prescribed in the act submitting the proposal or proposals to the qualified voters.

A Convention of the People requires a two-thirds majority of both houses of the General Assembly plus a majority of popular votes; delegates must be elected, and the product must be adopted at the polls. By contrast, amendment on legislative initiative requires a three-fifths majority of both houses of the General Assembly and ratification at the polls. The simpler procedure has been used for all amendments to the 1971 Constitution; indeed, the comparable provision in the 1868 Constitution was used exclusively ever since it was first adopted on the proposal of the 1875 constitutional convention, the state's last.

Although these sections draw a careful semantic distinction between a "new or revised Constitution," on the one hand, and a "constitutional amendment or amendments," on the other, the distinction vanishes in historical perspective: The entire 1971 Constitution was presented as an amendment to the 1868 Constitution.

Article XIV

Miscellaneous

SECTION 1

Seat of government. The permanent seat of government of this State shall be at the City of Raleigh.

Raleigh, named for the English explorer Sir Walter Raleigh who organized the first English settlement in North America (on Roanoke Island, North Carolina), was founded by the General Assembly in 1792 to be the state capital. Although all three branches of state government are in fact centered there, only the governor has a constitutional duty to remain in residence (Article III, Section 5, Subsection 1). No mention is made of a site for the sessions of the General Assembly. Sessions of the supreme court must be held in Raleigh "unless otherwise provided by the General Assembly" (Article IV, Section 6, Subsection 2).

SECTION 2

State boundaries. The limits and boundaries of the State shall be and remain as they now are.

The 1776 declaration of rights included a lengthy description of the state's boundaries, beginning at a certain "cedar stake" on the Atlantic shore; the 1868 Constitution shrank the section to its present laconic formulation, but left it incongruously in Article I. In 1971 the section received its present placement.

SECTION 3

General laws defined. Whenever the General Assembly is directed or authorized by this Constitution to enact general laws, or general laws uniformly applicable throughout the State, or general laws uniformly applicable in every county, city and town, and other unit of local government, or in every local court district, no special or local act shall be enacted concerning the subject matter directed or authorized to be accomplished by general or uniformly applicable laws, and every amendment or repeal of any law relating to such subject matter shall also be general and uniform in its effect throughout the State. General laws may be enacted for classes defined by population or other criteria. General laws uniformly applicable throughout the State shall be made applicable without classification or exception in every unit of local government of like kind, such as every county, or every city and town, but need not be made applicable in every unit of local government in the State. General laws uniformly applicable in every county, city and town, and other unit of local government, or in every local court district, shall be made applicable without classification or exception in every unit of local government, or in every local court district, as the case may be. The General Assembly may at any time repeal any special, local, or private act.

Although promising to define "general laws"—an oft-repeated phrase in the North Carolina Constitution—this section actually tells more about what they are not: They are not "special or local" and are "without classification or exception." The best definition is probably still the one Sir William Blackstone gave in 1765: "A general or public act is an universal rule, that regards the whole community. . . . Special or private acts are rather exceptions than rules, being those which only operate upon particular persons, and private concerns."[17] The present section was rewritten by an amendment, the same amendment that rewrote Article V on state finance, adopted at the time the 1971 Constitution was adopted; it brought the specific language of the section into line with the new finance article.

A long list of subjects on which local, private, or special acts are prohibited is in the legislative article (Article II, Section 24, Subsection 1). The present section adds the further rule, a rule of interpretation, that whenever the legislature is directed or authorized by the constitution to enact "general laws," it is thereby prohibited from adopting special or local acts on the same subject. "General laws uniformly applicable in every county, city and town, and other unit of local government" are particularly required in state and local taxation (Article V, Section 2, Subsections 2 and 3). "Local court districts," the domain of the district courts, must be governed by uniformly applicable laws (Article IV, Section 12, Subsection 4 and Article IV, Section 18, Subsection 2).

What cannot be done directly cannot be done by indirection: The General Assembly cannot pass special or local acts, nor can it create the same effect by

partial repeal of general acts. What valid local, private, or special acts there are
may be repealed at any time; this means, presumably, that no vested rights are
created by them. These two provisions repeat the substance of Article II, Section
24, Subsection 2.

Qualifying in practice its otherwise comprehensive ban on special or local
acts is the permission in the present section to enact general laws "for classes
defined by population or other criteria." Ingenious drafters have been able to
define classes with memberships of a few or only one, leading to questions about
the current vitality of the rules requiring only "general laws." In 1987 the North
Carolina Supreme Court recognized that "tortured classifications" were being
used and announced a new test for determining whether a law was "general":
whether it affects the "general public interests and concerns" (Town of Emerald
Isle ex rel. Smith v. State, 1987).

SECTION 4

Continuity of laws; protection of office holders. The laws of North
Carolina not in conflict with this Constitution shall continue in force until
lawfully altered. Except as otherwise specifically provided, the adoption of
this Constitution shall not have the effect of vacating any office or term of
office now filled or held by virtue of any election or appointment made
under the prior Constitution of North Carolina and the laws of the State
enacted pursuant thereto.

If specific authority for the proposition that the General Assembly may not adopt
laws in conflict with the constitution were required, the first sentence of this
section would provide it: A law contrary to the constitution is void. Desuetude,
long continued disuse, may in some of the world's legal systems abrogate a
statute. Such is not the common law rule and was not the law in North Carolina
even before the adoption of the present section, which is new with the 1971
Constitution, although the state statute receiving the common law does exclude
such parts as have become "obsolete" (North Carolina General Statutes § 4.1).
The second sentence of the present section underscores the continuity between
the state's second and third constitutions: Offices and laws continue unless expressly changed.

SECTION 5

Conservation of natural resources. It shall be the policy of this State
to conserve and protect its lands and waters for the benefit of all its citizenry,
and to this end it shall be a proper function of the State of North Carolina
and its political subdivisions to acquire and preserve park, recreational, and
scenic areas, to control and limit the pollution of our air and water, to control
excessive noise, and in every other appropriate way to preserve as a part of

the common heritage of this State its forests, wetlands, estuaries, beaches, historical sites, openlands, and places of beauty.

To accomplish the aforementioned public purposes, the State and its counties, cities and towns, and other units of local government may acquire by purchase or gift properties or interests in properties which shall, upon their special dedication to and acceptance by resolution adopted by a vote of three-fifths of the members of each house of the General Assembly for those public purposes, constitute part of the "State Nature and Historic Preserve," and which shall not be used for other purposes except as authorized by law enacted by a vote of three-fifths of the members of each house of the General Assembly. The General Assembly shall prescribe by general law the conditions and procedures under which such properties or interests therein shall be dedicated for the aforementioned public purposes.

The principal effect of this section, which was adopted at the polls in 1972, is to create the State Nature and Historic Preserve, into which property may be placed and from which it may be removed only by a three-fifths majority in the General Assembly. Without this section, a simple majority—all that is required in most cases—would be sufficient.

Notes to Part II

1. See *Ordinances and Resolutions Passed by the State Convention of North Carolina at Its Several Sessions in 1861–62* (Raleigh: John W. Syme, 1862), 174–75.

2. *Executive Documents. Convention, Session 1865. Constitution of North-Carolina, with Amendments, and Ordinances and Resolutions Passed by the Convention, Session, 1865* (Raleigh: Cannon & Holden, 1865), 39–40 (pagination begins anew with each document).

3. *The Federalist*, No. 47 (James Madison), ed. Benjamin Fletcher Wright (Cambridge: Harvard University Press, 1966), 342.

4. *Proceedings and Debates of the Convention of North-Carolina, Called to Amend the Constitution of the State, Which Assembled at Raleigh, June 4, 1835* (Raleigh: Joseph Gales & Son, 1836), 197 (hereafter cited as *Proceedings and Debates, 1835*).

5. William L. Saunders, ed., *The Colonial Records of North Carolina* (Raleigh: Josephus Daniels, 1890), vol. 10, 870f.

6. Edmund Burke, "Speech to the Electors of Bristol," in Edmund Burke, Selected Writings and Speeches, ed. Peter J. Stanlis (Chicago: Regnery Gateway, 1963), 187.

7. William Blackstone, *Commentaries on the Laws of England* (Oxford: Clarendon Press, 1765–69), vol. 4, 151.

8. Edward Coke, *Institutes of the Laws of England* (London: Society of Stationers, 1641), vol. 2, 55–56.

9. Blackstone, *Commentaries* 4: 342.

10. Henry G. Connor and Joseph B. Cheshire, Jr., *The Constitution of the State of North Carolina Annotated* (Raleigh: Edwards & Broughton, 1911), 46 (citing State v. Driver, 78 N.C. 423 (1878)).

11. Act of 1784, ch. 22, § 5, reprinted in Walter Clark, ed., *The State Records of North Carolina* (Goldsboro: Nash Brothers, 1904), vol. 24, 574.

12. Blackstone, *Commentaries* 1: 85–86.

13. *Proceedings and Debates, 1835*, 337.

14. *The Federalist*, No. 78 (Alexander Hamilton), ed. Benjamin Fletcher Wright (Cambridge: Harvard University Press, 1966), 491.

15. Proceedings and Debates of the 1868 Constitutional Convention (February 18, 1868), reported in *North Carolina Standard*, February 26, 1868 (hereafter cited as Proceedings and Debates, 1868).

16. 1 U.S. Stats. 52. See Proceedings and Debates, 1868 (March 6, 1868), *North Carolina Standard*, March 7, 1868.

17. Blackstone, *Commentaries* 1: 85–86.

Bibliographical Essay

For a masterful overview of North Carolina constitutional history, see John L. Sanders, "A Brief History of the Constitutions of North Carolina," in *North Carolina Government, 1585–1979: A Narrative and Statistical History*, edited by John L. Cheney, Jr. (Raleigh: North Carolina Department of the Secretary of State, 1981), 795–807, 1029–32. This volume also reprints the three state constitutions and all proposed amendments, both those ratified and those rejected, but its usefulness is diminished by a multitude of typographical errors, including in one instance the description of an amendment as ratified when it was in fact rejected (Amendment of 1891, 889). North Carolina constitutions also appear in Francis Newton Thorpe, ed., *The Federal and State Constitutions* (Washington, D.C.: Government Printing Office, 1909), vol. 5, and in William F. Swindler, ed., *Sources and Documents of United States Constitutions* (Dobbs Ferry, N.Y.: Oceana Publications, 1978), vol. 7, although in both cases a "Constitution of 1876" appears that was in fact only an amended version of the 1868 Constitution. The current constitution with amendments inserted and, if necessary, sections renumbered is printed at the front of the biennial volumes of the *Session Laws of North Carolina* (formerly entitled the *Public Laws of North Carolina*). A verified copy of the constitution as it was at the date of publication appears in the *North Carolina Law Review* 70 (1992): 1703–39. For a close study of the mechanics of the amendment process, see John L. Sanders and John F. Lomax, Jr., *Amendments to the Constitution of North Carolina, 1776–1989* (Chapel Hill, N.C.: Institute of Government, 1990).

North Carolina constitutional historians have been well served by state historians who place constitutional development in context. For the latest overview, see William S. Powell, *North Carolina Through Four Centuries* (Chapel Hill: University of North Carolina Press, 1989). The colonial background is described in a book by Jack P. Greene, *The Quest for Power: The Lower Houses of Assembly in the Southern Royal Colonies, 1689–1776* (Chapel Hill: University of North Carolina Press, 1963), and in a pamphlet by Robert L. Ganyard, *The Emergence of North Carolina's Revolutionary State Government* (Raleigh: North Carolina Department of Cultural Resources, 1978). The crucial issue of representation is covered in Lawrence F. London, "The Representation Contro-

versy in Colonial North Carolina," *North Carolina Historical Review* 11 (1934): 255–
70, and in Mary P. Smith, "Borough Representation in North Carolina," *North Carolina
Historical Review* 7 (1930): 177–91.

CONSTITUTION OF 1776

The basic documents have been collected in the massive volumes of the colonial and
state records: William L. Saunders, ed., *The Colonial Records of North Carolina*, vols.
1–10 (Raleigh: Josephus Daniels, 1886–90) (volume 10 covers 1775–76), and Walter
Clark, ed., *The State Records of North Carolina*, vols. 11–26 (Goldsboro: Nash Brothers,
1896–1906); a four-volume index, covering both sets, was prepared by Stephen B. Weeks
(Goldsboro: Nash Brothers, 1909–14). The drafting of the first constitution is briefly
sketched in Frank Nash, "The North Carolina Constitution of 1776 and Its Makers,"
The James Sprunt Historical Publications of the North Carolina Historical Society, vol.
11, no. 2 (Chapel Hill: University of North Carolina, 1912). Earl H. Ketcham, "The
Sources of the North Carolina Constitution of 1776," *North Carolina Historical Review*
6 (1929): 213–36, traces some of the sections to antecedent constitutions of other states.
A tabular comparison of the North Carolina Declaration of Rights with the earlier declarations of Maryland, Pennsylvania, and Virginia (and with selected British documents)
is in an appendix to John V. Orth, "North Carolina Constitutional History," *North
Carolina Law Review* 70 (1992): 1797–1802.

The delegates to the constitutional convention of 1835 speak for themselves in the
published *Proceedings and Debates of the Convention of North-Carolina, Called to Amend
the Constitution of the State, Which Assembled at Raleigh, June 4, 1835* (Raleigh: Joseph
Gales & Son, 1836). For a succinct account, see Henry G. Connor, "The Convention
of 1835," *North Carolina Booklet* 8 (1908): 89–110. For an assessment of the politics
involved, see Harold J. Counihan, "The North Carolina Constitutional Convention of
1835: A Study in Jacksonian Democracy," *North Carolina Historical Review* 46 (1969):
335–64. Ending the property qualification for voting in 1857 is traced in two articles by
Thomas E. Jeffrey: " 'Free Suffrage' Revisited: Party Politics and Constitutional Reform
in Antebellum North Carolina," *North Carolina Historical Review* 59 (1982): 24–48,
and "Beyond 'Free Suffrage': North Carolina Parties and the Convention Movement of
the 1850s," *North Carolina Historical Review* 62 (1985): 387–419. For a scholarly
overview of North Carolina developments in the context of surrounding states, see Fletcher
M. Green, *Constitutional Development in the South Atlantic States, 1776–1860: A Study
in the Evolution of Democracy* (Chapel Hill: University of North Carolina Press, 1930).

For a glimpse of the complexities of land law, reformed at the direction of the 1776
Constitution, see John V. Orth, "Does the Fee Tail Exist in North Carolina?" *Wake
Forest Law Review* 23 (1988): 767–95. The history of the North Carolina Supreme Court,
established on its present basis in 1818, is traced through its first seventy years in an
address by Kemp P. Battle, published in *North Carolina Reports* (1889), vol. 103, 339–
76. The same subject is canvassed as of the court's centennial anniversary by Chief Justice
Walter Clark in *North Carolina Reports* (1919), vol. 177, 615–35. The account is periodically updated: For the years 1919–69 by Justice Emery B. Denny, see *North Carolina
Reports* (1968), vol. 274, 611–30; for the years 1969–89 by Justice David M. Britt, see
North Carolina Reports (1990), vol. 326, 839–57. D. L. Corbitt, "Judicial Districts of
North Carolina, 1746–1934," *North Carolina Historical Review* 12 (1935): 45–61, dis-
plays the changing geographical basis of justice. An important reinterpretation of the case

of Hoke v. Henderson (1834) is offered by Walter F. Pratt, Jr., "The Struggle for Judicial Independence in Antebellum North Carolina: The Story of Two Judges," *Law and History Review* 4 (1986): 129–59, the two judges in question being North Carolina's renowned Chief Justice Thomas Ruffin and his brilliant associate Judge William Gaston.

The supreme court's practice of issuing advisory opinions, which began under the first constitution and continued under the second and third, is examined in Preston W. Edsall, "The Advisory Opinion in North Carolina," *North Carolina Law Review* 27 (1949): 297–44. The later history of the practice is reviewed and its discontinuance advised in a student comment, "The Advisory Opinion in North Carolina: 1947 to 1991," *North Carolina Law Review* 70 (1992): 1853–98. The religious test for office is examined in Gary R. Govert, "Something There Is That Doesn't Love a Wall: Reflections on the History of North Carolina's Religious Test for Public Office," *North Carolina Law Review* 64 (1986): 1071–98.

CONSTITUTION OF 1868

The constitutional convention of 1868, although the source of modern state constitutional development, is much less well documented than was the earlier convention of 1835. Something may be gleaned from the published *Journal of the Constitutional Convention of the State of North-Carolina, at Its Session 1868* (Raleigh: Joseph W. Holden, 1868), sometimes bound with and entitled *Constitution of the State of North-Carolina, Together with the Ordinances and Resolutions of the Constitutional Convention, Assembled in the City of Raleigh, Jan. 14th, 1868* (Raleigh: Joseph W. Holden, 1868). A day-to-day report of the debates which puts flesh on the bare-bones account in the *Journal* was published in a Raleigh newspaper, *North Carolina Standard*; an edition of the proceedings and debates of the 1868 convention is being prepared by Joseph S. Ferrell of the Institute of Government, University of North Carolina at Chapel Hill. One day's proceedings are available in John V. Orth, ed., "Tuesday, February 11, 1868: The Day North Carolina Chose Direct Election of Judges," *North Carolina Law Review* 70 (1992): 1825–51. For the career of a carpetbagger who left his mark on the constitution, see Otto H. Olsen, *Carpetbagger's Crusade: The Life of Albion Winegar Tourgée* (Baltimore: Johns Hopkins University Press, 1965). For a recent carpetbagger group portrait in which Tourgée figures prominently, see Richard Nelson Current, *Those Terrible Carpetbaggers* (New York: Oxford University Press, 1988).

An invaluable guide to the second constitution, as amended, is Henry G. Connor and Joseph B. Cheshire, Jr., *The Constitution of the State of North Carolina Annotated* (Raleigh: Edwards & Broughton, 1911). Robert D. W. Connor, son of Henry G. Connor, edited *A Manual of North Carolina* (Raleigh: North Carolina Historical Commission, 1913), a treasure trove of information that inaugurated biennial volumes, now prepared by the secretary of state. Amendments to the constitution from 1868 to 1958 are canvassed in Dillard S. Gardner, "The Continuous Revision of Our State Constitution," *North Carolina Law Review* 36 (1958): 297–313, which features a helpful table of all amendments and proposed amendments. The key issue of the franchise is examined in William A. Mabry, " 'White Supremacy' and the North Carolina Suffrage Amendment," *North Carolina Historical Review* 13 (1936): 1–24, and is placed in geographical context in Chapter 7 of J. Morgan Kousser, *The Shaping of Southern Politics: Suffrage Restriction and the Establishment of the One-Party South, 1880–1910* (New Haven, Conn.: Yale

University Press, 1974). One set of unsuccessful amendments is covered in Joseph F. Steelman, "Origins of the Campaign for Constitutional Reform in North Carolina, 1912–1913," *North Carolina Historical Review* 56 (1979): 396–418. Joseph S. Ferrell, "Local Legislation in the North Carolina General Assembly," *North Carolina Law Review* 45 (1967): 340–423, includes a helpful history of the successful 1916 amendments that greatly lengthened the list of prohibited local legislation.

The problems of the state debt, the subject of state constitutional amendment and litigation implicating the Eleventh Amendment to the U.S. Constitution, are sketched in John V. Orth, "The Eleventh Amendment and the North Carolina State Debt," *North Carolina Law Review* 59 (1981): 747–66, and are placed in a larger context in John V. Orth, *The Judicial Power of the United States: The Eleventh Amendment in American History* (New York: Oxford University Press, 1987). Practical problems of state finance, also shaped by Reconstruction, are set out in Albert Coates and William S. Mitchell, "Property and Poll Tax Limitations Under the North Carolina Constitution, Article V, Sections 1 and 6," *North Carolina Law Review* 18 (1940): 275–307. Escheats, for two centuries a source of revenue for higher education, is the subject of a useful pamphlet by Blackwell P. Robinson, *The History of Escheats* (Chapel Hill: University of North Carolina, 1955).

A pioneering study of state protection of an important civil right before the modern era, written by a justice of the North Carolina Supreme Court, is Harry C. Martin, "Freedom of Speech in North Carolina Prior to Gitlow v. New York [1925], With a Forward Glance Thereafter," *Campbell Law Review* 4 (1982): 243–78. The curious case of State v. Emery (1944) is noted in "Constitutional Law—Right of Women to Serve on Juries," *North Carolina Law Review* 23 (1945): 152–58.

The North Carolina Supreme Court was headed by the colorful jurist Walter Clark from 1903 to 1924. A dated biography is Aubrey Lee Brooks, *Walter Clark: Fighting Judge* (Chapel Hill: University of North Carolina Press, 1944). Some of Clark's papers have been published: Aubrey Lee Brooks and Hugh Talmage Lefler, eds., *The Papers of Walter Clark*, 2 vols. (Chapel Hill: University of North Carolina Press, 1948, 1950). A valuable profile of Clark, by a justice of the North Carolina Supreme Court, is Willis P. Whichard, "A Place for Walter Clark in the American Judicial Tradition," *North Carolina Law Review* 63 (1985): 287–337. Useful biographical sketches of public figures in North Carolina history, including many judges, are in William S. Powell, ed., *Dictionary of North Carolina Biography*, 4 vols. to date (Chapel Hill: University of North Carolina Press, 1979–). Memorials of judges, many containing valuable personal information, appear in *North Carolina Reports*, often on the occasion of the presentation of portraits; indexes of these memorials are in volume 206, 938; volume 266, 807; and volume 306, 804.

CONSTITUTION OF 1971

The drafters of the state's third constitution speak for themselves in *Report of the North Carolina State Constitution Study Commission to the North Carolina State Bar and the North Carolina Bar Association* (Raleigh, 1968). This slender volume includes, in addition to a valuable statement of the methods and objectives of the commission, an all-too-brief commentary on the proposed constitution and a section-by-section comparison of the 1868 Constitution as it was then with the proposed constitution.

Annotations of judicial decisions on the various sections of the constitution are included in volume 21 of the *General Statutes of North Carolina*, published by Michie Publishing Co. and periodically supplemented.

Every year the *North Carolina Law Review* (*N.C. L. Rev.*) publishes an issue surveying developments in North Carolina law. As attention has shifted in the last decade from federal to state constitutional issues, the section headed "Constitutional Law" has begun to include the subheading "State Constitution." In volume 70 (1992) the issue includes a Symposium on the North Carolina Constitution. Articles and student notes and comments on state constitutional law also occasionally appear in the *Wake Forest Law Review* (*Wake Forest L. Rev.*), the *North Carolina Central Law Journal* (*N.C. Cent. L. J.*), and the *Campbell Law Review* (*Campbell L. Rev.*). Arranged below under the various articles of the constitution to which they refer are the most significant of these items published since 1971, particularly those concerning cases cited in the present commentary.

Article I. Declaration of Rights

Valuable student materials on important cases include "State v. Felmet: The Extent of Free Speech Rights on Private Property Under the North Carolina Constitution," *N.C. L. Rev.* 61 (1982): 157–66; "Responsible Citizens v. City of Asheville: A New Analysis of the Taking Issue or a Step into Confusion?" *N.C. L. Rev.* 62 (1984): 1389–96; "Repose for Manufacturers: Six Year Statutory Bar to Products Liability Actions Upheld—Tetterton v. Long Manufacturing Co.," *N.C. L. Rev.* 64 (1986): 1157–78; "State ex rel. Martin v. Melott: The Separation of Powers and the Power to Appoint," *N.C. L. Rev.* 66 (1988): 1109–22; "Race-based Peremptories No Longer Permitted in Civil Trials: Jackson v. Housing Authority of High Point," *N.C. L. Rev.* 67 (1989): 1262–80; "State v. Cofield: Grand Expansion of Citizen Rights in Grand Jury Selection—The North Carolina Constitution Bars Discrimination in Foreperson Selection," *N.C. L. Rev.* 68 (1990): 1046–63; and "The Cause of Action for Damages Under North Carolina's Constitution: Corum v. University of North Carolina," *N.C.L. Rev.* 70 (1992): 1899–1915. See also "State Constitutional Law—Effective Limitation of Occupational Licensing," *Wake Forest L. Rev.* 13 (1977): 507–21, and "State Regulation of Public Solicitation for Religious Purposes—Heritage Village Church & Missionary Fellowship, Inc. v. State," *Wake Forest L. Rev.* 16 (1980): 996–1030. The North Carolina decision in State v. Carter (1988) received brief notice in the *Harvard Law Review*: "Criminal Law—Exclusionary Rule—North Carolina Constitution Does Not Contain a Good Faith Exception," *Harvard Law Review* 102 (1989): 724–29.

Articles address various issues in more detail. Separation of powers provokes perennial problems discussed in narrow terms in John V. Orth " 'Forever Separate and Distinct': Separation of Powers in North Carolina," *N.C. L. Rev.* 62 (1984): 1–28, and more broadly in Ran Coble, "Executive-Legislative Relations in North Carolina: Where We Are and Where We Are Headed," *Wake Forest L. Rev.* 25 (1990): 673–706. The right to bear arms must be reexamined as legislation regulating firearms is considered. Stephen P. Halbrook, "The Right to Bear Arms in the First State Bills of Rights: Pennsylvania, North Carolina, Vermont, and Massachusetts," *Vermont Law Review* 10 (1985): 255–320, marshals much of the evidence, but misses the important fact that the North Carolina drafters adopted the Pennsylvania provision, but deleted the guarantee of the people's right to bear arms for the defense "of themselves." The survival of substantive due process in state constitutional law is examined and lauded in Joshua A. Newberg, "In

Defense of *Aston Park*: The Case for State Substantive Due Process Review of Health Care Regulation," *N.C. L. Rev.* 68 (1990): 253–72. The relevance of substantive due process to a hotly debated issue is argued in Louis D. Billionis, "Liberty, the 'Law of the Land,' and Abortion in North Carolina," *N.C. L. Rev.* 71 (1993): 1839.

Article II. Legislative

A student note explores the troublesome topic of "generated laws": "Town of Emerald Isle v. State of North Carolina: A New Test for Distinguishing Between General Laws and Local Legislation," *N.C. L. Rev.* 66 (1988): 1096–1108. An article examines the interaction of federal and state law on the crucial subject of legislative apportionment: Robert N. Hunter, Jr., "Racial Gerrymandering and the Voting Rights Act in North Carolina," *Campbell L. Rev.* 9 (1987): 255–91.

Article III. Executive

Administrative agencies, hybrids in a system of separated powers, are the subjects of two articles: David L. Dickson, "Advisory Rulings by Administrative Agencies: Their Benefits and Dangers," *Campbell L. Rev.* 2 (1980): 1–91; and Charles Markham, "A Powerless Judiciary? The North Carolina Courts' Perceptions of Review of Administrative Action," *N.C. Cent. L.J.* 12 (1980): 21–95.

The office of attorney general is also twice addressed, by successive holders of that office: Rufus L. Edmisten, "The Common Law Powers of the Attorney General of North Carolina," *N.C. Cent. L.J.* 9 (1977): 1–36, and Lacy H. Thornburg, "Changes in the State's Law Firm: The Powers, Duties and Operations of the Office of the Attorney General," *Campbell L. Rev.* 12 (1990): 343–81.

Article IV. Judicial

Articles explore both judicial power and the problem of judges' misconduct: Raymond P. Mallard, "Inherent Power of the Courts of North Carolina," *Wake Forest L. Rev.* 10 (1974): 1–23, and Edward B. Clark, "The Discipline and Removal of Judges in North Carolina," *Campbell L. Rev.* 4 (1981): 1–40. One student note on In re Appeal from Civil Penalties (1989) asks "The Forty-Two Hundred Dollar Question: 'May State Agencies Have Discretion in Setting Civil Penalties Under the North Carolina Constitution?'" *N.C. L. Rev.* 68 (1990): 1035–45, and another analyzes "Baker v. Martin and the Constitutionality of Partisan Qualifications for Appointment to District Courts," *N.C. L. Rev.* 70 (1992): 1916–28.

Article V. Finance

Student notes explore the meaning of the "public purpose" requirement for state expenditure: "Municipal Ownership of Cable Television Systems: Madison Cablevision Inc. v. City of Morganton," *N.C. L. Rev.* 68 (1990): 1295–1316, and "Rejection of the 'Public Purpose' Requirement for State Tax Exemption," *Wake Forest L. Rev.* 17 (1981): 293–308 (noting In re University of North Carolina, 1980). Revenue bond financing is the subject of another student note, "Public Purpose—Restricting Revenue Bond Financing of Private Enterprise," *N.C. L. Rev.* 52 (1974): 859–75, now largely outdated by the constitutional amendments incorporated as Sections 8 to 13. For an article exploring the subleties the subtleties of the new regime, see William H. McBride and David Dreifus, "Industrial Development and Pollution Control Financing in North Carolina," *N.C. L. Rev.* 61 (1983): 419–49. An imaginative new form of public finance, installment purchase, is the subject of a student note, "Constitutional Expansion of Local Government Financing Alternatives: Wayne County Citizens Association v. Wayne County Board of Commissioners," *N.C. L. Rev.* 70 (1992): 1947–56.

Article VI. Suffrage and Eligibility to Office

A student comment, "State Durational Residence Requirements as a Violation of the Equal Protection Clause," *N.C. Cent. L.J.* 3 (1972): 233–49, canvasses the federal cases that made North Carolina's one-year residence requirement a dead letter.

Article IX. Education

For student comments concerning the troubled boundary between religious liberty and the state's interest in education, see "The State and Sectarian Education: Regulation to Deregulation," *Duke Law Journal*, 1980: 801–46, and "State Regulation of Private Religious Schools in North Carolina—A Model Approach," *Wake Forest L. Rev.* 16 (1980): 405–37. For a thoughtful student note on a trend that is further weakening public control of education (and that also implicates religious liberty), see "Delconte v. State: Some Thoughts on Home Education," *N.C. L. Rev.* 64 (1986): 1302–29. An article covering novel ways to increase revenues for public schools is David Lawrence, "Fines, Penalties, and Forfeitures: An Historical and Comparative Analysis," *N.C. L. Rev.* 65 (1986): 49–83.

Article X. Homesteads and Exemptions

Basic doctrine is usefully presented in William B. Aycock, "Homestead Exemption in North Carolina," *N.C. L. Rev.* 29 (1951): 143–67, and perceptively criticized in Rhoda B. Billings, "Does North Carolina Really Have a Homestead Exemption?" *Intramural Law Review of Wake Forest College* 2 (1966): 53–76. Modern realities are described in Ralph A. Peeples, "New Rules for an Old Game: North Carolina's New Exemption Act," *Wake Forest L. Rev.* 17 (1981): 865–909, and Ralph A. Peeples and Richard J. Votta, "The Legislature Strikes Back: Exemptions, Part 2," *Wake Forest L. Rev.* 18 (1982): 1025–71.

Article XI. Punishments, Corrections, and Charities

The chief justice of the North Carolina Supreme Court addresses the ultimate punishment: James G. Exum, "The Death Penalty in North Carolina," *Campbell L. Rev.* 8 (1985): 1–28.

Table of Cases

OPINIONS OF ATTORNEY GENERAL

Index